YOU'RE ENTITLE'

YOU'RE ENTITLE'

by Harry Golden

INTRODUCTION BY *Harry Golden, Jr.*

Cleveland and New York

THE WORLD PUBLISHING COMPANY

PUBLISHED BY *The World Publishing Company*
2231 WEST 110TH STREET, CLEVELAND 2, OHIO

PUBLISHED SIMULTANEOUSLY IN CANADA BY
NELSON, FOSTER & SCOTT LTD.

LIBRARY OF CONGRESS CATALOG CARD NUMBER: 62-9057

FIRST EDITION

Several of these essays have appeared in a syndicated column, distributed by the McClure Newspaper Syndicate.

"The Eichmann Trial" in Chapter 2 originally
appeared in *Life* magazine.

"Notes for an Autobiography" was taken from
the author's chapter in *Five Boyhoods* (Double-
day and Company, 1962).

"The Immigrant and the Children of Dixie"
originally appeared in the Washington *Post* and
other Scripps-Howard newspapers as one of a
series *Americans in Action.*

The lines from *The Prophet* by Kahlil Gibran
which appear on page 97 are reprinted with
permission of the publisher, Alfred A. Knopf,
Inc. Copyrighted 1923 by Kahlil Gibran; renewal
copyright 1951 by Administrators C.T.A. of
Kahlil Gibran Estate, and Mary G. Gibran.

I DEDICATE this book to the memory of my father, Reb Lebche, who emigrated to America from the Galician town of Mikulinz in the Austro-Hungarian Empire of Kaiser Franz Josef. All his life he spoke a halting English, though he certainly made his ideas clear enough. He was enamored of the phrase, "You're entitle'." This phrase not only recalls the humor that surrounded his life in the New World, but it reflects his strong juridical interest.

In my youth, I told him over and over again that the phrase was more correctly pronounced, "You're entitled." I kept telling him, "It ends with a *d*, Poppa," to which he nodded understanding, but the next time it still came out, "You're entitle'."

"Entitle' " was the expression of a free man. No one was *entitled* in Eastern Europe. You served in the army for ten years and it entitled you to nothing. Your taxes entitled you to no franchise. But in America men were free and *entitled*, or as my father insisted, "You're Entitle'."

HARRY GOLDEN

Charlotte, N. C.
June 10, 1962

Contents

CONTENTS

CONTENTS

CONTENTS

ACKNOWLEDGMENT

I am again indebted to Harry Golden, Jr.,
of the Detroit *Free Press* for this new
selection of essays from my
writings and for editing
the manuscript

I knew him when

"ONLY IN AMERICA" has become part of the language, and it is also the name of a race horse running at the state-fair tracks in the Great Plains stakes.

On menus in Miami Beach, New York, and Los Angeles, you will find offerings called, "For 2¢ Plain" (but the clear seltzer water referred to is listed at thirty-five cents).

And, in the Bohemian Gaslight Square section of St. Louis, there is a fine delicatessen named "2¢ Plain," engaged at the moment, incidentally, in a hot-pastrami price war with less worthy competitors.

"Enjoy, Enjoy!" has become an advertising slogan of the E & B beer people.

But the success of these books and his emergence as a national figure have not materially changed my father, Harry Golden. He did have a painter refinish the doors of the Victorian frame house in which he holds forth at 1312 Elizabeth Avenue, in Charlotte, North Carolina. The last time I visited him there, the doors were bright red. "Why?" I asked.

"I want my place to look like an old-time brothel I remember on Allen Street," he replied.

"Oh," I said.

And then he proceeded to invite me to write the introduction for this new collection of essays, and he indicated that he would like me to tell something about my work with him.

As it turns out, the most fascinating thing about editing books for my father is that you start from nowhere.

This, then, is how it happened: I was the City Hall reporter for the Charlotte *Observer*, and, in January 1956, Knight Newspapers transferred me to the Detroit *Free Press*. Some time later when I returned to Charlotte on a vacation, my father announced that he was finally going to have published the book we had been talking about for some years.

"Wonderful," I said.

"Buddy," he said, "you've been a copyreader on a daily and you know the fine points of punctuation and spelling. Will you read the manuscript for me?"

And so, when I got back to Detroit, I found a large parcel in my mail. It contained simply, and in no particular order, approximately one thousand clippings from my father's newspaper, *The Carolina Israelite* (never on Sunday, and you're quite fortunate if you see it every other month or so).

So I set about the task of selecting, organizing, editing, renaming many of the stories, and writing chapter titles.

And that was *Only in America*. In the case of subsequent books, my starting point was a file of *Carolina Israelites*, and my father air-mailed new, additional stories as he wrote them.

In the process of selection, I throw discarded material to the floor of the working room of my home in Detroit. Every third or fourth week during the operation, my pretty Southern wife, Bebe, invades the place to clear the floor.

What has been left, in *You're Entitle'*, you will find good reading.

On a subjective level, however, there is something more important than the fact that my father is a good writer. How many men can say—my father is a brave man?

And he is that—this fat little guy, short of breath, with his cigars and ideas in Charlotte; this immigrant and Yankee in the native-born South; this Jew in the citadel of Anglo-Saxon Protestantism; this integrationist in a land of segregation; this happy reformer among the complacent.

Ensconced behind a typewriter in the tumult of his office, he dwells on politics and religion and food and history and sex and the arts and a boyhood half a century ago in the southeastern corner of Manhattan Island. He is the champion of many causes —some lost—but many, like the cause of the Southern Negro, that will inevitably be won.

At this writing, I understand that the horse, Only in America, has yet to win a race. But he is still trying. And so is this writer. My father. My father.

HARRY GOLDEN, JR.

Detroit
June 1, 1962

1.

MORE COMPLAINTS
AND FREE ADVICE

A note in passing

I AM a reporter and, I hope, no sermonizer. But that doesn't mean I don't know something about this process of living. I shall soon see my sixtieth year and along with hundreds of thousands of other middle-aged men, I believe the good life, as the Greeks called it, is within reach. We only have to be careful about two things. First, don't get in trouble with the Internal Revenue people; and second, don't get mixed up with a woman.

Memo to Senator Goldwater

ONE of the things which the country could stand right now is a movement spearheaded by Senator Goldwater and Mr. William Buckley, of the *National Review,* to change the designation of the "liberal arts college" to the "conservative arts college." We might as well have this thing out in the open.

The only constants

THERE are religions on the face of the earth that are almost as old as civilization itself. There were religions that flourished for generations and generations before dying out. The dynasties of the Caesars, the Hapsburgs, and the Romanovs all

25

reigned for many centuries. Even during the kingdoms of David and Solomon; even during the terrible economic and social upheavals which have beset civilization from time to time; and despite the advent of science and the space age, which aims for the moon and Mars and Venus—there remain only three constants, only three things which have never diminished in value— three things which are the *only* constants of mankind:

> gold
> a woman
> irrigated land

Women in space

THE Golden Plan for Space Exploration provides that women should be included on the first journey to the moon. There are several reasons why they should go along.

It will be a long trip and everyone knows those fellows, once they get away from barracks discipline, aren't going to do too good a job of house-cleaning the spaceship. A woman is by nature neater and more efficient, and if anyone is going to sweep up cosmic dust, she ought to do the job.

Contrary to all malicious gossip and slander, the insurance companies tell us women are better drivers. Certainly they could steer the spacecraft if the fellows get hung up in a chess game or get behind in taking all the notes to satisfy the bureaucratic needs of congressmen back on earth.

Women will also insure that these astronauts eat a balanced diet. A balanced diet is a big preoccupation with women and not so with men. Anyone in the Army who lived off C rations knows the fellows used to trade off the cans of food they didn't like for the cans they did. One soldier would eat prune bars for months and another Spam. Anyone knows bachelors have no trouble with their weight, being able to subsist on hamburgers, steaks, and canned spaghetti, with an occasional meal of eggs thrown in, and nary a vegetable to bother them. It isn't until they are married that the weight problems come, what with the little women preparing tuna-fish casseroles and salads and green vegetables.

The last reason for including women is that space will be mighty lonely if you leave her and French pastry out. Mighty lonely indeed.

How to detect a bad cook

COOKING is so much a part of life that a young fellow who is going to get married ought to get hold of a good cook rather than a bad cook. "Good food is a moral fact," wrote Joseph Conrad who himself hired out as husband and provider to a wife who prepared excellent cuisine. But how, wonders the young bachelor, am I to tell a good cook from a bad cook? There are several distinguishing signals for the good cook. One, if her mother cooks well, she probably will, too. If the vegetables are always interesting, it's dollars to doughnuts the lady knows her way around pots and pans and recipes. Watch out for desserts and meat. Desserts are too easy and whipped cream is an excellent disguise for a fallen cake. And meat is simply not that hard to broil, bake, or fry. Good meat is the steer's doing, rarely the lady's, except when she ruins what the steer did.

There are, however, two criteria by which you can judge the bad cook. They are easily decipherable. The first is apparent if she doesn't know good cooking when she eats it. Good cooks are always gushing over the food and exchanging recipes, like philosophers gossip over a new idea. The bad cook is chary with her praise, for the simple reason she doesn't know that what she is eating has been prepared with love and affection.

The second is the dead giveaway. It is eggplant. Bad cooks are crazy about serving eggplant and invent every sort of excuse and plot and intrigue to make it a main course. Why bad cooks should have lighted upon eggplant, I don't know, but I do know they have an utterly strange attraction toward this bland and useless vegetable. If you meet a lady who serves you eggplant

I recommend, if you love her, that you be nice and kind to her, but don't marry her. She's no one to whom to bring home the boss.

I once set forth this idea and I never got so much mail.

Apparently there is a whole subspecies of Homo americanus who subsist on eggplant—eggplant fried, eggplant boiled, eggplant in the pot, nine days old.

Some people said I was a bigot, others said I was an unadventurous eater (I—who eat all day—unadventurous!). Also, I am in possession now of some sacred eggplant recipes which will enable me to prepare eggplant fritters, eggplant pizzas, eggplant knishes, eggplant appetizers, and another dish called, strangely enough, rat-a-tat-tooey or rat-atooey (the spelling isn't important, said my correspondent; the eggplant is), which is eggplant cooked in tomato sauce with chopped beef. The lady who sent me this must be on a salt-free diet because rat-atooey, if you will, was as bland a dish as ever I turned my back upon.

You see, I tried. My conclusion remains. Eggplant may be a dandy weapon for Neapolitans to hurl at tenors who sing flat, but it is no food for a growing boy or a growed man, as we say down heah in the South.

There were plenty of people with time to defend eggplant.

Anyone who will take the time to tell an aging writer that kasha has nothing on eggplant is indeed with it. I suppose some of my letter-writers wonder once in a while how the husband is making out at the office. Is he getting enough eggplant?

The stupidity of multiple choice

In the old days, the teacher asked, "Who discovered America and in what year?" When a kid rose to answer, either he knew or he didn't. No one asks questions that way today. Usually the question is worded: "Who discovered America? Choose one: (1) Bernard Baruch, (2) Christopher Columbus, (3) Nathan Hale, (4) Mickey Mantle."

These are called multiple-choice questions. I believe they have done more to discourage genuine education in this country than all the PTAs put together.

Once upon a time educators started to worry because all the kids knew were facts. They knew that 1066 was the year of the Battle of Hastings and that 1812 marked the second war with England, but they didn't know the consequences of these. *Ergo,* the educators thought it was the fault of facts that the kids didn't know and banished them.

But when you give up facts, all you can teach is that citizens ought to work together happily, and attend a church of their choice at least once a week.

To pretend to everybody that the kids are educated, the teacher passes everyone. It is true that some of the classes are called "remedial" and are composed of children who thought Mickey Mantle discovered America, and that others are composed of children who guessed correctly that it was Christopher Columbus. But this is not an appreciable difference. Both classes visit the firehouse, the newspaper, and make a tour of every church in the area except the witness houses belonging to the Seventh-day Adventists.

At the same time, all the churches are worried that the children will find out people die and the vice committees are imploring the police chief to pluck all the books off the stands because the kids might read them. Then all of us sit around and deplore the fact that children "go steady." But the kids are one jump ahead of us. They see us eager to edit the idea of competition out of education, worship, and literature; so they go ahead and edit out the competitive and contingent elements in love.

Jewish best-sellers

THE Literary Supplement of the London *Times* had a recent discussion of the "Jewish" best-sellers in America. Summing up, the critic for the *Times* wrote that the main characteristic of the Jewish writer in America "is his creative energy rather than his focus, and his tendency to flow outward to the American world rather than inward to the Jewish."

Just what the critic in the Literary Supplement meant when he said the Jewish best-sellers do not flow *inward* to the Jewish world, I leave to others. It is a meaningless statement to me. I can tell you how many buttons the American Jew has on his underwear, but I cannot imagine how I could flow inward to the Jewish world.

Which *Jewish* world?

The Jewish world contained in the Williamsburg section in Brooklyn? Or the Jewish world contained in Miami Beach? The world of the Jewish settlement worker in Spanish Harlem? Or the world of the Jewish executive director out in the fancy suburb? Or the world of the Jewish scorer of the Ryder Golf Cup Matches? Or the world of the Jewish pro-segregationist in Macon, Georgia?

It is hard enough turning out a paper every other month and a book every year; now I have to worry because I don't "focus."

The trouble with women

ASIDE from the fact that they are not philosophers, what is the trouble with women?

Number one: women are possessed of this terrible compulsion to move the furniture about. There is no end to the myriad number of mathematical arrangements of the furniture. You can leave the house one morning, off to the shop, to bring home the goodies for the wife and kids, and when you return that night you wouldn't recognize the place. You are reduced to a form of blindness, groping your way around what should be your own familiar home. But this is getting off easy.

Number two: no man has yet found the wife or secretary who is able to make the adjustment to either air conditioning or central heating. On the hottest day of the summer, you can return to the office after lunch to find the staff sitting there clothed in babushkas, shawls, and sweaters, teeth chattering and knees blue. It seems the air conditioner produces a draft. And in the winter they will burn you out of the place. They seem never able to understand that moving the thermostat up one degree will ignite the oil burner. Ah, no! They move it up twenty degrees and, to boot, will insist it does not work properly, that it's likely to explode.

Number three: no man does right by a woman at a party. If it is not asking for that extra drink which enrages and disgraces them, then it is putting salt on your salad before tasting it. Coming home from a party with a woman is worse than having the boss put you on the carpet for sheer negligence.

I remember an old *Saturday Evening Post* cartoon where the husband about to depart the party looks at his wife and remarks, "From your expression I can tell I had a wonderful time."

A kind word for drinking alone

ACCORDING to the medical experts who help staff some of our national magazines the most obvious and degrading symptom of disease is found in solitary drinking. They warn everyone away from drinking alone. The advice tendered to drink with groups, however, is perhaps some of the worst advice ever offered.

In the first place, no matter what the party or happy gathering there will always be at least one man who takes the drink he doesn't particularly want simply because everyone else is drinking. It may well be this fellow's mangled body the State troopers pull from behind the smashed wheel of a battered automobile some time later that night. People who drink in groups always have "one for the road."

The man who drinks alone is already home and not only he but another motorist is saved. Also, he is not in the bathroom heaving nor will he have morning-after regrets about vino veritasing. It is an absolute slander and a degrading canard to say the man who drinks alone is a sick man. He is drinking because he likes liquor —not because he wants to get as drunk as everyone else. He will avoid the wife-swapping part that takes place when everyone gets good and loaded, and all the virgins are safe from his depredations. The man who drinks alone is minding his own business, the way it should be.

Cures for a hangover

CATO's cure for a hangover which I documented in my book, *Only in America*, was received with great enthusiasm and considerable gratitude in many parts of the country. You will recall that Cato's cure was to eat raw cabbage leaves the morning after, and many people who tried it have reported that it works —for them. Cato was a pretty good man with the wine, besides having one of the great minds of antiquity, and he was more successful with his cure for a hangover than Caesar was with his cure for baldness. (The great Julius gave up finally. He came to the conclusion that the only "cure" for baldness is to become a conqueror and cover the bald spot with a laurel wreath.)

But "cures" work for some people and not for others. It may be a matter of what the medical men call metabolism, but I wouldn't know about that.

I was a clerk at the Hotel Markwell on West Forty-ninth Street in New York, and I shall be forever grateful to one of my permanent guests, Mr. Sam E. Sam came into the lobby every evening loaded to the gills, but a minute after he entered his room he picked up the phone. And after a while I was able to anticipate Sam's order, "Send up a quart of vanilla ice cream."

Less than one hour later Sam E. emerged from the elevator handsomely groomed and as sober as a judge.

I tried both raw cabbage leaves and ice cream, and as far as my own metabolism is concerned Cato the Roman was not as successful as Mr. W. C. Whitney's chauffeur, which was Sam E.'s very prominent and highly interesting position in life.

The old Irishwomen I remember in Hell's Kitchen were even better experts than Cato and Sam when it came to getting their men back to their jobs on Monday morning after a weekend bout with the grog. They fed them salted codfish in cream gravy. Thus these wonderful women by instinct combined the remedy of the natural salt in Cato's cabbage leaves with the relaxing smoothness of Sam's ice cream.

The doctors would give their hungover patients this salted codfish in cream gravy but they are too busy, and so they give them injections of salt and vitamin B_1. Salt and vitamin B_1 help the body to get going. But how did the old Irishwomen know that Pat needed salt and vitamin B_1 and that the salted codfish in cream gravy was the perfect answer?

How about whisky?

For years there has been a debate between prohibitionists and sociologists. The one has said, "He's poor because he drinks," and the other replied, "He drinks because he's poor," but basically this is nothing more than a play upon words. We are certain of this: He's slowly destroying himself because he drinks. No one can dispute that, and because he drinks he has filled our sanitariums, jails, hospitals, and insane asylums. I have less excuse to drink than anyone else. Why? Because I once saw a brilliant man bang his head against the wall of a cell and laugh uproariously every time his head crashed against the solid concrete.

Folks like me who drink whisky rarely surrender themselves to introspection, and the fact that I recognize it as an evil may be the beginning of a possible redemption. (Beware of the sinner who has seen the light.) As a writing man I believe I can deliver a fairly coherent essay of maybe five thousand words on the value of opium and its by-products, morphine and heroin, but I know, in all honesty, that I cannot write a single half-page, double-spaced, on the value of alcohol as a beverage.

We whisky drinkers rationalize the process in a million different ways. "It's a food." "It's stimulating." "It brings out the best in me." But mostly, "I can take it or leave it alone." This last statement is never made unless you are holding a drink in your hand. It's like playing the horses. Your logic tells you that *everybody* loses, but that you will beat it. "Him—not me."

All that I know about drinking is bad. Very bad. Fights, split lips, filth, blood running down a man's face, a man brutally beating his wife, his daughter, his friend—and spitting. Mostly spitting. Spitting is part of drinking, and you do not know the half of it unless you have gone to work early in the morning and seen the hundreds of wretches in the alleys clearing their throats after the night before, or unless you have tried to earn a quarter sweeping the sawdust out of a saloon on a Sunday morning.

There were men on Elizabeth Street who sold their shoes for the price of that early morning drink of whisky. They received sixty cents for a pair of good shoes or they would receive thirty cents plus a pair of "reliefers." Reliefers were shoes that were too far gone to be repaired, and so this human intellect, capable of building a bridge, a power plant, or writing a poem, was now faced with the momentous decision of whether to take the sixty cents and walk to the saloon in stocking feet, or take thirty cents and get that pair of reliefers.

And the women waiting outside the Family Entrance. It was Saturday night and their husbands were inside with the pay envelope. The women stood there like the chorus in a Greek tragedy. And soon the husbands came out, and each woman took her man home. She washed him, fed him, tucked him in, and got him ready for work Monday morning, to start the whole process all over again the following Saturday.

Of course, the younger men stood around bars laughing at all of this. The younger men spoke of all the great men who drank. Every drunk at the bar knew the story of Bourke Cochran, the famous Tammany lawyer, and how Cochran received five hundred dollars a day in court and how he never addressed the jury unless he had finished a full bottle of whisky. The drunks loved that story and if you got chummy with a barfly the first thing he told you was about Bourke Cochran; and of course, the story was a fake. It was a fake because for every Bourke Cochran there were five thousand other great "lawyers," "doctors," "writers," "mechanics," and "scientists" in the Bellevue Hospital psychopathic ward or in the alleys clearing their throats.

To some degree drink also involves the process of dehumanization. The art of conversation has been lost. Today the folks get together and immediately proceed to knock each other out with whisky—to avoid boredom. But I am a vocal man. Thus, when I, too, grab for the stuff in this "knocking each other out" process, I am literally dehumanizing myself. I am deliberately applying the leveler of stupidity, boredom, gossip, and wastefulness, to say nothing of the cost, which is considerable.

Converse and Winthrop

THE most enthusiastic audience I have ever appeared before was at Converse College, Spartanburg, South Carolina.

South Carolina? Amazing, isn't it! And I have been saying this all along. (One of my critics, *Commentary* Magazine, thought it made a big point when it asked how this fellow, Golden, can be a real "integrationist" when he keeps saying that he loves the South, and that "the South has some of the kindest people in the world," to quote these knuckleheads accurately.)

Converse College is a fashionable girls' school. Probably the *most* fashionable. The girls come from South Carolina, North Carolina, Tennessee, and Virginia mostly. At Converse (a campus of great beauty) there is an exceptional curriculum along with horseback riding, sororities, and all the other upper-middle-class social activities.

I said to these Southern girls that their fathers are the leaders of their respective Southern communities, and so, too, will their husbands be leaders of their respective Southern communities, and that they now owe it to themselves and to America to free themselves forever from the myths, superstitions, and legends which betray the dignity of 26 per cent of the Southern population, our Negro neighbors.

I told them that some of their political leaders are leading them up a blind alley, that instead of fighting Khrushchev, they are fighting such great Southerners as Frank P. Graham.

When I finished my lecture to these six hundred and fifty Southern girls I had the greatest experience of my entire career as a lecturer. The girls cheered and applauded and they did not stop applauding until the program chairman, Political Science

Professor Colonel Dixon (Ret.), held up his hand to call a halt.
The Colonel was so deeply moved that all he could say was,
"Good night." Both of us left the stage with handkerchiefs plainly
visible.

Dr. Frank P. Graham, former Senator from North Carolina and
for twenty-five years president of the University of North Carolina, had a somewhat similar experience a few months ago. Dr.
Frank, who is India-Pakistan mediator for the United Nations,
spoke at the well-known Winthrop College, in Rock Hill, South
Carolina. The South Carolina Legislature voted to censure the
officials at Winthrop College for having invited Dr. Graham,
who is about as subversive as the Sermon on the Mount and the
Declaration of Independence.

But what the press did not adequately report is that the Legislature did not censure the Winthrop College authorities because
they had invited a man who said a kind word for the Freedom
Riders. What they were really angry about was that the Southern
girls at Winthrop applauded and cheered.

How to beat the Japanese

THE North Carolina textile industry is fighting against
the cheaper textile imports from Japan. I have a plan whereby
I may save my fellow Tar Heels. It is a plan I came upon quite
by accident.

It seems the Japanese were also exporting to America not so
long ago a well-made talis. A talis is the prayer cloth used in the
synagogue. The old-timers up in New York who sell religious
merchandise were deeply chagrined and hurt by inroads this
Oriental product made against theirs. They could not possibly
meet the competition in price. But there is more than one way to
skin a cat. They enlisted the aid of the Rabbinical Association,
which issued an edict that all Japanese-made talisim were not
kosher. All religious objects, just as food, must be prepared and
manufactured under strict rabbinical supervision among Orthodox

Jews. Today, the Japanese product is piling up in the warehouses, non-kosher and unsold.

It will not be long, however, until the Japanese wise up and hire themselves a rabbi. Therefore, let me advise our Tar Heel textile tycoons to beat the Japanese to the punch regarding their own products and hire rabbis to supervise production at each of their plants. Better yet, each of the textile tycoons might do well to become a Jew. I would personally participate in Charlie Cannon's conversion. I think he would make a fine Jew and we would be glad to have him. We can then get him a rabbi to oversee the manufacture of all his sheets, towels, pillowcases, and blankets, and he will beat the Japanese at their own game.

The Golden Plan for Wall Street

United States News and World Report recently produced the most pertinent advice in the current dialogue about the post-bomb world.

What should you do if you have stocks and bonds and investments and the H-bomb does indeed drop? Among the guides for right financial action was the admonition not to convert holdings to cash. Everything will be rationed so money won't have its value and if, by some chance, that buried cash gets burned up, the Government won't replace it. Jewels are always good, says *United States News,* but you have to remember they don't return interest.

I think the average reader has a pretty good idea by now of what USN&WR is up to. It is warning that the insurance companies will not be able to pay off claims in case of death by H-bomb, which is bad, but the Government will restrict foreclosures on mortgages in case the local industry is up in smoke, which is good.

I cannot help feeling, however, that USN&WR omitted two crucial proposals. Immediately after the bombs begin to fall, the secretary of the local chamber of commerce should get on the air waves and recount the potential and actual growth of the town, the number of new industries it brought in up until that first bomb started descending, and the amount of the area pay rolls. This is an invaluable record and must not be lost. It will be a wonderful aid to the fellows who take up the project after the unpleasantness is over.

Second proposal: and this is indeed an important one. The last thing on either television or radio should be a fellow from one of the big brokerage houses calling off the high, low, and last price of the day. The last price need not necessarily be the last price of the preceding day but the last price paid before the trading was temporarily interrupted by the invasion.

While he sings out the high, low, and last, I recommend all of the 4-H clubs in the area band together and provide background music.

> In the sweet bye and bye
> We shall meet on that beautiful shore.

Stanley isn't happy

TRAVELING around the country lecturing, I get to meet all sorts. And the more of the sorts you meet, the more you meet the same people coming and going. Over and over, in California and New York, Miami and Charleston, Bangor and Scranton, people say the same things.

At the home of the program chairman in one of the Midwestern cities, the hostess interrupted pleasantries to tell me about her son. She said, "Stanley isn't happy." Stanley is fourteen years old and dresses beautifully and even has the luxury of weekly manicures.

"That's the best news I have heard all day," I told my hostess. "Stanley isn't happy. Does Stanley have his own bed to sleep in? Does he have to share a bed with two brothers? Does he have to sell newspapers? Does he have enough to eat? Does he have to contribute his share for the support of the family?"

But Stanley is unhappy. There are Stanleys multiplied by the hundreds of thousands. Yet their parents worry that they are not happy. Not only are the Stanleys unhappy, but their parents feel they aren't getting the best possible education and on top of this no one understands kids any more.

We Americans are child-oriented. Because we are unhappy, we imagine children must be unhappy. Happiness is a word bruited in the television commercials and the advertising columns and we imagine there must be a way to buy it. If one has a Waring blender and a two-car garage with three cars in it, one imagines that one ought to have happiness, too.

Now I am not one to insist that children laugh and smile all the time. There are indeed attendant worries in growing up. But as someone else once wisely said, "It is only in middle age that one understands the folly of youthful worry and what good does that do you."

Stanley has his own bed, all the latest styles of sports coats, and even his own car. But all over America I hear "Stanley isn't happy," which should give us a few clues. Fifty years ago you never heard parents discuss their children in terms of "happiness." They said, "Stanley is doing well in school," or "Stanley has a new job," or "Stanley has just been promoted." That is why I laughed when this mother said, "Stanley isn't happy." Stanley would be a lot less unhappy if his mother stopped asking him if he's happy.

How much are you making?

PEOPLE are always asking the actors and the writers how much money they make. This is a question these gentle people wouldn't dare ask of the laundryman, the retail merchant, the scrap-metal dealer, or even the Mayor, whose salary is a matter of public record.

They feel no compunction however with actors, song writers, writers, and creative people. An actor who has spent twelve years in his profession trying to master his craft at an average of one thousand dollars a year will always seem overpaid. He may have worked a sixteen-hour day for thirty dollars a week in summer stock; he may have landed a lucky job at fifty dollars a week in an off-Broadway show; he may spend twelve years selling neckties in Macy's during the Christmas season before he finally lands a good part in a Broadway show he knows is destined for a four-month run at best. But people whistle in admiration when, in stunned embarrassment, he confesses that he makes three hundred and fifty dollars a week. That's wonderful money, they tell him, for three or four hours' work.

But people are intensely interested in how much a creative man makes. Why?

Because the commercial society feels a guilt. And the creative man inspires this guilt. He is not inadequate in the way the commercial society knows and feels it is inadequate. The commercial society tries to relieve this guilt two or three times a year by going up to the schoolhouse and bullying the teachers, or sitting on the dais and throwing weight around, but it doesn't work. It is not enough.

The creative man, the actor, the song writer, the writer, or the professional golfer has it. His life is not empty. He does not have to run to the church supper, to the community center, or to the fraternal committee meeting to establish an identity. His time is his own. Being creative alone ought to be enough. There are a few million men in America who would gladly do what Mickey Mantle does, for nothing. Baseball is a joy and it builds the body and teaches good sportsmanship. People sense an impropriety in the fact that on top of all of this Mantle also gets more than eighty thousand dollars a year.

The commercial society takes on the pain of mercantile endeavor. Secretaries misfile important correspondence, the employees are demanding a new water cooler on the factory floor, the salesman loses his samples, the raw material or the new part for the busted machine is delayed in transit. For all of this pain, the commercial society needs to reward itself with money. The creative man creates, that's his reward. But when the creative man makes money on top of it—well, this is just too much to bear.

So they ask, "How much are you making?" And whether you reply or not, they think it is too much.

Carl Sandburg

WHILE I was on tour with Carl Sandburg, promoting my book, *Carl Sandburg*, we chanced to stay in Chicago, the city of the big shoulders; but the cathedral, too, of middle-class values. After a day autographing books we retreated with newspapers to the hotel dining room.

The walls swirled with velvet draperies, candles flickered helplessly on each table in little cups of melted tallow, the heavy rug admitted no footsteps, and you could barely see your hand before your face. This is a dining room with atmosphere.

Carl would have none of it.

"Never eat," he said, "in a place where you can't read your newspaper." And indeed, that is the sterling test of any eatery, dining room, or steak house. If you can't read the newspaper, abandon ship.

Pity the classicist

CONGRESS has extended the National Defense Education Act, which grants monetary benefits, to teachers of modern languages—but not to teachers of Greek and Latin.

This is a mistake. If there are no classicists—who will interpret the mottoes of most of our States, not to mention the mottoes of dozens of colleges and universities?

I expect a professor of the classics to write a book on the subject and I grant him forthwith the title "Future Less Vivid," which is one of the subjunctive constructions every young classicist learns how to identify.

The test of the sophisticated city

SAUSALITO is one of the suburbs of San Francisco. It has a city council, and this year one of the candidates for a council seat is Aunt Sally Stanford. Aunt Sally is an old-time madam but now she is running on a ticket much like herself—namely, reform. Show me another city which can turn its madams into political aspirants and I will show you a sophisticated city.

This is good news for Sausalito, for one of the activities in which Aunt Sally will not indulge is the eternal yammering of committees. Aunt Sally is probably used to cash-on-the-barrel-head activities and let us hail her political future.

My cold remedy

WHEN I have a sore throat, which happens two or three times a year, and it does not seem serious enough for a visit to Dr. Wheeler, I call him and he prescribes something from the drugstore. I dutifully swallow his pills, but I also do something I would not dare confide to my doctor. I apply a remedy used fifty years ago on the Lower East Side. I put a hand towel under cold water and soak it until my hand itself starts becoming numb. Then I wrap the towel around my neck and wind a dry wool wrapper around that and fasten the whole harness with two safety pins. When I arise the next morning, the cold towel is as hot as if it had been steamed and I am usually cured. Then again, I might be cured because of the wonder drugs. I'll never know. But I always use both.

Another effective East Side remedy I tried in later years was the use of hot packs on crying children when they could not get to sleep with a sore throat. First you applied a hand towel rinsed in warm water. Then a second hand towel, hotter than the first, was applied, and after that a third rinsed in still hotter water.

Over this went the wool muffler. The two outside towels were removed one at a time and reapplied, leaving the first one on. After an hour the child fell asleep and everything was all right.

On foreign relations

ONE of our crass stupidities is not realizing the strength of the most potent legislation of our times—social security. Spanish broadcasts could so easily voice the benefits of social security which they do not do now. Uncle José returns to one of the Latin-American countries after working thirty years in the United States and there he sits every month and Uncle Sam sends him a check—*magnífico!* Do Uncle José and his assorted friends hate Uncle Sam? Social Security—*sí;* communism—no! I do not have the time to undertake this public relations job for the Government, but I will gladly help. If they send a man down to Charlotte I will map the whole thing out—for free.

The Cub Scouts

TODAY, the Cub Scout pack never sees the woods. Gone are the days when the pack came back, one boy badly stung by bees, one with a deep cut inflicted while whittling, and still a third sporting the beginnings of poison ivy. None of the little Cubs knows how to tie a bowline or even blaze a path on the bark of trees.

It was my shock to learn about the institution of den mother. The poor kids today get too much of mother as it is, and she herds the pack into the warmth and comfort of the living room, turns on the television, passes cookies and lemonade around on a tray, and afterward discusses the program. This will really make men out of them.

How to register with another woman

WE HAD a motel raid here in Charlotte which tumbled some eminently respectable businessmen out of their beds and some even nicer ladies with them. While vice-squad raids are not common, nevertheless they are a constant source of menace. There is a way, however, to insure perfect safety.

When you register at a motel, hotel, or tavern with another woman, always use a Jewish name. This puts you above all suspicion and also thwarts any private detective scouring the area. No one makes up a Jewish name, or so people imagine. You're always safe at motels or hotels or taverns with such names as: Tom Ginsburg, Danny A. L. Levy, or Wallace Garfunkle.

Lincolnton, North Carolina

LINCOLNTON, North Carolina, is a textile town with about 6,000 people. The story is that the Southern Railway people debated a choice between Lincolnton and Charlotte for its terminal, and if they had picked Lincolnton instead of Charlotte, perhaps Lincolnton would now have the 200,000 and more people and Charlotte the 6,000 people. These things are always interesting to contemplate. There's a little puff of gaseous cloud in front of the sun. If it hadn't wandered into that position by accident, a few hundred million years ago, there'd be no Charlotte, Paris, nor Lincolnton at all, since life as we know it cannot exist in a temperature of 600 degrees Fahrenheit.

Protecting your car

IT HAS been remarked that human nature is so constructed that if a man tosses an unstamped letter out of his window, a passer-by is sure to buy the postage and mail it. People hold mail as a sacred trust and rarely desecrate its privacy.

There is another sacred trust we instinctively accept. We are an automobile culture and consequently a nation of automobile robbers. Cars are stolen every minute of the day and it is an inconvenience we have accustomed ourselves to. With one exception. No one ever steals a car whose motor is idling. It's as though we hold this to be unfair; it takes an unnatural advantage. To steal a car, you have to jump the wires, not simply release the brake.

The cruelest phrase

Don't mind me, I'm broad-minded" is the cruelest and most depressing of all phrases. It is the statement of an ego inflated with dreams of its own moral superiority. The phrase denies and dismisses art.

A good friend comes up behind you at the office party and you begin to explain that you were kissing the blonde only because it was her eighteenth birthday and he says, "Don't mind me, I'm broad-minded." Right away everything is sinful and there is no grace left in your explanation.

The only revenge you can hope for is to catch this fellow some day when he walks out of a brothel and, as he starts to say that the only reason he was there was to read the gas meter, you interrupt him with, "Don't mind me, I'm broad-minded."

The time is out of joint

I fear we don't take time seriously. I remember a debate some years ago between some intellectuals which had for its subject the question, "Is Iago a Liberal?" to which proposal one of the more common-sense intellectuals asked, "Does Desdemona buy her shoes at Bergdorf Goodman's?"

This is not the way it is

THE soap operas, which are the mainstay of television's daytime hours, are the most invidious of all the television genre.

They urge interference in the lives of others. The whole soap-opera idea is based on such intrusion. Every day on several networks, lines like the following are repeated:

"Why don't you tell Ellen to have a baby?"

"You know it will never work out between you and Jan."

"Claire is upset. I know you are both set on going, but you really shouldn't."

"Why don't you talk to her and tell her what's right?"

"There are two things you can both do . . ."

Will you tell me, please, who the hell lives like that?

A great experience

IF YOU hear that there is a naturalization process for new citizens at your courthouse, go. If a new citizen asks you to be his witness, agree. It is one of the pleasantest and happiest honors you can partake in. New citizens need two responsible witnesses, and never are people closer in good will. Hearing a new citizen take the oath of allegiance and swear his loyalty is like the happiness you feel about a baby's birth or the joy that surrounds a wedding. The judges who question the prospective citizens and confer citizenship upon them say they never tire of the work. They could do it night and day. There are mighty few great experiences in life; don't miss this one.

Progress in treating mental illness

THE scientists of the Western world have often said that Russian scientists, unlike their politicians, rarely lie. Anything their scientists tell us is invariably reliable.

The Russians have been experimenting with a new treatment for insanity. A long, drug-induced sleep has been found to aid materially in the treatment of mentally disturbed people.

Scientists at our own Lafayette Clinic in Detroit, Michigan, have taken the opposite tack. They have deprived normal, healthy, intelligent people of sleep and discovered that after a long period of wakefulness, the responses become those of the insane—there are delusions, desperation, an inability to concentrate.

Sleep, or the lack of it, brings about certain biochemical changes. As the personality alters, so does blood. As perception wanes, so does energy.

"The innocent sleep, sleep that knits up the ravell'd sleave of care."

How to improve TV

MARK TWAIN was wrong. He said, "Everybody talks about the weather, but nobody does anything about it." Mark Twain was wrong because he lived before the advent of television and the 6:30 A.M., noon, 7:30 P.M., and late-evening weather report. Everybody is doing something about the weather—on television, at any rate. Add up the number of people who appear daily and nightly to explain the barometer and the highs and the lows and they exceed easily the gigantic cast of *Ben-Hur*.

I do not understand it. I do not understand television's recurring, never-abating concern with the weather. After all, you have only to look out the window to tell what the weather's like. You hardly need a battery of toothy girls and weather experts to tell you that it is raining.

I live three hundred miles inland from the sea and twenty miles from the nearest river, and every night and morning, I notice that our television informers post me about the tides. High tide will be at six, they tell me, low at 5:49. It is not very interesting.

Nor can I say that the barometer readings absorb me. I am not even sure what a barometer does, except that in those South Sea Island pictures Hollywood turned out in the thirties, whenever the barometer fell, you knew Terangue was going to get caught in the hurricane.

From long experience, I have found that most of my views can often stand correction. My honorable secretary, the mother of three teen-agers, informs me that her brood watches the weather report on the family television set the first thing in the morning: the girls want to know what to wear.

Even if I grant this utility to the weather report, it still does not explain the long list of highs and lows, and the big map of the United States with all the arrows and cartoons, and the updrafts and the low drafts and the fronts—these things certainly don't indicate fashion changes. I don't think the people who describe it understand it, let alone the people who plot it.

If we took Twain's comment and made of it a moral dictum and did nothing about the weather, we'd all be better off and television would be immeasurably improved.

Do not get excited

AT LEAST ten billion years ago, a supernova exploded, just as other supernovae are exploding at this very moment. But this particular explosion involved a giant star, larger than our sun, and it resulted in the formation of our universe. Gases from this explosion flooded into space at the rate of two or three million miles an hour.

Then these gases began to condense. One of them was a molten body and, as it cooled, a thin layer of crust began to form around it. Surrounding this spheroid was a thick atmosphere of air and water vapors. As this sphere kept spinning, a bulge formed on one end of it and eventually ripped off and spun into space. The earth and the moon were now in place. The hole left by this rupture left a scar in the Pacific Ocean basin.

As Earth kept cooling, it began to take up gases and solids left in the wake of the supernova's explosion. These were rocks, none of which are more than two billion years old, and radioactive material, which we are just beginning to dig up.

For millions of more years, however, methane, carbon dioxide, nitrogen, and other gases blanketed the spheroid, effectively shielding its surface from the sun with a ring of dense clouds. Then the gases settled into the earth and allied themselves cata- lytically, and the sun broke through and great oceans were formed. Before this, our planet resembled the planet Venus—carbon di- oxide instead of oxygen filled the atmosphere.

But the settling of the gases let the carbon begin to combine into other forms and one day in the bottom of the ocean some material turned from inorganic to organic and the process of "life" had begun.

One day the air itself around Earth was clear and bright and ready for something to breathe. Eventually these growths in the ocean would come into the sunlight. They would change their form from one composed of jelly to one with rigid parts, and one of the things they would need on land would be something to feed upon.

There is strong suspicion that the first plant to nourish life was very similar to that material we call today reindeer moss. It is found all over the earth, at the equator and at the North Pole, in the brightest sunlight and in the densest jungle.

This life-making process never stops. Slime dredged from the ocean in our own time has revealed new types of organic if jelly- like molecules which in millions of years may enter upon the earth.

Contemplating all this enables me to remain calm in the face of the announcement that they've canceled the flight from San Francisco to Milwaukee, where I have a speech at eight o'clock.

2.
INNOCENT ABROAD—
CIGAR-FIRST

The universal foreign policy

I SPOKE to prostitutes in England, France, Denmark, Germany, Israel, and Korea, and found none of the girls interested in DeGaulle, Macmillan, Ben-Gurion, Nasser, Algiers, Gaza, or Red China. They all have one foreign policy. They worry about—the police. The policeman is the prostitute's calculated risk.

For these interviews a friend or a taxi driver guided me and served as interpreter, where necessary.

It was important that I came not as a customer. A business relationship would have cast a different light on conversation and my interview would have had no value. The girls spoke to me frequently because I was obviously not a local policeman and because I offered them in every case double the regular fee for the same time a customer would take.

I found the French are a particularly moral people. Even the imbibing of wine, which makes the rest of the world raise its eyebrows, is in many instances only a way to wash down some of their badly cooked food in the provinces.

The English, whose food is equally bad and whose wine is nonexistent in addition, have poorer morals. For years the English have permitted the myth of French immorality to persist while it is they themselves who have been getting away with murder.

In what the Frenchman calls "the love," the Englishman is the champ. The reason England had an empire is because they are the only people whose pattern of speech enables them to converse without the use of their hands, a trait which impressed the primitives and the Fuzzy-Wuzzies.

Do not, however, let that reserve fool you. They used it to impress the natives; they found they could fool the rest of the world with it, too.

Two years ago, new legislation took the London prostitutes off the streets. On my first visit there the girls had lined themselves up in Mayfair, not far from the American Embassy, but on my next visit the new law was in operation and the girls had to resort to other methods. The bulletin boards on store windows are filled with advertisements of prostitutes—"French taught" or "Dancing lessons"—and each notice includes a name and telephone number.

In the last twenty years, amateur competition has reduced the earnings of the prostitute among the unmarried young men, but she still does a good business with the middle-aged natives and with the foreign businessmen and with the tourists. The "amateur" girl, who works in office or factory, cannot be had for the beckoning; she must be courted. And this takes time and propinquity. The casual visitor to a city, businessman or tourist, does not have the time and cannot establish propinquity.

In London the call girl who works at the better hotels is available at pretty fancy prices not much lower than the going rate on New York's Park Avenue and, interestingly enough, these girls take American Express money orders, following the procedure of big-time gamblers and, I suspect, learning it from them. She asks her client to write hs passport number on the back of the money order. Prostitutes, in fact, prefer American Express money orders because a man is likely to be a little more generous with a money order than with cash. Why this should be, I don't know, but that's what the girls tell me. Sometimes the customer may be drinking heavily and give the girl two fifties instead of one. The girl sends a post card to the American Express Company the next morning saying, "I received the following money orders for services rendered," and she lists the numbers and amounts and signs her name and address. In the event the customer files a loss claim with the Express office, the clerk tells him he probably forgot that he had bought something and that the salesperson has notified them.

The interesting thing about prostitutes in Copenhagen, Paris, London, Athens, and Rome is that many of the girls hold regular jobs during the day. They work in factories or in offices and they use their nighttime oldest profession to supplement their earnings.

In Korea prostitution is much more than a matter of passing interest or sociological study. It is a serious political problem because it involves us, the United States. I am certain that one of the several reasons for the upheavals in Korea in the last three years has been this problem of prostitution.

A Korean newspaperman told me, "The Japanese did not make whores out of our young girls; they brought their own engineers and their own skilled workers in order to keep us as hewers of wood and carriers of water. They also brought their own women."

He told me that the American soldier has turned thousands of young Korean girls into prostitutes. Their presence and generosity and the intense poverty of the country combine to make thousands of little girls come from the rice fields and from the villages and from the hills into the cities.

In Seoul these girls gather around the Monument (statue of General J. B. Coultner), and, I do not exaggerate, for the first ten days after payday, a soldier cannot pass in his jeep because so many girls solicit him; they literally stop his forward movement.

Many of these Korean girls are young. All are very beautiful. After these girls are twenty-five or so it is an entirely different story, but from the age of twelve to sixteen, they have little chalk-white cameo faces, which they stick into the windows of the car, crying, over and over, "Good time, good time, good time."

The first ten days after payday the girls charge the soldiers seven dollars. The second ten days after payday, it is three dollars. And the last few days before payday there is a common understanding, an unwritten covenant, that a dollar, even fifty cents, will take care of it.

Since most American boys cannot pronounce the Korean names, the dance halls, night clubs, and brothels have adopted numbers. Each girl that a soldier sits with at a night club or a restaurant immediately gives her number, "I am number nineteen." There may be eight or nine girls sitting around and you tell the madam you want number seven or nineteen or whatever the case may be.

Prostitutes in Jerusalem? "Why should this surprise you?" replied my Israeli friend and guide. "We are a civilized nation. We have everything just like everybody else."

The Israeli Penal Code, based on the British law, does not forbid prostitution. But there are three punishable offenses connected with the oldest profession: soliciting, keeping a brothel, living on the earnings of a prostitute. And there is a fourth offense, indirectly connected: spreading a venereal disease.

On the other hand, a healthy girl, accepting an offer and taking the client to her own home, does not break the law. A brothel, according to Israeli law, is a place used for prostitution by at least two women. A place where only one girl "works" is not a brothel.

Still, there is a risk even for one girl working in an apartment: the landlord may ask the court for her eviction. This means financial disaster. Rents in Israel are very low, but for a lease you must pay a premium. They call it "key money" and it amounts to several thousand dollars, even for a small apartment. When the tenant leaves, he receives two thirds of his "key money" back. But if he is evicted by an order of the court, he loses his whole investment.

The Israeli police are not hard on prostitutes. Since there are few "brothels" as defined by the law, the most frequent accusation against them is "soliciting." Even this is used only if a girl is suspected of associating with criminals. The police, however, do not extend this leniency to panderers. The average prison term is three years for a man convicted of living off the earnings of a prostitute.

There are about three hundred prostitutes in the country, divided into three groups: The "French" prostitutes, who "claim" to be from Paris, but who are really Jewish immigrants from Morocco, Tunis, and Algiers. These are the girls for the "workingman," walking the streets of Tel Aviv, Jaffa, Haifa, and Beersheba. Quite a few of them are married and have children.

The second group, by far the majority, are girls who emigrated from Romania, Hungary, and Poland. They are the uprooted. Many of them lost their families in the Nazi holocaust. I was told they lack the enthusiasm for the hard work required of everyone in the building of a new country.

The third group and the smallest are the Sabras, the native-born Israeli girls and, surprisingly, most of them are of Yemenite origin. "Surprisingly" because the Yemenites are the most pious Jews in Israel. But there are reasons to explain this phenomenon: the girls grow up in large families (ten children is not unusual), they are very poor, and they live in an ultra-orthodox atmosphere.

(In Paris and Rome a few of the girls had pictures of the Bleeding Heart of Jesus over their beds. They told me they go to Mass regularly.) In the Yemenite family only the boys "count," the girls are "secondary." And the temptation is strong to escape not only poverty but also this lesser role in life. They go to the streets very young, about sixteen or seventeen, but they live in constant fear of the family. A police official told me that when a father or a brother finds out what the girl is up to, he beats her unmercifully.

The institution of the call girl does not exist in Israel. A telephone is still a luxury. It is expensive and you wait a year for the installation. Few girls stay that long in one place. They walk the streets or solicit in bars and night clubs. The majority of the prostitutes work in Tel Aviv, the biggest city, and in Haifa, the main port. A few stroll the streets of Beersheba and there are some in Jerusalem. Somehow, the atmosphere of Jerusalem doesn't fit with the profession, but during the tourist season many of the Tel Aviv girls descend upon the ancient Hebrew capital.

The prices vary according to the girl, the customer, and the place—"pornography is a question of geography."

The girls who solicit the "workingman" get fifteen Israeli pounds ($5.00). The same girl asks for twenty pounds from a man past middle age and anywhere from thirty to one hundred pounds from a tourist.

For years Tel Aviv was probably the only city in the world with a population of over one hundred thousand, without prostitutes. This was in the pioneering times, before the state was declared, before the big immigration started. Bialik, the great Hebrew poet, has been quoted often: "Tel Aviv, the first modern Jewish city in the world will not be a real city as long as it doesn't produce some criminals and prostitutes." Bialik may rest in peace. His wish has been fulfilled.

The "pioneer" of prostitution in Israel is an old Polish Jew known by everybody as Berele. He operated a "house" in Jaffa, which the police closed when Israel became a state. This fellow keeps Israelis in stitches with his arrogant letters to the Open Forum of the press. He demands legislation that will permit him to operate another brothel, and he says he is prepared to split his

income fifty-fifty with the government. He claims that public
health, the welfare of the poor girls, the well-being of the lonely
men, the future of the tourist industry, to say nothing of his own
well-being, all depend on the legalization of prostitution. To no
avail.

Jews make entertainment out of everything. The most popular
quiz program in Israel is a Bible contest. It is a well-organized
event, and the participants are scholars, farmers, soldiers, and
students. A panel of Biblical scholars ask the questions; such as,
"How many soldiers did David lose in the battle against the Phi-
listines?" Or, "How old was Jonah when he arrived at Nineveh?"

Abraham Shlonsky, one of Israel's best-known poets, has criticized the contest. He says that Biblical knowledge should go
deeper than statistics. "Next time," says poet Shlonsky, "the con-
testants will be asked the telephone number of Rahab, the whore
of Jericho."

Another story concerns the octogenarian founders of a kibbutz
on the Sea of Galilee. They were discussing some disturbing news,
allegedly that there are prostitutes walking the streets of Tel Aviv!
Jewish girls? Impossible! They simply refused to believe it, and it
was decided that the youngest of the group, Rachel, age seventy-
six, would take the kibbutz's milk-car to Tel Aviv and check on
the rumor.

In the evening she returned and sadly reported, "It's true."
"But," she added triumphantly, "none of them belongs to our
generation!"

In Teheran I visited a brothel numbering about eight girls, but
instead of the inevitable madam there was a man directing the
operations. And another surprise; one of the English-speaking girls
was from Brooklyn, of all places. How a Jewish girl from Brooklyn wound up in a Teheran brothel, I'll never know, for she was
vague about the whole thing. I told her she has an interesting
story to tell and she said what each of the other girls around the
world said to me: "I'll write a book some day."

This brothel caters to a high-class clientele, local businessmen
and visiting oil executives. The girls sit around modestly, well-
dressed, chatting with the customers, then one of them, with a

client, will walk slowly to the stairway as though she were a hostess showing off a suburban home. There is no piano.

The brothel in Teheran uses the same system as an upper-class brothel in Paris. The customer selects a girl and she takes him into a room with no bed. It is a kind of conference room for a "summit meeting." The deal is closed and the client pays the money agreed upon. The girl disappears, presumably to turn a portion of the money over to the manager, for which she gets a key to an empty room. She returns to the conference room and leads her client to the assigned room. Here she will also expect a tip and will ask in addition the inevitable, "How about a drink?"

In every brothel, the prostitute earns an additional commission on the sale of drinks. The price around the world is uniform, more or less—the equivalent of one American dollar.

In Germany I looked upon the most interesting prostitution system in the world. The same thoroughness and efficiency goes into prostitution in Germany as goes into the rebuilding of an economy or of a military organization.

Some restraint, humor, and even charm characterize the prostitutes around the world. But it is a pretty cold business in the city of Hamburg. There is nothing to match it anywhere, not even in the Far East. The district spread along the waterfront is called St. Pauli and there are at least four hundred bars, night clubs, brothels, and strip-tease joints as well as clubs openly catering to lesbians and homosexuals.

Two streets constitute main thoroughfares, the broad boulevard called Reeperbahn, and Grosse Freiheit (Great Freedom). It is Great Freedom Street which can boast of wall-to-wall brothels, with but one exception—the majestic St. Joseph's Roman Catholic Church.

In this district there are also the two blocks of brothels on a street called Herbert Strasse which the Germans have nicknamed, "The Meat Market." These two blocks are barricaded at both ends by heavy steel fences, so high that no one passing the adjoining streets can see what is going on inside. The fences are solid, without peepholes, but they have an opening on each side for pedestrians. Once you are inside there are two rows of old three-story brick houses, each with a large store-type display window at street level. In these windows, exactly like displayed merchandise, sit the women, offering themselves at a fixed price based on quality.

The average price is twenty marks, or five dollars, not counting, of course, the commission on drinks. In these display windows are women who by dress and motions indicate that they have something for everybody.

Even the most famous restaurant in the area, Café Keese, is part of this system. The proprietor spoke to me with great pride of the respectable clientele. But when you go to the men's room in this high-class restaurant, conspicuously displayed in glass cases are every sort of phallus and sexual contraption, some of which I am sure would have astonished the late Dr. Kinsey. Also displayed are pictures of nudes and advertisements for sex pills supposed to awaken sexual desire "within three hours."

Germany has full employment today and actually imports Greeks, Italians, and Spaniards by the thousand to fill the manpower need. Yet prostitution thrives. My German newspaper friend shook his head sadly. "No, it's not poverty, it's something else," he said, adding, "every single one of these hundreds of prostitutes on the Reeperbahn goes home in a taxi, while the working people around her take the streetcar or hike to their jobs."

One of the interesting ladies of easy virtue I talked to was an English girl living and working in Paris. She had been born in Wales, lived at Swansea as a young girl. She told me matter-of-factly that, after the usual unhappy marriage, she hied herself to London where she walked the streets.

London, she said, is a prostitute's nightmare. After two years, she came to Paris where she has worked ever since. No less than one-half of her English customers, she told me, came along with whips and boots with spurs and contraptions and fiendish ingenuity of all kinds. But in France she lives a decent, well-adjusted life with her normal French clients.

This particular prostitute also told me the easiest mark in Europe is an American, who brightens perceptibly when a prostitute asks him, "Hi there! You from Texas?" Almost all Texans are millionaires and I suppose there is no more subtle form of flattery than to let some fellow believe others figure him for millions.

Anyway it appears that every American wants to be taken for a Texan.

She said another gambit that works well with Americans is to tell them they are the first customer of the day, explaining she had two other offers but they were Algerians and "I don't sleep with coloreds." She says this always brings a smile of happiness and an extra ten dollars. She told me her Negro lover gave her this advice.

The prostitute with the best sense of humor is in my own home town, Charlotte, North Carolina. When I asked her about her profession she said that she took to hustling the hotels because she had become fed up with her social position. Her father, she said, was a steam fitter, and the only men she ever met as a young girl were steam fitters. "But now I meet bankers, doctors, lawyers, salesmen, dentists, editors, and publishers."

The best story of this entire experience came from one of three call girls I spoke to in a San Francisco apartment. Her name was Nova, a delicately beautiful girl about twenty-six years old. She told me her husband had an agency for a line of paints and varnishes and it was a struggle to get the business on a paying basis. Nova found it expedient to start a little business of her own, and when her husband became aware of it he kicked her out, closed up the business, and took off for his former home in the East.

Nova then went into the business seriously and with one purpose in mind. She wanted money, and saved every penny with a single-minded penuriousness that would have done justice to old man Scrooge. Nova would walk before she would spend fifteen cents on a cable car; and she had her shoes resoled and bought simple dresses in the bargain basements.

Her clients found this appealing and were generous to her— "Here is a poor kid down on her luck." Nova told pathetic stories about illness in her family—all of whom, as a matter of fact, were phenomenally healthy except for her grandma who got a slipped disc at eighty when she fell off a bar stool.

And so Nova saved her money until it amounted to a small fortune. "Nova," I asked, "were you saving your money with some investment in mind?"

"No," she answered frankly. "I just liked the stuff; it was a game to see how much I could stack up." Then, sadly, "Did the other girls tell you I don't have it any more?"

"No, they didn't, Nova, what happened?"

And here is her story word for word:

"Well, I never saw any future in tipping. This laundryman received commissions on the side from the other girls, but I just paid him what he had coming each week. He had a record of how much business I gave him and turned me in to the Income Tax people for the informer's pay. From his list they figured how much business I had done and after penalties and everything, I figure the first guy to the moon will get there on my money."

I persuaded Nova to have a drink with me. We silently drank a toast to the space program.

Parking meters in the Holy Land

IN ISRAEL, which gave the world Judaism, Christianity, and Islam, you now can find parking meters. Where once the prophets trod as they wended toward Mount Tabor, now a car may park for one-half hour for fifty agorets (about two and a half cents). And where the prophet Elijah mounted his fiery chariot for the heavens there's now a one-way street.

But the modern Israelis take parking tickets in their stride. They adjust to them as they adjust to hostile Arabs and friendly American tourists. That is not to say a bitter struggle did not accompany this process of resignation. Indeed it did. The Israeli police had a tough time. But like policemen everywhere, eventually they prevailed. Serving a traffic summons was, in the beginning, a rough proposition, especially with the new immigrants.

The cop would signal the car to pull over to the curb. The occupants within were invariably surprised. Is this possible, they said, arresting a Jew in Israel? Immediately they recited to the policeman their long, sad history. They told him about the uprooting of their native communities, about the terror of the concentration camps, about the demeaning and hopeless life they led as DPs, about the struggle to arrive safely in Israel.

The Israeli cops were tolerant. They listened. When the motorist was through, the policeman said gently, "Here is your ticket. Everything you've told me, tell to the judge, too."

Israel has made some excellent advances in the science of traffic safety. The first step is the quick disposition of traffic violations. The traffic ticket lists all the violations and the fines levied for each. If it is a first offense, a guilty driver can attach his payment to the ticket and mail or deliver it to the court. A second offense costs exactly twice as much money for each violation. For a third offense, a violator must present himself before the court. The result is nearly always a suspension of his license.

The judge usually says, "The suspension will give you a chance to think over all your mistakes. When we decide to give you your license back, you can start a brand-new life. Next case."

Simpatico

IN RELATIONS with the rest of the world, it is not a matter of needing Republicans or Democrats, but rather needing a complete about-face in our attitudes. We need to accept humanity, and understand that these are people like ourselves. What we are getting in Cuba today is a result of our failure through the years. "Banana republics" is what we called them; not a country of people with problems and hopes, but "banana republics," which has produced the fierce hatred directed at us from Cuba and several other Latin-American countries. It was easy to lick Mexico, to send the Marines to Paraguay, to patronize the Panamanians. And we never paid the slightest attention to many Latin Americans of considerable stature we had among our own people. Instead we sent New Englanders as ambassadors, men who had no sympathy for these people. Behind them came the big companies, vast mechanized monsters systematically removing the oil and the sugar and the raw materials. With friendship and a sense of partnership, discarding the "banana republic" attitude, we could have built a tremendous moral force among our neighbors that would have been a model for the world.

Nothing else perhaps is as inflexible as a contractual relationship. It is sound but it isn't warm or comforting, and it has weights and measures in the nature of it that have no appeal to the emotional Latin.

The contractual agreement makes us cold, precise, and calculating. We make a bargain and stick to it; the contractual relationship is sacred.

The Latin gives his word, and shrugs at all the fine print. To stir him emotionally is to find him either a fierce enemy or a devoted friend. It is up to us to see that all two hundred and twenty-six millions of our Latin-American neighbors are stirred favorably toward us.

All the upheavals and protests around the world have been triggered by one singular need—this need for human dignity. This is true in countries where the most unbelievable poverty exists, where whole families never see more than one hundred and fifty dollars a year in hard money, where sanitation conditions are as primitive as they were in the twelfth century; yet when the students get out on the square to do their snake dance and shout slogans it is not for wages or shorter hours or for increased foreign aid from the United States. In every case it has had to do with their status as human beings, their need for acceptance as part of the open society of mankind, as equals.

It is on this basis, I believe, that President Kennedy's Peace Corps has one ingredient missing. I believe that this ingredient is a Peace Corps from "them" to "us" in exchange for our students and technicians from us to them. This is our most immediate problem in Latin America.

We can say of the peoples in the Far East as well as in Eastern Europe that they have been intimidated, threatened, and subverted by the Kremlin.

But can we say this of our neighbors in Latin America, seven thousand miles from the Kremlin?

If many of these peoples, traditionally the most ardent Christians in the Western world, suddenly find the philosophy in the Kremlin desirable, is this not the time to go deeply into the subject to find out why and to do everything possible to avert what might become our greatest tragedy?

Without peaceful progressive democracies as neighbors, how can we impress the nations of the Far East and Africa to emulate our way of life? Every American should take time out from his daily duties and learn something about Latin America.

We should exchange literature and invite students by the thousand, and welcome visitors and demonstrate plain old-fashioned friendship and hospitality. If we show that we wish to learn as well as to teach, we will find this a most rewarding experience.

We should have dozens of students from each country below the Rio Grande studying and working in our country for a year or two.

Unless the South Americans are given a wider and ever-increasingly broader view and share of our way of life, a new fascism will continue to flourish throughout their continent.

Around the world people have heard of Kim Novak but not of Dr. Jonas Salk. We do not need to ban Miss Novak from the screen, but we do need to show people the image of the thousands and thousands of compassionate men and women in America who would gladly, if but given the impetus, exhibit their natural *simpático* feeling for South America. That word means more in Spanish than one can imagine. It is here, in the American breast, and we need to give it full expression.

It is not too late.

Reading and Rivington Streets

READING STREET is about to disappear. Reading Street is one of the oldest streets in Liverpool, England, but it is earmarked for demolition under a new slum-clearance program. Eventually, new two-story houses will take the place of the balconied tenements that string along this famous thoroughfare. While living accommodations in the new English corporation dwellings will be better and more sanitary, many of the people who have lived their lives along Reading Street leave it with regret.

Reading Street is where the immigrants to Liverpool moved as soon as they landed in England. Thus the street used to resemble

Rivington Street on the Lower East Side of New York. Perhaps it looked grimy and dirty, but immigrant sections always hold within them a sense of life and purpose that seems often strangely absent from the green-lawned suburbs. Places like Reading Street in Liverpool and Rivington Street in New York exist in anticipation. They offer hope and promise, and these two qualities make them more than places to live; they make them an idea.

The immigrants who lived along Rivington Street in New York were for the most part Eastern European Jews. The immigrants who lived along Reading Street were the Irish who fled famine and depression in their homeland and came to Liverpool to make a new life. There the differences ended.

Pushcarts and peddlers and signs advertising "Lecture tonight" decorated Rivington Street. They were proof of a great vitality. Along Reading Street there were handcart girls who sold fruit. Street singers, that venerable British institution, strolled along and the children tossed pennies from the balconies. Rag-and-bone men made their weekly collections and, from Brownlow Hill, the Jewish section of Liverpool, came the eyeglass salesmen. The Jews also sold needles, thread, yard goods, and panes of glass to repair broken windows.

The immigrants along Reading Street clothed themselves with a "clothing cheque." They would place a down payment on a book of cheques (coupons) for a complete outfit at a designated clothing store and then they would pay so much a week to have one coupon punched. When the coupons were all punched, the clothes were free and clear. The immigrants on Rivington Street also bought on the installment plan: a solid gold watch, a trousseau, and steerage passage for their relatives to join them in America. On Reading Street the fellow selling on the installment plan was called the "cheque man," and on Rivington Street he was called the "customer peddler."

The delights of Denmark

IN DENMARK, the folks are always eating. They serve oysters there that are so plump they have to be cut in two with a knife, and over these oysters they squeeze the juice of one lemon. After the oysters come the whole smorgasbord and cheeses of all colors and shapes, including a green cheese that resembles Port du Salut. After the cheeses, the whitefish, and after the whitefish— steak. They have all kinds of steak in Denmark, from beef to reindeer. The desserts are beyond description. Accompanying all of this is the excellent Danish beer, Paaske beer.

The Danes' gusto for food carries no guilt with it. But there are countless Americans who enjoy shrimp pan roast for lunch and rise from the table with terrible guilt about calories.

The Danes are one and one-half missile-minutes away from the Soviet Union. Yet in Denmark there is absolutely no fear of the Soviet bombs or of "Reds" in general. No writer or editor has to plead first that he hates "Reds" before he says what he thinks. Denmark has no investigating committees. There are no pressures against public expression of any kind, and no penalties against the "wildest" talk.

In the last election, the Communists failed to garner enough votes to seat the Communist Party representatives in the Danish Parliament. Under Danish law a political party must receive enough votes to seat five candidates.

All the Danes I talked to regretted this Communist defeat. A Communist delegation in the Parliament had its uses. It provided the Danes with a forum in which to answer Communist philosophy and also gave them a chance to analyze Soviet policy, which could hardly make the Communists look good to the Danes.

The Communists did not know how to exploit their loss. During elections all parties must receive equal time on television and they get space in the newspapers by tradition. After this devastating defeat, the Communist Party leader said, "We were beaten badly but it merely means the Danes are too stupid to see how right we Communists are." You can imagine what the Danes think of that fellow's political future.

In view of Denmark's precarious proximity to the USSR, it is worth investigating why they should have this uninhibited freedom of expression.

The Danes have free enterprise, socialized medicine, and the workers are completely unionized. Denmark is almost the perfect Social-Democratic society in miniature. Except for the postal system, of course, and roughly one-half of the transportation system everything in Denmark is privately owned and the profit system is the basis of the economy.

Denmark has apparently struck the proper balance. I have written often of this idea—that if the Communists, God forbid, came to America, the first people they would liquidate would be the trade unionists and Social-Democrats. These are the worst enemies of communism. Denmark is a country populated almost wholly by these enemies.

Danish socialized medicine started around World War I. It is based on the principle, "Pay according to your abilities, receive according to your needs." If you want, you can engage a private doctor. You pay for the program through a social security system. It is deducted weekly from your salary check. A man who makes the equivalent of forty dollars a week would pay fifty cents for medical insurance every payday.

I spoke to a panel doctor who has a list of 2,100 patients and to a laboratory scientist and both men agreed on the practicability of socialized medicine. The practitioner told me, "Socialized medicine means we are scientists, that we can devote all our energies to the profession for which we were trained." The biochemist said, "I look all day into my microscope with no worries about competing for patients or about collection agencies."

The Danish doctor averages eight thousand dollars a year in American money, which puts him in the upper reaches of the Danish middle class.

The income tax is high in Denmark, higher than in the United States. The average skilled worker makes 33,000 kroner a year, which would be approximately $4,500 in American money. But he pays 25 per cent to the government, while the skilled worker in America pays 17 per cent.

There are 4,500,000 Danes occupying 16,000 square miles. It is thought of as a dairy country but this is not quite correct. Fifty per cent of the Danish national income comes from industry, 45 per cent from agriculture, and 5 per cent from fishing. The country has no natural resources whatever—no iron, no coal, no oil. Thus, for generations, they have trained their workers for highly skilled precision work. The Danes export locomotives to India, and almost half the merchant ships at sea run on Danish Diesels.

Shipbuilding is a great industry. Though Denmark has only the population of North Carolina, it has one of the six largest merchant fleets.

Prostitution is legal in Denmark but there are no brothels. Most of the prostitutes hold down daily jobs in industry or offices. The extra money these girls make is never confiscated nor are they ever annoyed, except for laws against rape and impairing the morals of a minor. The going rate for a prostitute runs between seven dollars and twenty dollars a visit. The seven dollars is for the Danes, the twenty dollars for tourists.

The Danish Income Tax Bureau is sterner than the American Internal Revenue Service. The prostitutes are taxed, no maybe about it. The Danes have a great sense of humor and when the prostitutes do not declare their income, they are haled before the tax collector who makes a pretty educated guess at what the girl is earning. Even if he overestimates, no one's feelings are hurt.

There is no guilt about sexual intercourse in Denmark but this does not mean the Danes are salacious. Not at all. The Lutheran Church sanctions trial marriage and premarital relations are quite normal. I asked the Danish father of two teen-age girls what he thought about it. "Do you discuss it with your daughters?" I ventured.

"Yes," he said, "but not in terms of morality, only in terms of wisdom. I ask each of them if she thinks the boy with whom she might consider sex experience has honorable intentions and is the sort she would want for the father of her children."

Despite this uninhibited sex, young Danish girls are aware of the basic fact; no young Dane with good prospects will marry a promiscuous girl. Promiscuity is not considered immoral in Denmark, only stupid.

In the history of public understanding, probably no country ever made a less-informed attempt than Germany when she tried to Nazify Denmark.

There was one time during World War II when the whole Nazi establishment in Denmark decided on a gigantic parade. For eight hours, storm troopers and soldiers and Nazi bands marched through the streets of Copenhagen in an attempt to impress the Danes.

At one point in this parade, a Dane walked across the street, breaking right through one of the Nazi formations and continuing on to the other side.

The Nazis arrested him and brought him before the court. The Dane's defense was a classic one. He said he simply didn't see the Nazis parading.

They fined him forty dollars. I suspect they knew he was telling the truth.

Denmark did indeed have its native-born quislings, but its sense of democracy sustained its citizens. The Gandhi idea of passive resistance worked, even against the Gestapo. In fact, when victory came, dramatic events took place in thousands of Danish homes. Here, Danes lit candles and put them in the windows and they protected the German occupation force. They rounded them up and guarded them against violence. They were less kind to the few Danish renegades who had co-operated with the Nazis. Traitors were executed swiftly but no Germans were lynched.

Today, not a single German tourist comes to Denmark who occupied the country during the war. All the Germans who come say, "I was on the Eastern Front, fighting the Communists." The Danes laugh and drink beer.

Psychiatry around the world

THERE are more psychiatrists in one square block of Brooklyn than there are in all of France. One doctors' building in Beverly Hills, California, will produce more psychoanalysts than ever attended one of Dr. Freud's Congresses.

In Israel the folks are building a new country, from forests and meadows to dams and universities. They are always busy there, thinking of new ways to employ their time, and in Israel psychiatry is not a big thing, even though Jews discovered the science. The busier you are, the less psychiatry you need.

It is very interesting that the Anglo-Saxon world took to psychiatry like a duck takes to water. We have produced countless movies about the psychiatric experience and even employ the mother or father complex in our television Westerns. Yet I have never seen an Italian, a French, or a Japanese picture in which psychiatry was even mentioned.

The progress of Puerto Rico

I HAD a call from Government House inviting me to dinner at La Fortaleza, the fortress-palace of Don Luis Muñoz-Marín, the Governor of Puerto Rico. But the date set, March 13, was the eighth wedding anniversary of my son Bill and his wife Judy. I had promised them an evening. I explained this to the secretary who said he'd call me back. A few minutes later, Governor Muñoz bid me to bring the family and celebrate at La Fortaleza. (Bill, a Ph.D., teaches English at the University of Puerto Rico. Bill's wife attends one of his classes—modern poetry, three days a week —and is studying Spanish.) Judy rattled off instructions to the baby sitter like a native and in her mantilla and black dress looked like a Puerto Rican princess when we started out.

La Fortaleza was the first fortress built by the Spaniards in Puerto Rico, in time for the ships that made up Columbus's second expedition to sail before it, and though it was fired once, by the Dutch in 1625, it stands today much as it did when galleons sailed the Spanish Main.

Doña Inez, the Governor's charming wife, dined with us along with the daughters; one son-in-law, a psychiatrist, Dr. Efren Ramdrez; the Governor's grandchildren; and Professor and Mrs. Antonio J. Colorado. Professor Colorado, an old friend of Muñoz, teaches at the University. There was something both poignant and satisfying to see the grandchildren racing through halls where once conquistadores stored their gold and silver.

Doña Inez has a deep and abiding interest in the affairs of the world and she travels constantly with Don Luis Muñoz. She makes it a point to study the women's organizations in different countries and tours as many of the institutions for children as her time allows.

The Governor and I discussed the progress of Puerto Rico, which is so phenomenal that this beautiful island promises to become the democratic showcase for all Latin America.

"Some of our people now have ulcers and obituaries are full of heart failure," said Muñoz.

Thus Puerto Rico is the first Latin-American country to fall victim to middle-class diseases. Even in the most remote villages the children now have shoes and the debilitating hookworm disease has been effectively controlled.

The Puerto Rico Industrial Development Company (PRIDE) reports that one hundred and forty-eight new plants came into operation during 1961. All the plants helped by this PRIDE number more than seven hundred with direct employment for 50,500 and annual payrolls of one hundred million. This is a fantastic development for an agricultural society with practically no natural resources.

I had delivered a speech that day before the Puerto Rico Exchange Club in which I said communism is a political answer to a social problem and that the only effective countermeasure is an expanded program of social legislation.

The Governor was generous in commenting, "You are right, the cry of 'land and bread' hypnotized the hungry but this Communist slogan has failed wherever there is in progress a good program of social legislation."

By way of confirmation Muñoz pointed out that there is no law in Puerto Rico against Communist agitation, and the Reds had exactly two hundred and fifty-three write-in votes out of an electorate of seven hundred thousand.

"One of the tragedies of our present political life," said Muñoz, "is that in Europe and Latin America the word 'socialist' and 'social-democrat' are good words, words which connote a philosophy at opposite ends of the pole from communism, yet, in the States these words are now evil words, and this is very sad."

Some time before my visit, I had written an article urging statehood for Puerto Rico. I believe now that my article was a premature and uninformed judgment. Statehood would not be advantageous at this time. To achieve her own prosperity Puerto Rico must remain a commonwealth for the present generation at least. Her needs are entirely different from those of the fifty States.

We talked into the night with the help of excellent Puerto Rican brandy. Muñoz speaks a beautiful English. He spent his early boyhood in America and is reputed to have lived in Greenwich Village for a while, although when I asked him about this he said simply, "I visited there often."

Late that evening we took our brandy into the private projection room of La Fortaleza to see a movie. The chairs were very comfortable and to my deep chagrin I fell asleep. When I roused myself and realized what had happened, I looked around sheepishly. But I soon regained my composure. Don Luis, God love him, was sound asleep, too, and so I went back to sleep to be in shape for the next round.

A little after midnight we shook hands with the Governor and bid him good night and good health. I am certain my son and daughter-in-law will never forget their eighth wedding anniversary.

Only in Israel

ISRAEL is an exciting, ever-changing civilization. Its days are not filled with humdrum but with struggle. Israel is like what the frontier in America was one hundred and fifty years ago, perhaps even one hundred years ago. Pioneers are exciting people because they are excited about their land. The New Englanders at the beginning of the eighteenth century were excited, the folks who came from Ireland and Scotland to North Carolina were excited, and so, too, were the Mormons who crossed the great deserts.

Here is a typical day in Israel. In the morning the usual package arrives from Greensboro, North Carolina. John Simons mails it from his Postal Box 204. This John Simons has a delightful hobby. He collects all the free literature available from the United States Government bureaus, from life insurance companies, steel companies, and large industrial concerns, packages them, and mails them to different places in Israel. Ein Hashofet, my favorite kibbutz, is one of the recipients of Mr. Simons' largess, and the folks there tell me this literature is very valuable and has helped them in their work.

After Mr. Simons' package is opened and disseminated, some farmers in a kibbutz in the Jordan Valley discover a skeleton over half a million years old.

About four in the afternoon, Mr. Otto Preminger, the Hollywood producer on location in Israel, complains about all the tsores (worry) he is having. Mr. Preminger is rushed for time because he's supposed to open this superstarred production in New York in December. A storekeeper is suing him for five thousand Israeli pounds, because Mr. Preminger sealed off the street where this storekeeper does business and this caused not only a loss of trade but a severe case of nerves.

Only in Israel.

The Hawaiians are vigilant

THERE'S no trouble like the trouble you can stir up with Hawaiians. They watch you like a hawk. They never forgive. Now they're mad at me. But I join select company. I join James Michener, George Bernard Shaw, H. Allen Smith, the State Department, and the Historical Society Museum of Oregon.

George Bernard Shaw refused to wear one of the flower leis when he arrived in Hawaii. James Michener said he didn't like the muu muu. H. Allen Smith declared against the aloha shirt. Each of these actions called forth a spate of angry letters to the editor, inspired mass movements, and brought round condemnation from the citizens on that long-extinct volcano.

Hawaii makes more trouble for the State Department than Nikita does at a vodka party. The State Department recently reclassified Hawaii by changing the average temperature for the tropics from 75 to 76 degrees Fahrenheit. Hawaii has an average of 75.2 degrees. This means the Hawaiians will catch pneumonia. They are very near secession.

Not content with this, the Hawaiians are also directing heavy abuse against the Historical Society Museum of Oregon. The Oregonians recently displayed the first printing press west of the Mississippi. Not only does Hawaii claim the first printing press west of the Mississippi, but it also maintains the Oregon printing press was donated to a Portland newspaper by a missionary in Hawaii.

In my book *For 2¢ Plain* I had a story about Queen Liliuokalani, Hawaii's last monarch. In the course of the story I confused James B. Dole, the pineapple king, with Sanford B. Dole, Hawaii's first governor. Oy vay iz mir (Woe is me). The mail from indignant Hawaiians almost broke the backs of laboring Charlotte postmen. More people in Hawaii knew the differences between the two Doles than knew the words of the "Star-Spangled Banner."

Also, the mailing list of my newspaper inadvertently had been carrying the Hawaiian subscribers as "foreign." It's hard to explain that this wasn't my fault, and there is nothing for it except to apologize. I am sorry *The Carolina Israelite* called residents of the fiftieth State "foreign." From now on, subscriptions to my paper will cost Hawaiians three dollars, not four dollars (the extra dollar that is charged to foreign lands). I will do better than that. I'll make the subscription rate retroactive. I'll gladly refund a dollar to every subscriber in Hawaii with my sincere apology. I'll do anything to make peace with the Hawaiians.

The Scotsman

CHARLOTTE is the citadel of the Southern Presbyterian Church in the United States and my readers will understand my deep interest in both Presbyterianism and Scotland.

When I spoke over the BBC in London, a reporter for *The Scotsman*, one of the most influential newspapers in Britain, asked me on what basis I suggested that the Presbyterians are one of the Ten Lost Tribes of Israel. I told the reporter that this was merely a humorous attempt to express my affection for my neighbors, but the reporter would have none of that. He insisted on

handling the story straight, and I fell right in line with his thinking and enumerated a dozen "facts" to support my idea.

After the interview was over I realized that there are probably
many other "facts" which we accept as history, and which are
based on a foundation just as flimsy as the idea that the Scots
were originally Hebrews.

But I do not relax in my efforts to learn as much as possible
about Scotland and the Presbyterians (Queen Victoria believed
that the entire British nation were members of the Ten Lost
Tribes of Israel), and here I want to give some advice. Do not
ever say, "Scotch Presbyterian," if you have any respect for these
people. There is no such thing as a Scotchman. They are all
Scotsmen, and no self-respecting Scotsman will stand still when
dubbed "Scotchman." This "Scotchman" designation was foisted
on the Scots by the English centuries ago and the Scots have
resented it ever since.

Only when it comes to drink is the word allowed—Scotch
whisky. If any of you need further proof, look to the anthem of
that wonderful land from the pen of Bobby Burns:

> Scots, wha hae wi' Wallace bled,
> Scots, wham Bruce has aften led . . .

And we have, of course, Mary, Queen of Scots, and lastly and
probably most important of all, is the great newspaper loaded
with my friends, *The Scotsman*.

The Russian ransom

THREE times during my travels in the last six months I
have come across the same story. I have met men who have paid
five thousand dollars to get a relative out of the Soviet Union and
into Israel. All of these men were widely scattered individuals.
None of them knew the others. But the details were identical and
the price would seem to be a "standard" five thousand dollars.
The deals are handled through an agent in Canada. Whether the
Soviet Government is behind this or not is irrelevant. Bureaucrats

everywhere, including Communists, have their own way of satisfying greed.

As a matter of public policy, Israel does not publicize the number of its immigrants from countries behind the Iron Curtain. Were they to do so, the Government feels, even this trickle would be stopped. No, apparently the only way to effect some emigration from the Soviet Union to Israel is through secrecy, because the payment of a "ransom" appears definitely to be involved. Nothing has made me so mad at the Soviet Union as this knowledge that people are paying five thousand dollars to get an elderly parent out of the country.

And you don't need mountains of propaganda to tell you the difference between the two civilizations, America and the Soviet Union. The simple fact that one will not permit any of its citizens egress is enough. Mr. Khrushchev made two widely publicized visits here and talked his head off, but no common Soviet citizen can do the same.

Thomas Jefferson, after a tour of Europe, wrote a letter to his friend, James Madison: ". . . the pleasure of the trip will be less than you expect but the utility greater . . . freedom to travel everywhere will make you adore your own country . . . My God, how little do my countrymen know what precious blessings they are in possession of, and which no other people on earth enjoy . . ."

Mr. Jefferson was right. You "adore" your own country only when you are free to travel to foreign lands. When you are not permitted to travel to other countries you must continue to sit in darkness in your native land.

Library Week in Korea

I ACCEPTED an invitation from Agnes Crawford, chief librarian at the Pentagon, to visit Korea as a guest of the United States Eighth Army and speak to the men in each of the installations during National Library Week.

In the meantime came the Eichmann trial.

The trial opened on April 11 and on April 19 I told my friends, Robert St. John, Martin Agronsky, and Meyer Levin, that I was going to Korea the following day. "Korea? What's in Korea?" they asked. I replied, "Haven't you fellows heard? It's National Library Week."

Here was Eichmann no more than thirty yards away in one of the great dramas of the twentieth century and I was off for Korea. Before anyone gets any ideas about "the show must go on" tradition, I have a confession. I considered asking for a postponement of the Korean tour. But now I am prepared to advise one and all that you just cannot cancel anything on the United States Government.

Whom do you call up?

We have all had to cancel a speaking engagement; and while it is never pleasant, it is fairly simple. You find the name of the program chairman, call him up, and say, "I cannot come, and so forth," and that is that.

But there is no program chairman of the United States Government. In the first place the invitation comes from one source, and the acknowledgment of acceptance from another, and the itinerary and other arrangements from a third. If you were foolish enough to call any one set of these people, they would probably tell you that they have nothing to do with it, or that they never heard of you.

The conclusion was to go to Korea on the next day as planned.

And I am not so sure that this assignment was not really more important than Eichmann. After all, everything is transient in this world, except libraries and books.

I made twenty speeches in Korea, visiting every Eighth Army area from Pusan to Panmunjom. In the demilitarized zone the Communists up on the hill kept binoculars trained on our party. Our officers told me that they watch every bit of activity on our side. Even the visit of a Library Week lecturer is important.

At each installation I was the house guest of the commanding officer. As I was traveling light, General Francis T. Pachler of the Seventh Infantry Division lent me a bathrobe and slippers. The next day General John A. Seitz took off his red (artillery) scarf to send to my second son, Harry, Jr., who was once in charge of three 155-mm. guns.

Brigadier General and Mrs. Walter A. Huntsberry invited me to their home for a pleasant evening.

I visited with General and Mrs. Guy S. Meloy and discussed philosophy with General Carl Darnell far into the night. (General Meloy will soon succeed to the command of the United Nations forces and the Eighth Army.)

Korea is a hardship tour of duty and the officers and men serve their thirteen months without their wives and families, except those who must deal with their Korean opposite numbers, both military and political. At this level there must be an exchange of the social amenities in order to make any headway at all. Thus out of fifty-three top American military and political officers I met, only eight, including the commander in chief, had their families with them. But the eight wives I met confirmed a suspicion I have had for some years—that Army officers do marry the handsomest women in America.

My escort was Major Joseph D'Amico, an Italian from Milwaukee, who entered the Army as a private and won his commission in the field. He belongs to the Seventh Infantry Division, which he described to me (at least a million times) as being, "In War Invincible, in Peace Prepared." Every time I seemed to be impressed with an army command, Joe curled up his lip—"Wait till you get to my outfit." His outfit reckons time in terms of service in Korea. Thus the masthead of the division newspaper *Bayonet* proclaims, "5,097 days in Korea," etc.

When the United States Army asks you to do a chore they give you a rating so that you will receive the privileges which will make you as comfortable as possible. I was rated GS 16—a simulated brigadier general. My escort, Major D'Amico, never left my side, but this was solely for my personal welfare. He never intruded when privates and sergeants asked to speak to me alone. It was a little embarrassing when we arrived at the various living quarters, and particularly at the Sanno Hotel in Tokyo. Being a "brigadier general," I was given a suite of two or three rooms, with a servant to press my clothes and run errands, while this battle-scarred veteran, Joe D'Amico, had to be content with a small room and do many things for himself.

The Army feels that you are still in their "service" until you return to your home base. Thus I was a brigadier general until the moment I entered 1312 Elizabeth Avenue, Charlotte, North Carolina. I often wonder if I had continued to percolate around without touching home base whether I would still have this rating.

Major D'Amico's superior and the man directly in charge of my visit was Colonel William W. Rossing, Special Service Officer, whom the Koreans call "Papa." He is a tough soldier but a kinder man you'll rarely meet. Colonel Rossing has a magnificent head of white hair, but I do not recommend that you engage him in a wrestling match or a foot race.

The most impressive aspect of my visit was working with the corps of librarians headed by Miss Dorothy Goddard. In some areas, and particularly with the front-line combat divisions, you will find an American woman in charge of a small library, often alone, or perhaps with another girl in the Red Cross or Family Service. Their facilities, I assure you, are not up to the standard of the Waldorf-Astoria. In some places there are no inside rest-rooms, and the six-month season of humidity and dust are not pleasant. Yet I have rarely seen a group of more dedicated people, devoted to an idea of getting books to the men, and providing a library in each sector where the men can gather to read books, hold discussions, and listen to the latest recordings from the States.

And yet I can understand this dedication. It exists not only in the librarians but also among the officers and men. There is a certain quality about the Korean people and Korea itself that finally grips you. I "catch on" very quickly wherever I go because I am not a "scenery" man. Of course I miss a lot not taking pictures or slides, or looking at exhibits, or examining the terrain, but I trained myself long ago to catch only the words everywhere, which transmit attitudes and ideas. With such an intense concentration it is surprising how much can be achieved. I have found that I can talk to three hundred people a week, including maybe forty solid conversations.

After each of my speeches I went to the library for a question-and-answer period. Nearly always one soldier would whisper, "Don't let the brass kid you too much." Without revealing the man's identity I always tried to draw him out during the question period. But on one occasion I had to be direct.

In one of my speeches I said that no segment of the American society is as "color blind" as the Eighth Army in Korea. There are Negro helicopter pilots and Negro officers sitting in their proper places at the dinner tables. The Pacific *Stars and Stripes* faithfully reported each of my speeches. The day after this particular speech, a boy handed me a clipping of it across which he had written—"Crap." I showed this to a dozen other soldiers, including a Negro captain and three Negro privates. They said there was no basis for what the fellow had written. During that day's question-and-answer period I told the assembled men about the clipping which had been handed me and said that I genuinely wanted to know if I was wrong in my estimate. The man who gave me the clipping spoke up, and all credit to him. He admitted what he had done but explained that he did not refer to the "integration" problem; he objected rather to the fact that some GIs call the Koreans "Gooks." Well, that was an entirely different matter and one which I had not discussed at all because I knew nothing about it. I have to give credit to that soldier because he walked over to a Negro private, put his arm around him, and said, "I did not mean this kind of integration."

Other messages were handed to me, but of a less controversial nature, such as the one from Sergeant Rothblat, "Tell Max Asnas of The Stage [the celebrated delicatessen on New York's Seventh Avenue] to send me a salami—tell him I was his bookie for a while." (Max complied immediately with two salamis.)

I spoke of the fascination of Korea and its people. The Koreans are a great people. We better not lose them. I feel terrifically drawn to the place and I must get back soon—and perhaps extend the visit to Japan.

I was told at the farewell banquet at the Officers Club in Seoul that it was the first social event attended by the Commander in Chief, General Carter B. Magruder. I did not mean to act coy, but I told the officers and civilians at the dinner that it was embarrassing to have such a fuss made over me by men who had been in battle.

General Magruder in his reply said that he could understand my embarrassment but, he added, "Perhaps we think that you too have been useful."

I do not know what more a man wants out of life after he has had such a sentence spoken to him by the Commander in Chief of the United Nations Forces in the Far East and General of the United States Eighth Army.

The Jeromes of Brooklyn

THE remarkable Sir Winston Churchill has written millions of words. Like Julius Caesar, he has made history and written it, too. And he has written it brilliantly.

Among all his millions of words, however, Sir Winston never mentions anything about his mother's marriages subsequent to the death of his father, the great Lord Randolph. Nor does he go into any history of his mother's family, the Jeromes of Brooklyn.

Someone should one day put into literature that stormy moment when the Duke of Marlborough learned his son Randolph wanted to marry Jenny Jerome of Brooklyn, and that equally stormy moment when Leonard Jerome of Brooklyn learned his daughter wanted to marry a titled English dandy who never worked a day in his life.

The Jews of London

EVERY time I visit London I am thrilled. I have studied English literature and history all my life, and the places I visit are familiar to me, even when I am seeing them for the first time.

Through such books as Winston Churchill's autobiographies and biographies, the *Memoirs* of Consuelo Vanderbilt, and Lytton Strachey's *Queen Victoria*, I became familiar with the lives and habits of British royalty and the great families that flourished during the Victorian era. The names of the places where the families lived have become familiar names—St. James and Connaught Place, Marble Arch and Grosvenor Square. It is in these sections that the English Jews live today, the rich professional men and merchants and financiers whom I have been visiting since 1958. It is a wonderful story of how they have succeeded to these places. It tells us much about the history of our times and it parallels the population movement in our own country.

I have described the movement of American Jews from the ghetto to Riverside Drive and then out onto Long Island. A similar movement by Jews took place in England, except in London the Jews went from east to west by northwest to Hendon, Finchley, and Golders Green, and some have town houses in London, in the vacated Victorian mansions, while in America they went from east to west to further east and south by east.

I suspect these movements will go on forever and that thirty years from now there will be similar stories to write about different places and different streets and different names.

On my last visit to London in December 1961, I stopped at the town house of a good friend in the Marble Arch section. My host has a delightful sense of humor and he gets the point. I am never bored with people who get the point. As we passed through his great hall, he stopped at a large oaken table on which were arranged hundreds of Christmas cards. He nudged me and wickedly whispered, "Let's you and I riffle through these and see if we can find one from a Christian."

The little dramas that are played out in London have the same plots as the little ones played out in America. There is one that exactly duplicates the drama of the Jews in the South immediately after the Supreme Court ended segregation in the public schools in 1954. The Jewish merchants, salesmen, and manufacturers of the South felt they were "on the spot." Invariably they were Northerners removed to the South and invariably a crucial tension makes Jews vulnerable. They decided to reflect the surrounding culture. They petitioned their national rabbinical and social-action organizations to stop supporting the integrationists, to keep amicus curiae out of the courts.

I told the Jews at that time nothing would help, and indeed I was right. Jews throughout the South are blamed by the White Citizens Councils for having fostered integration. I advised these Jews years ago that the best choice was the humane choice, a vigorous support of the Supreme Court decision, but my advice did not make them happy. The urge to be like the rest is strong, but the Jew of the South remains a most unconvincing segregationist.

In England the Macmillan government is involved in a big debate concerning the Commonwealth Immigrants Bill. This bill is a result of the problem that vast immigration has brought to the British Isles. Until now, any citizen of a Commonwealth country was free to enter England unimpeded. While the bill does not specifically bar colored people from entering England, there is no doubt that this is what the Comomnwealth Immigrants Bill is intended to do. It is aimed at barring Negro immigrants from Jamaica, the other West Indies, and Africa.

This is indeed a break with old British traditions, particularly as these traditions affect the Commonwealth. The Labour Party has signified its opposition to this measure and Macmillan may have to risk a vote of confidence.

The British Board of Jewish Deputies which represents, at least unofficially, the Jewish Community of Britain, held a meeting, the result of which was a decision to keep "hands off." This is essentially a middle-class decision based on middle-class fears.

Though the Jewish homes on the great streets of London have a long and honorable history, the conversation within them is the same as that heard in the Jewish homes in Great Neck or Dallas. Always there is the story of some slight, a description of the extent of anti-Semitism at a country club, at a public function, or at a fashionable luncheon society.

A member of one of the richest Jewish families in London told me that when his Christian community was having trouble raising 170,000 pounds for the constructon of a new home for boys and girls, a director of the project approached him for help. The name of this home is The Purley House. The director who appealed for help said: "I know there are no Jewish boys or girls in the home, but this is a community project and we need your help."

The Jewish businessman went to work and among his friends and associates he raised 100,000 pounds. The businessman told me that when the director announced this amazing contribution at his annual meeting, another director said, "Why shouldn't they? *They* have all the money."

I told my host and his guests what I tell my Jewish audiences here: "You can't win," or as my father said, "Gurnisht helfen" (Nothing helps), and the best remedy is to do the best you know how at the job you have. Eat good, drink good, buy books and phonograph records, and do everything you possibly can for the children and grandchildren.

My visit to Teheran

THE propagandists call our civilization a materialistic one. We have not countered this propaganda successfully and we have every right to do so. Everywhere in the world you see clinics and hospitals, restored churches, paintings, and tapestries, with little copper tablets or markers which say, "Restored by so-and-so or such-and-such organization—American."

One of the most amazing evidences of successful philanthropy may be seen in the city of Teheran in Iran.

Here live some eight thousand Jews in a voluntary ghetto, 80 per cent of whom are totally illiterate, contending against a dire poverty. I hasten to add that this is not because they are Jews or because they live in a voluntary ghetto; they merely reflect the condition of the entire country. The Moslem Iranian who lives down the road has no more of the world's goods nor is he any less illiterate.

To this ghetto has come the Joint Distribution Committee headed by a remarkable man named Theodore D. Feder. He directs the operation and brings not only the latest developments in medicine and science, but also good will, kindness, and genuine affection.

Another great man working in the ghetto of Teheran is Dr. Jules Lewis, an Australian Jew who is medical consultant and director of the combined Family Health Center and Hospital which the Joint Distribution Committee has established.

It was heartwarming to go through Dr. Lewis's hospital. For the first time in their lives or in the history of their ancestors, these people are receiving medical care and advice as good as they might expect in Tel Aviv, New York, or Miami.

The doctors' tasks are difficult because the patients have to be educated. For example, Dr. Lewis and Mr. Feder show slides to the mothers, teaching them the most primitive concept of sanitation. One film shows a mother dipping a spoon into a jar of yogurt and feeding her baby who has measles; then she dips the spoon into the jar again and offers it to another child who is healthy. Here the film is stopped and a doctor warns mothers not to do this.

The Iranians are a bit ambivalent concerning their Moslem religion. They belong to the Shiite sect and go out of their way to explain that they are not Arabs. In fact, they changed the name of their country early in this century from Persia to Iran, which means "Aryan."

Iran is an absolute monarchy under the rule of the Shah. One of the few Jewish intellectuals in Iran told me that he'd much rather have the absolute rule of the Shah than the Socialist rule of the late Sir Ernie Bevin.

The Jews here still make a yearly pilgrimage to the tomb of Esther and Mordecai, only a few miles from the ghetto.

An insight into the history of the Jews in Persia is provided by the community at Meshed, an area in the northeastern part of the country between the Soviet Union and Afghanistan. These Jews of Meshed lived under a benevolent Shah for several hundred years, but bad times came in the middle of the eighteenth century and they were forcibly converted to Islam. Under threat of death they worshiped as Moslems but secretly kept the laws of Judaism. In recent years, the Reza Shah took a realistic view of these neo-Moslems in Meshed and told them to go about their business. They immediately reverted to Judaism. Some of them came into the open and settled in Teheran, and quite a colony of them went on to Jerusalem.

There are Jews in Teheran who live in the open society. These Jews are the newcomers, dating from only about one hundred and fifty years back. While some of them are wealthy, most are small merchants, peddlers, and manufacturers. I was in Teheran during the April twentieth celebration of Israel's Independence and the Jews of Teheran had a party at the leading hotel. When I arrived I was highly gratified although surprised to see the Israeli flag beside the Iranian flag and a portrait of David Ben-Gurion hanging beside a portrait of the Shah. Iran is a Moslem country and probably the only Moslem country which allows such a display.

As I left Teheran it occurred to me that Dr. Lewis and Mr. Feder with their hospital may have had something to do with all of this. The Joint Distribution Committee, supported principally by money from American Jews, has materially helped the Iranians, Jew and Moslem, by furnishing doctors, nurses, and medicine. They are saving the lives of Jewish and Moslem children around the clock.

The Common Market

BECAUSE Napoleon Bonaparte conceived of establishing a common market on the continent of Europe, he thought a suitable reward was for him to serve it as Emperor. But England had access to the sea and wanted no part of a Continental market, particularly one presided over by a Corsican. While Germany gave Europe its royalty, the House of Hanover could not guarantee *Der Vaterland* a share of the world-wide trade. No common market was established and World Wars I and II were the dreadful result of Germanic frustration.

Perhaps England's entry into the common European market will mean peace, prosperity, and plenty for Europe. Napoleon had a pretty good idea, but the idea had to wait until England was forced to liquidate her Empire. To have England working in harmony with her vigorous Continental neighbors is the most hopeful development so far in this post-world-war-we-hope world.

The Seventh-day Adventists abroad

AN INTERESTING community has assembled in the village of Gan Yavne in southern Israel. This colony is composed of about thirty souls—children, parents, and grandparents—all of them Seventh-day Adventists. They have migrated to Israel from America in order that they may observe the Sabbath—Saturday— as dictated by Biblical custom. For Seventh-day Adventists Israel is a Holy Land and they live in absolute obedience to Biblical precepts. They do not, however, keep dairy and meat dishes separate, as they say this is not enjoined anywhere in the Old Testament. But their meat is slaughtered by a shochet and soaked and salted as in the Orthodox Jewish rituals. They do not cook on Saturday and perform only the most imperative tasks—like feeding the animals.

All of them are farmers. They believe in one God, the God of Abraham and Moses, and to Him they pray daily. Their coming to Israel fulfills a dream of several generations. One of these new immigrants, Mary Levenson, had planned to enter Israel ever since her grandfather was denied a visa by British mandate authorities after World War I.

Another, Norman Werner, and his wife Jenny, who came from Oregon, say that there are many more Adventists back home in America who are still waiting for their opportunity to live in Gan Yavne.

May they prosper!

Bingo in England

THE English have gone bingo mad. Never mind that wall in Berlin or the dissolution of the Empire. The Englishman is really concerned with the Rugby scores, which the English newspapers never fail to print on page one. An American in Piccadilly Circus is surprised to see a huge neon sign flickering on and off with the name and address of a bookmaker, just like our advertising signs flickering on and off in Times Square.

The English have the right idea. Two billion dollars a year goes into the pockets of American gangsters, thugs, and thieves in control of gambling and betting. The English have diverted some of this money to the government coffers by legalizing gambling and making bets available to everyone. What they have done in essence is recognize a fact of life—that everybody wants something for nothing and the easiest way most people can think of to get something is by gambling. But no English gambler corrupts a policeman and no bookmaker pays off to a syndicate.

We Americans believe that if we don't legalize a thing it doesn't exist and won't cause us trouble—like Red China with one-sixth of the earth's population, or the narcotics traffic with its crime, horrors, and billion-dollar gangster empire.

Under the Public Health System which the Labour Party put into effect in the late 1940s and which the Tories have not only approved but extended, there is no narcotics traffic in England. There are no smugglers, there are no pushers, there are no schemers. Any addict receives free narcotics from the Government. The addict in England must, of course, submit to a medical process of rehabilitation, but, once he does, the health officer gives him a certificate which enables him to get his shot at the drugstore.

Narcotics and narcotic addiction is a great sadness in our country. Hundreds of millions are made by smugglers and gangsters and pushers. The narcotic addict who needs that twenty dollars a day for his shot commits every imaginable crime. Every female addict has admitted that sooner or later she has resorted to prostitution. In addition to filling the pockets of criminals we have increased our crime rate and made no substantial advance in the cure of addiction.

It is true that the British are no more advanced than we in effecting a cure for addiction. But those people who say legally administered narcotics is no answer forget there may well be no final answer to narcotics addiction. Certainly the British are more humane in dealing with the problem than we.

The British are more civilized because when they want to solve a problem, the first thing they do is admit it exists.

We're closer than we think

"SHOES alone know if the stockings have holes." Thus Haitians tell us secrets are known only to their keepers. Tribes in Africa say, "It is the sea only which knows the bottom of the ship."

"Three helping each other will bear the burden of six," say the Spaniards, while the Italians have, "A single finger can't catch fleas."

The English say, "God helps those who help themselves," and the Spaniards say, "God helps him who gets up early."

The Caesarea golf course

ISRAEL'S golf course is located at Caesarea, a port where once Roman centurions landed. Herod ruled Judea from here. The curious thing about this Caesarea golf course is that it is not restricted. I recognized the names of at least twenty Christians on the membership list.

The balance of nature

THERE have been many who insist that atomic and hydrogen bomb testing has disrupted the normal course of the weather. Whether such a charge is true or not, I do not know. But if the testing ever erupts into a war, I know that the bombs will upset nature's balance. Man would not survive but it seems probable that ants and rats would. Both are particularly fitted to take over since both live underground and are particularly good at scavenging and organization. Nor should one forget the resourceful cockroach, a survival expert second to none. The cockroach was an old-timer long before the first pyramid was built.

Subscribers in Lebanon

I HAVE subscribers to *The Carolina Israelite* in Lebanon. Most of them are in attendance at the National College at Choueifat. All of them receive my paper in a plain wrapper with no return address.

The Italian businessman

THE overpowering fact about the American businessman is that he has no time. The harder it is to get to see him, the more successful you know he is. If you never see him at all, you know he's at the very top; he is always busy. In Italy exactly the contrary is true. If you can't see the businessman it means he is in the dumps, struggling hard. Once he becomes successful, he becomes more accessible. When he tells his most menial employee, "Come in, spend an hour, tell me everything that's on your mind," he has reached the pinnacle.

The sign in Tel Aviv

THERE are two signs in a Tel Aviv Hospital which read: "No Smoking" and "On the Sabbath POSITIVELY No Smoking."

The Eichmann trial

WHEN Gideon Hausner, the Israeli attorney general, began, "I stand before you, judges of Israel," I felt a sudden chill. A quick glance around the courtroom convinced me most of the five hundred journalists and writers shared my experience.

What Mr. Hausner told us when he said, "I stand before you, judges of Israel," was that we were witnessing one of the great dramas of history. Precisely because that opening phrase was spoken in Jerusalem, the Holy City, to which mankind looks for its earliest beginning, the phrase was spoken as part of the unbroken thread of history. We were sitting only a few miles from the fortress Betar which fell to the legions of the Roman Emperor Hadrian in the year 135 A.D. Later Hadrian plowed under the land so that Jews would never live here again.

I feel a sense of dismay that this man Eichmann had, in common with the rest of us, birthdays, schooldays, celebrations upon the birth of a child, fear, sorrow, wonder, and joy.

And I am distressed that he shared our generation.

What was most remarkable about Adolf Eichmann, sitting in his booth of bulletproof glass, was that he was so ordinary looking. He might have been a waiter, a window cleaner perhaps, or an insurance agent. But the defendant's very drabness was an advantage for the Israelis. A man of overwhelming personality, such as the late Hermann Goering, might have intruded himself upon the story, and the Israelis were intent upon telling the story. It is part of their four-thousand-year history. More than that, it is a religious obligation: "And thou shalt tell it to thy son."

Yet despite his ordinary appearance, this Adolf Eichmann was really a stranger, a stranger to the human race, who had come among us as the central figure in the greatest of all murder trials. And what were the charges that brought this stranger into a courtroom in the Holy Land among people who for centuries have repeated the hopeful prayer, "next year in Jerusalem," and who were now willing to risk the prestige of their hard-earned sovereignty on this single trial?

The indictment was staggeringly unlike any ever heard before in a courtroom of any nation. It alleged that Adolf Eichmann issued the instructions for the extermination of the Jews of Europe to Gestapo commanders and other Nazi officials, that he directed the use of poison gas for this purpose at Auschwitz, that he helped devise measures to prevent childbirth among the Jews and among the children of Jewish-Gentile marriages, that he robbed the Jews of untold millions, including the personal properties of the extermination camp victims: the gold from their teeth, their artificial limbs, their clothing, their shoes, all of which were sent back to Germany—presumably in the same freight cars which had brought the victims to the gas chambers and incinerators.

And now this stranger was on trial for these things, and Israel had turned over to his defense bales of documents, including the names of all prosecution witnesses, so that Eichmann would be defended in accordance with Anglo-Saxon law, upon which the Israeli law is based.

One amazing fact about this event was that it marked the first time in centuries the Jews themselves had ever tried a man for persecuting and killing Jews. Eichmann was far from the first of his kind. Standing in ghostly array behind him in his bullet-proof booth were the many godfathers of Auschwitz, the official persecutors, beginning with the Roman emperors of the fourth and fifth centuries A.D. who decreed that a Jew must not marry a Christian on pain of death and imposed rigid restrictions on a Jew's everyday life.

In the opening sessions of the trial both sides roughed out their positions. The defense counsel, Dr. Robert Servatius, challenged the legality of Eichmann's capture in Argentina, disputed the law on which the trial was based, questioned the court's jurisdiction on grounds that an alleged criminal could not be tried by his alleged victims, and indicated doubt about the impartiality of the judges. He gave the key to his strategy when he referred to the accused as a mere cog in the machinery of a "predecessor" state of the modern Germany.

Hausner responded by citing a whole series of United States court decisions establishing that a court may try a defendant regardless of how he was caught or brought to trial. He cited particularly Pettibone vs. Idaho, in which the court ruled that, even though Mr. Pettibone was taken out of Colorado against his will and without the knowledge of that State's authorities, the courts of Idaho thereupon had a right to try him for murder. Colorado had a grievance, the United States court held, but Pettibone did not. As for the legality of the Israeli law under which Eichmann was being tried, Hausner noted that no fewer than seventeen nations have passed similar laws since 1945 pertaining to crimes against humanity.

Yet the trial was not without its serious risks for Israel. (It reminds me of the warning the fathers gave their growing sons on the Lower East Side of New York concerning relations with the women of the streets: "It begins all right. But you never know how it will end.") One of the chief dangers for Israel was that the revelations of the trial were likely to prove embarrassing to some of her closest friends in the Western world. The defense claimed that, a year before the war ended, Eichmann had offered to let hundreds of thousands of Jews out of German-occupied territory if they were accepted elsewhere. But (as the story goes) all the doors were shut tight and the only place where they could go, Palestine, was effectively sealed against them by Britain.

There was also testimony that as early as January 1944 carefully drawn maps and diagrams of the railroad facilities leading to Auschwitz were placed in the hands of the Allies. But the roadbeds over which the daily boxcars of Jews traveled to extermination were never bombed—because the Russians said that these railroad tracks were too important to their advancing armies.

Some of this is doubtless true, but a philosopher with whom I spoke in Israel was quick to discount much of it as hindsight. "Even we Jews did not produce any Jeremiahs between 1939 and 1945," he said, adding, "The Jews themselves, on their way to the gas chambers, could not quite get themselves to believe what was happening to them."

The point of the matter is that the Western Allies were not aware that the Nazis were fighting two separate wars, with two separate general staffs—one war to conquer the world and the other war to kill all the Jews. Because the West was not aware of these two wars, the Jews could gather to themselves no allies.

In this regard one of the most important witnesses for the prosecution was a Mr. Joel Brand. I spent a day with Mr. Brand and saw for myself what others had told me—that he is a man who lives in the shadows with a broken heart, haunted by the dream that if his mission had been successful one million Jews who died in the gas chambers might be alive today.

Joel Brand was the representative of the Jewish community in Budapest. Eichmann gave Brand the mission of opening ransom negotiations with the Allies, through the Jewish Agency, a sort of shadow government of Palestine under the British Mandate: one million Jews in exchange for ten thousand trucks and a few carloads of coffee, tea, and soap. But Brand was unable to make personal contact with anyone who could negotiate. The British took him into custody in Syria, transported him to Cairo, and kept him incommunicado.

At this moment President Roosevelt heard of the possibility of saving some of the Jews from the gas chambers and he dispatched a personal representative, Ira Hirschmann, to seek out Brand. Mr. Hirschmann was given the run-around from Istanbul to Aleppo and finally to Cairo where only his personal credentials from President Roosevelt persuaded Lord Moyne—the British resident minister in the Middle East—to grant him a visit of one hour with Brand. Brand says that Lord Moyne's position was that the release of all those Jews "would pose a great problem." The Brand mission failed with Lord Moyne's final word that everything would have to be cleared with the Foreign Office in London and there was no telling how long that would take.

The past fifty years produced greater technological advances than the previous five thousand. The paradox is that these advances have proved more destructive than beneficial.

When the Crusaders under Count Emicho entered the city of Mainz on May 28, 1096, they planned to kill all the Jews. They wanted the Jewish property for traveling expenses to help them wrest the Holy Sepulcher from the Saracens.

But it took some doing to kill eleven hundred Jews in the year 1096. At least six thousand others escaped death, because the killer had to confront his victim personally. He had to wield a heavy sword, a knife, or a bludgeon, all of which involved risks. A young fellow, for example, could possibly duck the first blow, even kill his assailant. A potential victim could run and hide. There was also the posibility that a murderer would lose his nerve, or get plain dog-tired slashing people. It was not simple and that is why the Dark Ages were a fairly pleasant era in which to live.

And take the Kishinev massacre in 1903. On the Lower East Side of New York the immigrants hung out black crepe from their windows. President Theodore Roosevelt sent an undiplomatic protest to the Czar; Luigi Luzzatti in the Italian Parliament was able to arouse the entire intellectual community of Europe in stormy protest. I hope that wherever the little Czar Nicholas II is now that he forgives me for my past contempt of him—forty-six Jews were killed.

Genghis Khan, who has had a very bad press through the centuries, started far up there in the cold wastes of Mongolia and swept across the face of the earth, winning battles and killing people. But Genghis Khan gave you a choice. When he came to the city of Samarkand in 1220 (where he killed all the adult males) he proclaimed, "Give up, come under my sovereignty and everything will be all right." So the Samarkands did not give up and they died. A man elects to defend his city and dies for it—there is some dignity in this kind of dying.

Nearly two decales ago, however, with the advances in communications and transportation, Adolf Eichmann was able to sit at a desk with dictating machines, telephones, and push buttons, and kill by remote control six million men, women, and children in twenty-six months. And they had no choice. None at all.

An interesting phase of the Eichmann trial took place outside the courtroom in the reaction of the people of Israel, many of whom knew of Eichmann in another world twenty years ago. But in Israel there was a surprising lack of passion about the trial. A woman who survived Auschwitz expressed the opinion of many Israelis: "I was happy when they caught him. But I was also very sad." Another said to me, "Our brains are being opened again." As these reminders of the past came back to these people they were forced to relive an experience which is beyond human understanding, even after the mountains of literature that have been written about it, and even after the testimony of the Nuremberg trials.

There was also in Israel a considerable body of conservative opinion. It expressed itself in terms of "don't rock the boat" and would have preferred that one of the commandos who captured Eichmann had shot him in Argentina, and thus avoided all further complications.

A cynic in a coffeehouse stopped his game of chess long enough to answer my question. "What do I think of the Eichmann trial? Well, the Gentile world will watch it carefully to see if we are liars—to see if maybe there were not six million Jews massacred by the Nazis but only 4,999,400." Then he turned from me and said to his partner, "Your move."

One segment of the Jews in Israel remained unimpressed with the whole procedure. I visited Mea Shearim, the ultra-Orthodox section of Jerusalem, and had an audience with Rabbi Avrom Blau. The rabbi was seated at a long bench in the old synagogue Beth Joseph. He was surrounded by some of his disciples, all of them wearing the traditional black gowns and round black fur hats. Speaking in Yiddish (these ultra-Orthodox Jews believe that it is blasphemous to speak Hebrew except when addressing God in prayer), I asked him what he thought of the Eichmann trial. There was a long pause while all the others looked toward the rabbi. Finally he said, "It does not matter who is the accused or who is the accuser. These affairs are beyond our understanding which is only to read the law and await the Messiah."

But the Prime Minister himself expressed the opinion which seemed to be the general atmosphere surrounding the Eichmann trial. "Our concern is not one of vengeance but only of documenting an era in which genocide became a policy of a political state." And on this basis the Israelis were willing to shoulder all the risks involved in the attempt to bring this ordinary-looking man to justice for the most incredible crime in history.

While the trial is still fresh in our minds, it might help us to listen for a moment to Gibran, a poet from the Middle East:

Then one of the judges of the city stood forth and said,
Speak to us of Crime and Punishment, and he answered saying
And a single leaf turns not yellow but with the silent knowledge of the whole tree
So the wrong-doer cannot do wrong without the hidden will of you all.

Israeli short story

THE doctor bent over his patient. Dispensing with his stethoscope, he pressed his ear against the man's chest, as he had done years ago, in his native Yugoslavia, before he had dreamed of emigrating to Israel. He could hear the wheezing breath. As he knelt there he wondered whether the darkness meant a late-afternoon storm or whether it was his eyesight that was, ever more progressively, fading away.

The patient, Police Sergeant Ya'akev Mizrahi who hailed from Iran, tried to raise his head and asked expectantly:

"Shall I be all right?"

Before Dr. Yitshak Hameiri could answer he felt as though somebody had struck him on his forehead. He wanted to turn around and rise up, but at that moment he felt a black veil drop over the room. He knew he was blind.

It came as no surprise. Dr. Hameiri had contracted the terrible eye disease in a concentration camp in German-occupied Serbia. After the war he had emigrated to Jerusalem. Now his blindness seemed the end of his medical career.

But his wife promised she would be "his eyes." She was able to drive the doctor to and from his house calls.

The light in Dr. Hameiri's home clinic is on every night.

Orientals do not like their wives to be examined by a doctor who can see them in the nude, and Oriental Jews are no exception. The blind, sixty-year-old Dr. Hameiri is preferred to a younger, sighted doctor at the Sick Fund Clinic. Proud of his ability to save a human life, the aging doctor, blindness or no blindness, continues to make his contribution, despite all the difficulties, day and night, in wind and rain, in heat and cold— a friend and a healer.

3.

IN A PLAIN
WRAPPER

Empathy

THIS is the phoniest of all the phony words.

Who could have invented this atrocity?

What's the matter with the old words, like "mercy," "compassion," and—let's face it—"sympathy"?

But now the wise guys sit around with a Scotch mist in their hands and talk about "empathizing."

No one knows what he is talking about. "Empathy" to me has always sounded as ugly as the words, "colonic," "emetic," and "emphysema," which is a horse disease.

I realize my campaign against such words as "dichotomy" and "empathy" may put magazines like *Commentary* out of business, but it cannot be helped.

If we have almost five million unemployed Americans, let us at least have some unemployment among words which are simply featherbedding.

This goes for trite and meaningless phrases, too.

Of all the English phrases that have caused needless confusion I believe that "in other words" is the champ. It is an indulgence, and not only an indulgence, but a wicked indulgence to try to say the same thing two different ways. There is only one way to describe Hamlet; that is the way Shakespeare did it in five acts of poetry. You cannot modify the Constitution nor modify the Magna Carta. You may derive rules to govern new situations, but every Supreme Court justice has always come back to one of the first ten Amendments to say exactly what he means. When a lawyer tells you how he is pleading your suit for damages and in reply to your question about your rights says, "in other words"—you need a new lawyer.

While I'm on the subject, you might as well know about a communication I received recently from Professor Simon Sonkin out in Stanford, California. He says that in one issue of my journal I misused the word, "epitome." The professor says the word means a summary, an abstract, a concise statement of the main points of the work, a representation in miniature; such as, "Brussels is an epitome of Paris."

It does not mean the highest point or the apex. Professor Sonkin goes on to assure me that hundreds of thousands of educated and literate people misuse "epitome" daily. I would be perfectly willing to observe propriety and use the word correctly from now on except for one fact: I used to know a girl named Epitome and conceived quite a fancy for her. Indeed, not a day goes by that I don't recall fondly my liaison with Epitome—Epitome Garfunkle of East Twelfth Street.

To be remembered

THE thundering events of our time usurp all the newspaper space and all the publicity. Every two years the world relaxes as the statesmen and diplomats convene at the Summit; and every other two years the world shudders as scientists invent and develop new nuclear systems.

But in a few decades all the publicity will seem overemphasized, and I mean the scientists and the statesmen no disrespect.

What will seem equally important and perhaps even more important than these events will be some poems, a symphony, and a book here and there.

Between 1780 and 1800 the British Isles was becoming the storehouse for more than half the world. There were shopkeepers, importers and exporters, bankers, traders, and salesmen; and all of these millions of men had families and hopes and ambitions and private lives. We know nothing about them. Some of us know of George III, a few others even recognize the names of Pitt and Burke, but all of us have had some association with Bobby Burns. "Auld Lang Syne," perhaps "Flow Gently, Sweet Afton," or even

What tho' on hamely fare we dine,
  Wear hodden-gray, and a' that;
Gie fools their silks, and knaves their wine,
  A man's a man for a' that.

And at the Battle of Lepanto in 1571 the Christian world broke forever the threat of the Turks as a maritime power. All the Christian powers combined with a fleet of nearly four hundred ships and thousands of seamen and soldiers to win this battle. But the Battle of Lepanto has also become famous because one of the soldiers out of the many, many thousands was Miguel de Cervantes. He was wounded in that battle, and after writing *Don Quixote* he became known as the Cripple of Lepanto.

Yoo-hoo, Fenimore!

THIRTY years ago if you went to Coney Island on a hot summer's day and yelled "Abie" or "Jake" through a megaphone, you could collect every lost kid on the beach. In fact, this is the way it was done. A policeman kept patrolling the boardwalk yelling "Abie" and "Jake" and the kids were found even before their parents knew they were lost. But today no kid would turn his head.

You have to yell "Scott" or "Kingston."

About the only family that still sticks by the old stand-bys is the British Royal Family. They still rely on Charles, Mary, Elizabeth, and the like. The rest of the families in Britain and America name their children Elliot, Candy, Robin, Ainsley, Brooks, Penny, or Fenimore.

There's a sort of depressing romantic sameness about them. Practically no child is named after a maiden aunt who owns three hundred shares of A.T.&T. Either the thrifty maiden aunt is a thing of the past, or our prosperity is so great that no one wants to accurse a child with Abigail just to get three hundred shares of A.T.&T.

A secret of long life?

THE secret of a long life is there for all of us to discover. Obviously, it consists of involvement. Winston Churchill, Carl Sandburg, Robert Frost, Bernard Baruch are men whose interest never flags. They are all involved in the world, the events, and the people around them. I think this was my father's secret (he lived well into his eighties). When he came visiting he did not ask the grandchildren, "Do you love me?" Nor did he ask me, "How's everything?" The moment he entered the door he was pulling newspaper clippings out of every pocket—"Let's answer this ignorant editor . . . let's do it now."

The old man who sits around complaining he hasn't had a letter from his married daughter is unhappy, not because his daughter has forgotten him, which she hasn't, but because he is uninvolved. He has let go the wheel of life. He needs to forget himself in the history which surrounds him on all sides. He needs to become involved.

Women and pool

"PROFICIENCY at billiards," wrote Herbert Spencer, the English philosopher, "is indicative of nothing but a misspent youth." This statement is probably one of the most judicious ever made. But despite Mr. Spencer's wry view, billiards and pocket billiards are the most maligned of all sporting endeavors.

Billiards, a game played on a slate table covered with a green cloth, involves three balls, one red, two white. The object of the game is for the shooter to cue one white ball so it hits first the red ball and then, after caroming off the sides of the table, the second white ball. This is called "three-rail billiards." The game of pocket billiards is played with one white cue ball and fifteen numbered colored balls, and the object is to sink the colored balls, one at a time, into any of the six pockets of the table.

In his musical, *The Music Man*, Meredith Willson has his hero, Harold Hill, declare, "That game with the fifteen numbered balls is the devil's tool."

But the game is here to stay.

The real complainers against it are proof of its virtues. The people who don't like pool happen to be women, particularly mothers and sweethearts. And they don't like pool because it is an activity which does not admit them. The day may come when women will pass freely into the Harvard Club but no woman is ever comfortable in a place where spittoons line the walls. Moreover they can't shoot pool, any more than they can play polo. I understand from a doctor friend of mine—ordinarily I wouldn't take this quack's word for anything but this seems reasonable enough—it's because their collarbones are a little bit longer than men's and they don't get that free swing. Morever, you can't lean across the table to put that six ball in the corner pocket wearing skirts or even slacks. At least you can't look decorous doing it. Pool is still a man's game. Let us hope the women never invade the poolroom as they have invaded the bowling alley.

The man on the sidewalk

THE other day outside my office, a man stumbled and gripped the lamppost. His feet could not gain a purchase and he fell to the sidewalk and rolled into the gutter. Two girls who were passing by started giggling. By the time they had passed the man, they were actually laughing.

The immediate assumption of course was that he was drunk. Why this should be, I do not know. The common alcoholic will get himself home before he commences his drinking, knowing that he will consciously seek the unconscious and that he had better be near a bed when he passes out. The drunk will rarely stumble and fall but rather secure himself in a doorway, so that when he passes out he will have at least minimum shelter.

Even if he were drunk, certainly this was no cause for laughter. Even less a cause for neglect. The man on the sidewalk was sick, even if he was drunk, and he needed help.

Yet everyone knows most of us walk by the man on the sidewalk.

Someone in our office called the police and my office manager and I went out to see what we could do. We pulled him back to the grass and my office manager dug out the fellow's wallet.

The first thing we saw was the carefully printed note which said, "I am not a drunk. I am a diabetic, probably in shock. I will need sugar."

How terribly sad it was! Here was this poor fellow who probably lived in constant fear that he would go into shock out alone in the street and that if anyone helped him at all they would immediately take him for a drunk.

How well he understands the world in which we live!

In a plain wrapper

I REMEMBER the ads I used to read for books with titles like, "The Secret of Human Relations." The ad always promised that if you ordered the book it would be delivered in a plain wrapper with no return address. These books were nothing more than sex hygiene books, but they disguised this fact by pretending to be pornographic tracts.

Now the situation is reversed. You can send for a thirty-day supply of High Potency Capsules and these capsules are guaranteed to put pep and energy back into your marriage. Despite the fact that these capsules are described as vitamins, the truth is that they are aphrodisiacs.

The ad shows a picture of an attractive, matronly sort of woman sadly staring into space under the bold caption, "Are You Suffering From Tired Love?" This handsome matron soliloquizes that, after fifteen years of marriage, love has grown tired. If this lady had ordered those books that were once advertised, she wouldn't have had this worry. Those books would have told her that after fifteen years she didn't have a squawk coming.

I hope that the combination of glutamic acid, choline, inositol, methionine, citrus bioflavonoid, liver, and blood-building B_{12}-plus gets that old zing back into her marriage. And I hope the manufacturers of these capsules remember the trick of making the love philter. It won't work unless you mix it at midnight under a full moon with the right incantations.

Early adulthood

THE bar mitzvahs which took place on the Lower East Side of New York City years ago made a thirteen-year-old boy not only a member of the congregation, but a male adult with all of the consequent responsibilities. It could not help but do this, since the children on the Lower East Side were surrounded by adults. Children today are surrounded by adults, but there is this difference: there was no special or unique world for the East Side boy. There were no Bo Diddley teen-age jazz concerts, no Bobby Darin cliques, no special teen-age movies. There was one world: the adult world with all its pain and happiness, and if the child wanted social contact and love, that was the world in which he achieved it.

The East Side boy wanted working papers as soon as he could pronounce the words; the East Side girl was immediately impressed as a surrogate mother.

I think this made it a better world for children.

It did not necessarily make better humans out of them, but all children must enter the adult world sooner or later; the world where you don't get everything you want—where there are such things as vain toil, crushing disappointments, stern and fierce competition, praise and blame. The earlier a child partakes in that world, the better adapted he is to survive its defeats and challenges and make a place that is his own.

It is no coincidence that the Anglo-Calvinist world, inheritors of the Judaic ethic, once shared the tradition of early adulthood.

Englishmen put a topper and tails on a thirteen-year-old when they send him off to prep school. It's not that way now.

If you expect a boy to be a man, the sooner you let him start practicing, the better.

You had to have baggage

WHEN the Raines Law was passed in New York State it was designed to improve morals, especially the morals of hotel-keepers and their guests. One of the provisions of this law was that you could not rent a room to a couple unless they had baggage. A day after this law went into effect, a dozen luggage stores opened up along Sixth Avenue with big signs, "*Baggage Rented.*" A fellow with a girl walked into one of these stores and for a two-dollar deposit and a fifty-cents-an-hour rate got a bag filled with newspapers, and they went off together happily to the hotel. When they were through they returned the bag and got the deposit back.

Another provision of the law was that saloons were required to serve meals to their patrons after regular closing hours but the law forgot to mention just what constituted a meal. In the back room of each saloon a slice of bread and a piece of dried beef reposed on a table. Every three months or so, when he got around to it, the bartender removed the moldy bread and beef, replacing them with fresh meat and a fresh slice of bread.

The best job

THE woman's page of a metropolitan daily introduced its readers to the problems of emancipated womanhood recently in an article by-lined Phyllis Lee Levin and entitled, "Road from Sophocles to Spock Is Often a Bumpy One." It seems the presidents of the women's colleges, themselves often female, have come upon the thorny problem that sixteen years of education is not a realistic preparation for motherhood and running a family.

"Housewifery is undignified and unrequited," writes Miss Levin, "some women complain. The housewife is reduced to screams and tears in order to have kitchens installed, electric outlets drilled, and roofs mended. No one, it seems, is appreciative, least of all herself, of the kind of person she becomes in the process of turning from poetess to shrew."

The educated housewife is a threat to herself. She has had to make too radical a change from career to family to allow happiness. This is the constant argument of ladies: it is very hard to be a lady.

Of course, one solution is that we could give up educating women, but this would necessitate dumping thousands of teachers on the unemployment rolls. Or we could give up having families, but that won't help us win the Cold War. Or we could examine the argument.

Reason tells us it is a specious argument. Being a mother is pain-racked and wearying. But it is not competitive. No mother has to pass tests, face examiners, or for that matter answer interrogators or justify herself. A man's life is filled with competition. The big-leaguer worries about being sent to the minors, the lawyer about losing the case, the advertising man about getting the account. A mother can abdicate if she chooses and somehow the kid will grow up. Many a boy with a slovenly mother has graduated from the jute mill and become the head of the big soft-drink distributing plant. But if a man abdicates, no one eats.

Women who complain about parenthood would do well to remember that not every editor, ballplayer, or garage mechanic thinks his work is man-worthy. A lot of jobs are plain pointless. In worthiness no job compares to motherhood, not even those important jobs the women complain about having to give up, like being assistant to the fashion editor or secretary to the media director.

Admittedly the women aren't able to contribute their unmetered poetry to the quarterly *avant-garde* magazines, but what gives a human more expression than nursing a child through his first bout of measles? The woman who says the accident of her sex took her away from important things has her values mixed up (but it's understandable with all those labor-saving devices blowing up in her face).

In the long run a housewife has probably the best job in the world: she's an executive, administrator, communications expert, and owns her own business all at once.

Reviewing the movies

Thirteen Ghosts and *The Electronic Monster*, double bill though they were, was a much better movie experience than watching the agonies of Paul Newman, Joanne Woodward, and Ina Balin in *From the Terrace*. It was just too hot to worry about who was bedding down with whom. The persona in *From the Terrace* switched marital partners with the indifference of bored guests switching seats in a game of musical chairs at a dull party, but the foursome in *From the Terrace* weren't enjoying themselves as much. You never saw such pain and emoting. If adultery brought this much unhappiness and inconvenience, the world would be filled with faithful men and the triangle that animates all of Western literature would be no more. The movie missed the point. No one can tell me that married ladies who dally don't giggle. But Joanne Woodward spent the whole picture biting her lips in the deepest anxiety. Paul Newman seemed so unhappy about Ina Balin's submission that it was comforting to know he still had a job and was getting paid and was building up his social security. The program changes tomorrow. *Brides of Dracula* is coming. That should keep the audience awake. It's so confusing to fall asleep while Paul Newman is getting married and wake up just as he's discovering new love with a new girl friend and his wife has her old psychiatrist back.

Trouble in the colleges

THE President of Yale University, A. Whitney Griswold, convened a special faculty committee to recommend to him what might be done to improve the University. The committee's prime suggestion was that Yale admit women undergraduates. This is bound to cause consternation on the campus. While 95 per cent of the conversation among undergraduates probably concerns the female of the species, I doubt they will welcome this innovation. While it is true that the women's colleges of America welcomed returning veterans to their classes after World War II, I suspect the men's schools are less generous. I rather suspect the committee made this recommendation because they were bored looking at nothing but the narrow lapels of the "Ivy League" attire.

On the same day, the students of Trinity College presented their professors with a seventy-eight-page report card which, among other things, criticized the professors for being "ineffectual, not strict enough, and maintaining poor curricula." The professors who failed were as angry as, if more articulate than, the students they flunked.

As if this weren't enough, the students at the Columbia School of Architecture picketed the ground-breaking ceremonies for a new seven-million-dollar School of Business, charging the building was "ugly, and of poor design." One of the silent pickets bore a placard which read, "Columbia, the fluke of the Ocean." Everyone was ruffled apparently, except the architect, who wrote down the wording of every placard and confessed to wonder at what college kids will think of next.

I believe all this heralds a new dawn in college education. The annual spring panty raids are over, and while this is bad news for lingerie manufacturers it will do the dean's blood pressure a lot of good.

Rejoicing in Richmond

JACK KILPATRICK, editor of the Richmond *News Leader*, had himself a ball. He gleefully reported in a big editorial that he had caught me in an error about the sale of Black and White Scotch whisky in the South.

I had said that Black and White Scotch whisky is not sold in Dixie because it suggests integration. I was wrong—my apologies to Black and White. It was an awkward attempt at a bit of satire. It didn't come off. You can't win them all.

The *News Leader*'s editorial noted: "If Harry Golden had made so much as a phone call to check the facts he could have found that Black and White Scotch is widely sold in the South."

The Virginia editor says that he wrote to the Fleischmann Distilling Corporation, which wrote back, "We are completely unaware of any racial prejudice with reference to Black and White Scotch. . . ."

But you never saw such rejoicing in the editorial offices of the Richmond *News Leader*. My, my! In Virginia, you know, they closed down the public schools of Prince Edward County. The white children are going to private schools, the Negro children, except for a few who can afford it, are not getting any schooling. (The American Friends Service Committee is doing all it can.)

But, I prefer not to start a feud, even when I'm right, and in this instance I was wrong.

What I was driving at, Mr. Kilpatrick, is that there are Southern cities where mobs collect to hoot and howl at four little colored schoolgirls.

The unasked question

IN ALL our modern fiction which subjects infidelity and adultery to a minute, soul-searching, almost microscopic examination, why is it that the adulterer never asks the adultress how much money her husband makes a year? Probably the writers don't mention it because they don't want to touch the real nervous core of our society. Most men guard the facts of their income a lot more jealously than they guard their wives (judging from our fiction). The ultimate betrayal is not a wandering wife, but a wandering wife who tells her lover that her husband doesn't make as much as everyone thinks.

We are a people with a great and overpowering love for the inauthentic. CBS used to have a rule book for the subject matter of television dramas. A script about adultery was all right on two conditions: (1) the wife's lover was never to be seen; (2) he mustn't be the husband's best friend.

Adultery has an economic base in our society. In a classless society where income is patent and known, fidelity would be the nature of things.

The undependable diamonds

DIAMONDS are a girl's best friend. The slogan was perpetrated by Anita Loos to suggest that a girl should insist on diamonds so that when her "daddy" leaves her, she will have security. The diamond is her recompense. But it is just not so.

Diamonds are useful to someone who is fleeing a country. They can be hidden easily and are not so bulky as money. They are bought advantageously for cash, but even so they are still not a girl's "best friend." The moment the girl puts the diamond on her finger, it depreciates 50 per cent, just like a new car that is driven around the block.

If a girl wants "security," or indemnification for a broken heart or for the surrender of her honor, she is better advised to take some United States Defense Bonds, or a few shares of A.T.&.T.

The age of innocence

I READ many things when I was a boy, including the society columns of the New York *American*, where I read all about the "coming-out" parties among the rich. I had an idea that a young lady's breasts "came out" at a certain age, and that it was fitting and proper for her parents to honor her maturity. There was nothing risqué or humorous about my thoughts on this matter. I merely believed it to be a sort of female bar mitzvah practiced among the Christians.

This led to reflections recently on whether there ever really is an "age of innocence." I doubt it. In the Orthodox Jewish tradition you never spoke about "such things." And "such things" of course meant one thing—sex. In all my years I never saw my father kiss my mother. I wouldn't make such a statement unless I was sure that hundreds of my contemporaries were able to make the same statement. And of course this was all the more remarkable when you realize that we lived in a five-room flat in a tenement where you could look into the open windows of a dozen other flats at the same time.

But "not speaking" did not mean "not knowing." That was an entirely different story. Children never discuss it with you no matter how close you may be to them.

The academic deadbeat

THE deadbeat is a man who doesn't want to pay his own way. In my lectures around the country I have found a growing body of deadbeats populating the colleges. These are the boys who switch courses and drop math and then plan for graduate school. They want to stay in college because they are willing to deadbeat it for the allowance they get from home or for the pittance they earn at after-school jobs. They are willing to mark time to avoid meeting that big real world that lies in wait. It is not generally known, but there are literally thousands of boys and some girls whose profession is going to college.

In most of the colleges, the students who are preparing for law, medicine, architecture, the ministry, or one of the other professions are the ones who get down to business and want to get out.

The deadbeats are the ones who are out for romance and love. The college girls tell me they can recognize the deadbeats right away. Deadbeats are courtly and make of the girl a precious object. They have plenty of time. But when the boy says to the girl after their first date, "Let's go to bed," this is the evidence that he is in a hurry, he is going to be an engineer—and soon, too.

The unwed mother

THE women's magazines are handing out some gratuitous advice to unwed mothers. The girls are told by the careerist editors: Give your baby up for adoption.

The magazines offer this advice as casually as though a newborn baby were a surplus pup or kitten.

This is the current neo-paganism.

William the Conqueror's mother didn't give him away, and today there are thousands of folks who would spend a small fortune for some proof that they are descended from this illegitimate child. Another mother who did not give up her illegitimate child was Miss da Vinci who stuck it out with her little boy Leonardo. Some boy, too.

Diana and John

DIANA SURRAH and John Vargo were married on August 5 at 10 o'clock at St. Gertrude's Roman Catholic Church, McIntyre, Pennsylvania.

They sent me an invitation and a letter telling me of their romance.

I had delivered a lecture at Pennsylvania State College, Indiana, Pennsylvania.

After the speech they, among others, came up to greet me. It just so happened that John and Diana remained alone with me for a few minutes, and they laughed at the coincidence that they were both subscribers to *The Carolina Israelite*. John asked Diana whether he could take her home. They talked about me for a little while, and during the next few months they talked a lot not about me.

And so two paid subscriptions have now become one, and may God bless them.

On birth control

IT SEEMS to me most of the adherents of a strict birth-control program are men and women over sixty. Now if you haven't been able to solve the population explosion by age sixty, the chances are you will never solve it. But that does not mean that people yet unborn won't solve it.

In the late 1890s the experts began scaring the pants off everyone with the prophecy that "by the year 1920 there will be insufficient arable land in the United States to raise grain and fodder necessary to feed the draft animals required to pull the wagons, drays, and plows which move the goods the United States must have."

The experts were absolutely right.

They just didn't foresee that we wouldn't need arable land for mules, horses, and oxen. They did not foresee that machines would take over their function and not only provide enough food and grain for the populace but indeed for the whole world.

Similarly, the experts of 1962 are probably right. The earth, as presently constituted, does not have room for its growing population. But I can hardly wait to see what little equation these 1962 experts have overlooked, what new invention will befuddle their predictions.

Where are the nymphomaniacs?

I'VE been reading a lot of the best-sellers, the ones about those curious women who go in and out of beds like other people go in and out of restaurants. It occurs to me that if there were as many nymphomaniacs in life as there are in American literature, we would be the happiest race of men in history.

Only-in-America Department

ALL of this happened within the last fifty years. Fifty years ago there were signs all over the country: "Irish Keep Out." "No Irish Need Apply."

But the Irish did not keep out and the Irish kept applying for the job. And now they hold down *the* job.

Sensible shoes

A WOMAN says goodbye to youth when she starts to wear sensible shoes. When comfort becomes so important that she climbs down from stiltlike heels, she is out of the charmed circle of youth. Romance flickers out except for movies and perhaps a remark to Mrs. Kohn that the new clerk in Spiegel's delicatessen looks a little bit like Tony Curtis.

The loser in love in perspective

I'M STILL thinking about the fellow who loved the pretty girl and who thinks of her at least once a week the rest of his life. She's had her hands full contending with children and bridge parties and never thinks of him at all.

It's not as sad as all that.

Now and then a young man will grow old, sentimentalizing about the great love of his life, the girl who married the football coach and had six children and never gives him a thought. But this sentimental old man wasn't allowed to face the responsibility of raising a family and he enjoyed his bachelorhood. Of course he can't tell this to people, so he creates a romantic little story about having loved and lost. This fills the bill and even sounds good after the third cocktail.

A cure for insomnia

FROM Dr. Crane's syndicated column, "Worry Clinic," in answer to a question concerning a cure for insomnia: "If you are a single person take a walk before retiring. Drink a glass of milk, either hot or cold. If you are a married woman, send for my booklet, 'Sex Problems in Marriage.'"

A favorite quote

A GRAND jury recommended that Philadelphia legalize prostitution. The legalization of this profession isn't designed to liven up the town, but rather to quiet it down. In a recent month there were 102 rape cases in the City of Brotherly Love, which, as one lady on the grand jury put it, "is a lot of rape needlessly going on."

Eleven notes in passing

• AFTER all the shooting is over in the movie and TV Westerns, the good guy rides over the hill to collect his unemployment check.

• Writing a letter to a newspaper editor is the easiest way to gain prestige in America.

• All during the voting hours in a recent election to determine the issue of prohibition in a western North Carolina county, the church bells kept ringing to remind the folks to stick to the straight-and-narrow and continue to drive that twenty-two-mile stretch to get the stuff in the adjoining county.

• The exact words of a telephone inquiry made recently at a library in a large Southern city—"Is it all right for colored people to use this library? Thank you. I would like some good books on existentialism."

• A big worry always drives out a smaller one. Perhaps that is why humanity survives so many threats. A man can sit in pain with an abscessed tooth and if someone yells "fire," his mouth is well again and you have to remind him when the fire is put out that he has a toothache. No one on a sinking ship has ever been reported seasick.

• A tablecloth restaurant is still one of the great rewards of civilization.

• Now that Jews are in their third and fourth generations in America there is a growing need for the Society of Half-Jews. My own survey indicates that, counting the Jews, half-Jews, quarter-Jews, and eighth-Jews, our population would be greater than the Catholics and conceivably greater than all the Protestants in the country combined.

• My first impresion of my city, Charlotte, North Carolina, was that everything was "on the level." In New York you have to go up and down—up to the subway, down to the subway, hills and dales, up and down. In Charlotte I stood that first night on the main street and the whole works was right there—the banks, movies, restaurants, even the homes of friends. This sold me—forever.

• The saddest aspect of old age is not necessarily the imminence of death, but the realization that we have outlived our contemporaries.

• The cocktail lounge differs from the saloon in that the saloon used to provide a free lunch, or at least a hard-boiled egg for a nickel. But at a cocktail lounge all you get to eat are those cellophane-wrapped peanuts.

• We need to emulate the English and create an American equivalent of the British knighthood. I do not mean we should go around calling people "Sir" and "Dame," for that goes counter to the American grain. But the worth of individual achievement should be formally and publicly recognized. How else can we substitute the honest respect of a Fritz Kreisler for that of an Elvis Presley, no matter how transient?

The absence of a ritualistic government acclaim or government recognition leads to great frustration. It leaves everybody to his own devices, running hither and yon looking for a dais to sit on or a letterhead to put his name on.

4

BEI MIR BIST
DU SCHOEN

Caruso at the Met

THE performance which made the most lasting impression on me was Verdi's *La Forza del Destino*, with Caruso, Rosa Ponselle, and Antonio Scotti. I've heard the opera many times since, but I always remember it the way Caruso sang it. Others may remember *Pagliacci* because the aria "Vesti la Giubba" became synonymous with Caruso. When Caruso came onto the stage he brought a whole world with him. When he came out of the stage door, too, a whole entourage gathered around him to walk a few blocks to an Italian restaurant. They wanted nothing more than to follow the greatest tenor in the world.

Caruso was to the Metropolitan and opera what Babe Ruth was to the Yankees and baseball. Inevitably Caruso stamped the Metropolitan as the best. People who had never heard the word "aria" before Caruso, suddenly became wild devotees when he sang. He had a personal magnitude, stage presence they call it, of such proportions that he didn't need press agents or publicists. By himself he was enough.

And it's curious, too, the people who remember Caruso. I was in a Southern city recently and a lady and I were talking and she mentioned casually that she hadn't been in New York City for forty years. "My husband and I went to New York City on our honeymoon," she said. "We heard Caruso sing at the Met."

Thousands of people all over the world still speak of Caruso. For them he represents a milestone. At the height of his fame, when he could have demanded anything he wanted from the Metropolitan, he yielded opening night once to Geraldine Farrar, who was just starting on her career. But one night in 1920 while he was singing *l'Elisir D'Amore* at the Brooklyn Academy of Music, he spat blood. By the time he had to sing *Samson and Delilah* he had to hold a heavy towel to his lips whenever he

123

came offstage to stop the flow of blood. *La Juive* was his last performance. After that he lay sick at the Vanderbilt Hotel, and even had the last rites of the Catholic Church. I was one of those who went there every day to read the doctor's bulletins. But Caruso said to the officiating priest, "I want to die in Italy," and he got up and within a week or so he was photographed as apparently recovered. He sailed to Italy and a few weeks later he was dead. That glorious voice was stilled.

Arthur Brisbane wrote a great obituary; he said that the Archangel Michael had gone to the heavenly choir of angels saying, "Quiet everybody, Caruso is coming."

The white badge of courage

President John Fitzgerald Kennedy recently told the pressmen of the country that he intends to drink more milk, to be photographed drinking milk, and to serve milk to his guests in the White House. The President warned that neither the fear of strontium 90 nor the guffaws of the press would deter him in this purpose, which is indeed the statement of a brave man.

A milk drinker must be, above all, a brave man. Think of Pierre Mendes-France, when he was premier of France, and he, too, had himself photographed drinking milk and how people howled at him. The premier of France drinking milk! And Mendes-France's purpose, which was to help reduce incipient alcoholism in French citizens under ten years of age, was lost in the laughter.

We are sure that primitive men knew of milk before they even looked at the moon. No metaphor has ever been as expansive as the Biblical metaphor which called Canaan a land of milk and honey, and what suggests human kindness so well as milk?

I spent quite a bit of time in Paris and London with that excellent movie actor, Richard Widmark. Mr. Widmark is a steadfast and undismayed milk drinker and a real man. I know of no one else who could go into the Crazy Horse Café in Paris, a beatnik hang-out, and order milk and wait for it to be served.

Mr. Widmark says he likes milk well enough to have invented

several gambits to overcome the hilarity. In the jet plane when the stewardess comes down the aisle and asks everyone what he'd like to drink, Mr. Widmark sticks to his guns. Each passenger gives his order: "Martini"—"Bourbon"—"Scotch"—and as usual Mr. Widmark says, "Milk please." The stewardess drops her pad and her face falls like the middle of a city street in Scranton, Pennsylvania, and she says, "Milk?" Mr. Widmark bends over as though in pain and says, "Upset stomach," and the stewardess is all commiseration and kindness. Mr. Widmark settles back with a heavy sigh, and drinks his milk in peace.

Hemingway the hunter

ERNEST HEMINGWAY did something of a disservice to young writers when he had himself photographed with a bottle of gin and a fishing pole, and when he talked of how he cheered at the bullfights and of the adventures he had in Spain, in Cuba, in France, and in Africa. Hemingway was a great writer, one of the greatest of this century, and it would have been just as nice to have had as many photographs of him reading as fishing or hunting. For he did more reading than he did fishing, he did more reading than he did drinking. He read every day of his life in a soundproof room for at least three hours. Pictures of him reading would have done young writers as much good certainly as those pictures of him standing triumphant over a fallen water buffalo. Ernest Hemingway read everything of consequence as fast as it came off the presses.

There are no primitive writers, there are only writers who read. Without books, there are no devices for writers.

Wolfie Gilbert and the chairlady

I MAKE many speeches in Los Angeles and the surrounding area for a variety of causes—Bonds for Israel, women's societies, Conservative synagogues, Reform temples, and college lecture series. When I am in California I always see my pal, Wolfie Gilbert, the fellow who wrote "Waitin' for the Robert E. Lee," "Ramona," "Jeanine, I Dream of Lilac Time," and a thousand others which, year after year, have captured the public's imagination. Wolfie writes songs you can recite twenty-five years later.

When the chairlady phones me at my hotel, I always ask if she would mind my bringing my old friend Wolfie along to the lecture. Generously, the chairlady accedes. Then I say, in a kind of offhand way, "If there is a place on the dais for Mr. Gilbert . . ." and again, charitably, the chairlady says, "Of course."

I go nowhere in the Los Angeles area without Wolfie. To be sure, Wolfie is occasionally in New York because he is the West Coast representative for ASCAP. If that's the case I nevertheless report to his wife, Rosie, so that no matter what end of the country Wolfie is at, he is well informed of my activities.

When Wolfie does accompany me, I wait until the chairlady is almost through with her report and at that moment I hand her a little slip which asks, "Will you please introduce Mr. Wolfie Gilbert?" This is perhaps cruel because the whole agenda is on a sheet in front of her—the slightest intrusion could throw the whole thing out of gear—but the request is from the guest speaker so she nervously says: "And I want to introduce to you Mr. Wolfie Gilbert, the song writer."

Wolfie rises modestly, but, instead of bowing, he walks directly toward the microphone with hand outstretched as if to grab it. The chairlady is taken by surprise and retreats in panic. She does not know that for the first forty years of his life Wolfie was a vaudevillian, a song-and-dance man, and he can no more resist the chance to stand before an audience than he can resist the chance to breathe.

Once he lays hands on the microphone, Wolfie says, "This is my seventy-fifth birthday."

Wolfie doesn't hide his age, but his birthday falls on any day he gets his hands on a mike.

Wolfie continues: "Yes, this is my seventy-fifth birthday and next week is Mother's Day. In the dim past, before Mother's

Day was famous, I did a lot for motherhood with my song, 'My Mother's Eyes.' I helped make mothers famous." Wolfie begins to hum his composition, but cuts himself off with the interjection, "Sorry, I do not have an accompanist."

At a recent lecture, I saw some of the leaders on the dais shrugging as Wolfie talked, while the chairlady cringed and stared at the agenda which she held in both hands. I, too, was the recipient of dirty looks, but the audience as always was wholly fascinated.

"In addition to writing 'Waitin' for the Robert E. Lee,'" says Wolfie, "on a certain day in 1927, I had a song plugger standing by at Station WMCA with instructions to wait for the dispatches. As soon as he heard, 'Lindbergh lands at Le Bourget,' he was to sing my song, 'Lucky Lindy,' written especially for the occasion. He had other instructions in case the dispatches were unfavorable."

Wolfie begins fishing in his pocket and extracts a crumpled piece of paper. "Remembering this," he says, "I will sing my new song for you in commemoration of Alan Shepard's flight. It's called 'Astronaut of Space.'" The chairlady is now holding her head in her hands with the agenda on the floor, as Wolfie recites, with his finger characteristically waving on high:

> Who brought new glory to America?
> In the hall of fame he takes his place.
> The world is proud of young America
> And Alan Shepard, the Astronaut of Space.

Whenever the world looks black to me and I sit brooding in a lonely hotel room, I begin to wish I was near Wolfie so I could ask him to hum the refrain, "Waitin' for the Robert E. Lee," to the accompaniment of a soft-shoe tap he does—seventy-five years and all.

Wolfie Gilbert is not what is wrong with this world.

They cheered his passing

THERE was a Federal judge in Kentucky by the name of Judge A. M. J. Cochrane who was so violent in his hatred of likker that he almost succeeded in sending half the State of Kentucky to prison.

This Judge A. M. J. Cochrane had the help of a prosecutor named Sawyer Smith who was just as "deaf" on Prohibition violators as the judge. Both judge and prosecutor were terribly bored by murder, bankruptcy, or embezzlement, but they sat straight as ramrods when they had before them a man who had run a still up in the mountains.

In some cases Judge A. M. J. Cochrane sentenced a fellow to five years' imprisonment on evidence that the accused had a mash stain on his vest.

In those days there weren't many Federal judges in a State like Kentucky and so the violators were herded into local jails until the judge reached the district. By that time there were two or three hundred brought into the courtroom, and Judge Cochrane would always say, "Those pleading guilty on this side and those pleading not guilty on the other side." Usually about one hundred and eighty-five went on the left side, pleading guilty, and about ten or fifteen hardy souls, Elizabethan individualists, went to the right side, "not guilty."

The judge would then order the "guilty" ones out until sentencing day, and he would turn his attention to those who pleaded "not guilty." He would look at them for about fifteen minutes; he would stare at one of them until the little fellow came up to the bench and said, "Judge, I'm changing my mind and pleading guilty." Usually this timid fellow was followed by five or six more and they were taken out for sentencing a few days later. This left six or seven heroic mountaineers. Judge Cochrane would then beckon to one of the last-ditch "not guilty" fellows and say, "If we convict you here, young fellow, I'm going to give you five years in the penitentiary." At the end of the first hour of court everybody had pleaded guilty and thrown himself on the mercy of Judge A. M. J. Cochrane, which was no mercy at all, because the most lenient sentence for possession of a pint of whisky was two years.

It was not the prison sentence that bothered these wonderful Kentuckians. What annoyed them so much was the inconsistency of the handling of the Prohibition Law. While A. M. J. Cochrane was giving a fellow five years for a still run-off of three gallons a day capacity, Federal Judge Francis J. Coleman in the Southern District of New York, who hated the Prohibition Law, was giving Big Bill Dwyer a fine of one thousand dollars and a suspended sentence of thirty days for a multimillion-dollar rumrunning business.

The one thing Judge A. M. J. Cochrane never knew was that the night the radio announced he had died, three thousand Kentuckians, all in one Federal pen, set up a howl and a cheer that was better than the Fourth of July or New Year's Eve on Times Square.

What is Jack Paar really like?

JACK PAAR was successful for two reasons. One was that he was spontaneous, off-the-cuff, unrehearsed.

Mr. Paar managed his element of spontaneity by the simple process of interviewing people. He had a certain ease of communication, "effortless communication," as Thoreau put it, and in this century of sputtering inarticulateness, it is a supreme gift. I do not mean that Mr. Paar in his interviewing can compete with an Edward R. Murrow, or a Howard K. Smith.

Nor can he even compete with the average newspaper reporter who meets a minor Belgian official at the airport. But Paar was a different type of interviewer. He was an interviewer who interrupted with impunity. Several times on Mr. Paar's show I was asked what I thought on certain matters. I drew in my breath and tried to arrange my thoughts and, before I could answer, Mr. Paar said, "Don't you think it's this way? . . ." This communicated a complete spontaneity to the audience. I was on the program when the camera cut to a commercial and Mr. Paar signaled his guests frantically: "Think of something, someone. We have three minutes left." But the fact that this plea was made out of range of the camera was irrelevant. Somehow the idea was communicated to his vast audience, millions of whom had the same trouble the next morning in classrooms, offices, factories, and PTAs.

Along with this ease of communication, Mr. Paar had an infectious good nature. Irritation was only momentary on his program.

Paar's ability of expression was not without its faults. He was a persuasive man and completely took you in. Sitting beside him and hearing him tell the audience why he didn't like Dorothy Kilgallen, Steve Allen, or Walter Winchell didn't make you cringe. He had the happy faculty of creating a family atmosphere which is all to the good; but after a recital of a petty hate you sat there wondering how you could convey the impression that you did not share all of Mr. Paar's viewpoints.

The second reason for his success was one that Paar seemed to be completely unaware of: he was following in the footsteps, and improving upon, some of the very people he criticized—the personal journalists.

Paar was the first personal journalist on TV; he was in effect an editor commenting on news and human interest—with a byline.

It was the by-line that was important. Paar said this, Paar said that. And that is the precise reason the columnists have enjoyed popularity in journalism.

The collective opinion of an anonymous editorial staff has no value. None at all. Except when it discusses new county taxes or parking meters.

Paar used vaudeville methods to get a message across. We still do not know how much education he has or how much knowledge he has of world affairs, and this is his great artistry. He shrugs his shoulders and gives the impression that he's just a boy in these matters. "Harry, I know nothing about this integration business," he'd say, "tell us a little about it."

There was a bit of preparation before you went on the Paar program. The producers sat with you for a few moments and went over some questions Paar would ask you. One time my "preparation" called for a few questions about my book, *Carl Sandburg*, each question to lead to a story, a quip, a joke. But earlier on the program, Bill Buckley, Jr., was making his pitch for the Ultra-Radicals, as he calls the members of his right-wing movement. When I came on the program later, Paar leaned across the desk, off camera, and said, "Harry, forget selling books, let's give this guy Buckley some hell."

On another occasion, Paar asked, "What is this about Red China? They have a lot of people, don't they?" I've heard dozens of questions of this kind from Jack Paar, and I will say now that this man gave us the only forum on TV we have had in the last ten years, the only forum on which people could say something.

James Byrnes and Al Smith

THERE is a singular parallel between the careers of the late Governor Alfred E. Smith of New York and Governor James Byrnes of South Carolina. Both men were drawn full length by William Shakespeare in the character of Harry Hotspur. Hotspur was a decent, brainy man with fine instincts and a good heart. He was the man who put Bolingbroke on the throne, but then turned on him and did everything in his power to tear him down, ending his days in bitterness and disappointment. Harry Hotspur lived again in the character of New York's Governor Alfred E. Smith, and in James Byrnes, former Supreme Court justice, former Secretary of State, and former assistant to Presidents Roosevelt and Truman. Al Smith did not become bitter against President Roosevelt because the latter won the nomination in 1932, when Smith felt that the party owed it to him. The break actually came some four years earlier. When Smith was nominated on the Democratic ticket in 1928 he did everything in his power to get Roosevelt to run for governor of New York. Smith felt he needed Roosevelt to help him carry the State.

Smith recognized that he'd be identified as the Tammany Hall Roman Catholic Democrat, and he wanted a Protestant who had never been identified with the political machine. Roosevelt was a natural. Everybody knows the story; how they had to beg Roosevelt to run, and how he refused because he had just invested a quarter of a million dollars of his mother's money in Warm Springs, and finally how Smith, John J. Raskob, Mrs. Roosevelt, and Louis Howe prevailed upon F.D.R. to accept the nomination for governor. Smith was defeated by Herbert Hoover and lost New York State while Roosevelt became governor. This was not a pleasant dose for Governor Smith. The day after Roosevelt's inauguration, former Governor Smith told him "not to worry," that he (Smith) had left a good staff behind, especially Mr. Robert Moses and Mrs. Henry Moscowitz; and furthermore that he had taken an apartment in an Albany hotel to be near the new governor and help steer the new administration. "In fact," said Smith, "you can go to Warm Springs any time you feel like it, and stay as long as you want. Everything will be taken care of here in Albany."

What happened in the next day or two marked the end of the friendship between Roosevelt and the man whom he had named "the Happy Warrior." It was a bitter man who checked out of the Albany hotel and went back to New York City. Roosevelt fired the entire staff, and set out to carry on the business of the State of New York on his own. The fight over the nomination in 1932 was really an anticlimax. Smith never had a chance and he was a smart enough politician to know it. He knew that the delegates would never nominate him again, but he fought desperately to keep Roosevelt from securing the nomination. The chances are that if he had thrown his votes to Newton D. Baker after the first ballot, he might have forestalled the McAdoo and Garner switch to Roosevelt, but he acted too late. As Roosevelt was flying to Chicago to accept the nomination, Smith was returning to New York. Four years later, this great man, a product of the Lower East Side, who had written the first workman's compensation law into American life, wore a huge sunflower in support of Alfred M. Landon. The picture of Al Smith with the brown derby, a "graduate" of the Fulton Fish Market, wearing the colors of the Kansas prairie politician was a sight to remember.

James Byrnes was called to Washington by President Harry Truman the day after the death of Roosevelt. Like Smith, Mr. Byrnes felt that President Truman did not have to worry, everything would be handled all right—by him. The disappointment of Byrnes came when Truman indicated that he expected to be the President of the United States. Instead of taking his place as an elder statesman wearing the toga of wisdom which is his by right and experience, Byrnes is eating his heart out in disappointment and bitterness. First, he feels that, but for an accident, he would have been chosen Roosevelt's Vice-President in 1944; and second, he feels he should have had greater freedom of decision when Truman called him to help.

Mrs. Roosevelt has written that her husband never lost his affection for Al Smith, and I am sure that by the same token if you pinned him down, President Truman would say he has a warm spot in his heart for James Byrnes.

Bei Mir Bist Du Schoen

JOHN MILTON sold his epic poem *Paradise Lost* to a publisher for five pounds (about twenty bucks in those days). Stephen Foster sold "Oh Susanna" for five dollars to the great minstrel, Dan Emmett. Toulouse-Lautrec tossed off dozens of posters for nothing.

History is filled with the story of men who did not realize the fruit of their labors.

Sholom Secunda does not fancy himself a great artist, but he wrote a song which has earned three million dollars in royalties. And his share was thirty dollars. Mr. Secunda, who was a composer for a Yiddish theater, wrote the song "Bei Mir Bist Du Schoen." Five years after the song made its first appearance, a music company which published Jewish songs offered Mr. Secunda thirty dollars. Mr. Secunda considered this found money since most of the composers published at their own expense.

Not too long after this Mr. Secunda heard his melody sung by an unknown trio called the Andrews Sisters, who made the song an immediate hit. Along with the sale Mr. Secunda had surrendered his rights. A sale is a sale, and Mr. Secunda explained that the loss of royalties bothered others more than it ever bothered him.

The Federal copyright law says that only the author may renew a copyright after twenty-eight years. Mr. Secunda will renew his copyright on "Bei Mir Bist Du Schoen" and share in all its subsequent royalty earnings. Mr. Secunda says that his song does not compare favorably with his symphonic compositions. But no American who was around in the 1930s can forget:

> Bei mir bist du schoen
> Please let me explain
> Bei mir bist du schoen
> Means you are grand.

What a woman!

THE greatest of all my letter-writers is my long-time friend and fellow liberal, Lorena Willis of Sacramento, California. I do not know what I would do without Lorena.

Now there's a woman.

How many women have been rolled at the age of four?

Lorena's Uncle Tommy took her to the saloons on the Barbary Coast of San Francisco. He sat her up on the bar and she sang while he passed the hat. Around three in the morning she fell asleep and he rolled her for the dough she had earned.

Today Lorena runs a Residence Club in Sacramento. In Bombay and Damascus and Teheran and Ghana, when young students are scheduled to study in the United States and their itinerary calls for them to be in central California, the word is passed along: "Be sure to visit Lorena Willis on P Street, Sacramento."

What most Germans do not know about Bach

MUSIC lovers are celebrating the 277th anniversary of the birth of Johann Sebastian Bach, but what most Germans don't know about Bach is that he had been obscure for many years, and the man to whom the world owes a debt for reviving an interest in this great German composer was Felix Mendelssohn-Bartholdy, a Jew.

Mendelssohn's grandfather was Moses Mendelssohn who helped the Jews of Europe enter into Western culture. Moses' son, Abraham, became a Lutheran and added the Christian name Bartholdy to his own to distinguish himself from other Mendelssohns who preferred to remain in the Jewish faith. After his son Felix became a great composer, the Lutheran Mendelssohn once said, "I used to be the son of my father, but now I'm the father of my son."

It was Felix Mendelssohn and a handful of others who had to overcome hostility and indifference to promote Bach and were finally able to put on the St. Matthew Passion on March 11, 1829, with Mendelssohn conducting. It was the first performance of the St. Matthew Passion outside of Leipzig since Bach's death eighty years earlier. For the rest of his life Mendelssohn was very proud of his accomplishment and once remarked, "It was an actor and a Jew who restored this great Christian work to the people." It is the only time that Mendelssohn is known to have referred to his Jewish background.

A young woman with a voice

I KNOW a family which includes a young daughter gifted with a beautiful voice. Whether that voice is beautiful enough to carry her to the New York stage or under the proscenium of the Metropolitan Opera I am not qualified to say. I doubt it.

The girl is seventeen, very pretty, and right now she has two roles in college-type theatricals. Her mother daily searches the local newspapers in their town to see if her daughter is mentioned.

But it is all a question of motivation. For this girl to make a career of that voice, the dedication and hard work of a unique individual will be required, and it has been my impression that women don't want to build a bridge, they want to produce a bridge-builder. Probably this young girl will have few clippings to show her children one day, for the odds are against her having a full-fledged musical career, and it may be just as well. Let us hope she bears the children who will write the sonatas.

Doc Rockwell's son

GEORGE LINCOLN ROCKWELL, the führer of the so-called American Nazi Party, has helped inspire countless anti-Semitic tracts, displayed the swastika, and worked constantly for the world-wide resuscitation of the Nazi Party.

What makes a man an anti-Semite? I have gone into this thoroughly in my writing, but it still remains one of the curious maladies of Western civilization, particularly when one thinks of George Lincoln Rockwell.

George Lincoln Rockwell is the son of Doc Rockwell, one of the most talented performers in the days of vaudeville. More than a man of genius, Doc Rockwell is a kind man. I used to know him well. In the days of big vaudeville, he lived at the Jefferson Hotel on Sixth Avenue and Thirty-eighth Street in New York, a sixty-room theatrical hotel which was my brother Jack's first hotel. Jack had been the night clerk in the Jefferson when he bought a one-half interest in the lease in 1915. I got to know Doc Rockwell when I visited my brother at the hotel and I found him a man of humor, kindness, and tolerance. My brother, an Orthodox Jew, had Doc at his table for many a Sabbath meal.

When vaudeville failed, Doc Rockwell became famous to millions of radio listeners, as "Old Doc" in a program of homespun philosophy. He lives in Maine now and he has had many offers to return to show business. But Doc Rockwell craves anonymity and has indicated that he is the bearer of a great sorrow. His sorrow is a psychotic son.

The congressman with an accent

ONE of the greatest representatives to sit in the Congress was an immigrant with an accent so thick you could cut it with a knife. But you listened to him with admiration and respect.

Meyer London was the first Socialist congressman from New York City. He was a champion of labor and an even greater champion of democracy.

Meyer London was an immigrant Jew who put himself through law school and directed his early practice to the aid of the emerging labor unions. He helped organize the bitter labor strikes that started some time just before 1910 and culminated in the formation of the garment unions by 1914.

In 1916 London campaigned against a Tammany candidate and won. His victory anticipated Truman's surprise victory in 1948. The morning after the election every newspaper had the Tammany candidate, Mr. Goldfogel, elected from the Lower East Side District.

In Congress, Meyer London urged passage of a minimum wage law, advocated unemployment insurance, and asked for a GI bill in 1918.

He was one of the first modern congressmen to urge equality and franchise for the Negro.

He was the first Socialist congressman to write legislation which a President signed into law. The law he authored stated that when an employer is discharged in bankruptcy he is not relieved from the debt he owes his employees, even though he may be purged of all other obligation.

In order to beat London, the third time out, Tammany Hall and the Republicans combined in 1920 and put up a joint candidate. London beat him by a few votes. The congressman sent a message to Tammany inquiring whether Tammany wanted a recount. Tammany replied, "Hell, no recount."

So just before the next election, the politicos gerrymandered his district. They cut away half of it, putting some of his constituents in Chinatown and giving the rest to the West Side Irish On the last day of the New York State Legislature they sneaked this gerrymander through by a voice vote.

London decided against making a race for it. He retired from Congress and politics, but not from socialism.

In 1926, while crossing the street on his way to the park with a copy of Chekhov stories in his pocket, London was struck and killed by an automobile. Fifty thousand people attended his funeral. It is curious to note that most of the reforms he advocated, which brought him enmity and contempt, were made into law in the 1930s and 1940s.

In 1920, Congressman London outlined a Socialist peace program to the House of Representatives.

"Our international program should involve first, cancellation of all war debs among all Allied nations. That must be done in order to establish economic stability. Next, we should revise or wipe out the treaty of Versailles. We should initiate an association of nations based upon democratic principles. We should convoke an international, interparliamentary congress to consist of delegates elected on a democratic basis to meet and discuss the basic principles of all peace. We should create an international fund out of which might credit be extended in food, raw materials, and machinery for the people in need of such aid. We should demand universal disarmament. We should recognize Russia because no peace which refuses to take into consideration a country with a population of 140,000,000 occupying one-half of Europe and one-half of Asia, can be a lasting peace."

How many tears, how much anguish, how much suffering, and how many lives would have been spared if we had followed this program in 1920, so brilliantly outlined by Congressman Meyer London, an immigrant Jew who spoke from the floor of Congress with a "foreign" accent.

America's feudal barony

Not long ago, Charles A. Cannon, on behalf of the Cannon Mills, raised the minimum starting wage for the workers. This was headline news in North Carolina and South Carolina, for it meant that there would be a minimum wage of $1.25 for journeymen mill-workers.

Mr. Cannon is the last of the feudal barons of the twentieth century. Because of his vast holdings in the Cannon Mills, he owns the material town of Kannapolis in the same way that William Faulkner owns the imaginary town of Jefferson in Yoknopawtapha County.

Kannapolis is North Carolina's eleventh largest city, numbering over 34,000 inhabitants. It is also the world's largest unincorporated city. It is a city owned lock, stock, and barrel—police, firemen, and parking meters—by the Cannon Mills (towels, blankets, sheets, and pillowcases). The guards in front of the company gates are deputized and belong to the police force, whose salaries are paid by the company.

Twenty thousand men and women work at Cannon Mills. A good proportion of them live in Cannon-owned homes. Mr. Cannon protects these investments of the company with a new coat of spanking white paint every other year and redoes the interior in whatever color the lady of the house chooses. The lawns here are clipped and green, the streets straight and clean, and adequate fire hydrants line the block. Leave the area called Cannon's square mile and the first thing you miss are the fire hydrants. It is not that the folks who live outside of the Cannon domain are sloppier; it is that they have no aldermen to float a bond for sewerage or enact drainage laws.

In the downtown area of Kannapolis, where Cannon Mills owns all the office buildings, the businessmen have thirty-day leases. As long as you stay out of the company's way, the lease is automatically renewed.

There are about sixty churches in Kannapolis, only one of

which owns the title to its land. The rest lease from the Mills.

Mr. Cannon inherited this barony from his father, who laid it out in 1906. Owning a barony is not a matter of holding title simple. Indeed not. Only certain men qualify for the role of seigneur. The men who work in Cannon Mills tell me that Charlie Cannon often walks through the factories in his shirt sleeves. He claims that all of his twenty thousand employees are his friends. He knows who has been sick in the family, who has graduated from high school, and who has just married. Many of these work at the same looms their fathers' worked. There is no doubt of Mr. Cannon's fellowship with his workers, but "the company" also relies on a tightly organized system of supervision which penetrates into the social, political, religious, and fraternal life of the community.

There are some unarticulated laws in Kannapolis of which everyone is aware. Every clergyman, for instance, avoids the phrases, "The *wages* of sin is death," or "In *union* there is strength," and all other words that might possibly suggest "collective bargaining."

Years ago, the officials of the CIO textile unions decided to make a concerted attempt to organize Cannon Mills.

The Kannapolis venture was an expensive one. First of all, the union was forced to rent a headquarters five miles out of Kannapolis on the Cannon Highway. A highly experienced organizer named Tom Gallagher, now retired, was sent to the area with a team of fourteen men, who signed up 4,435 Cannon employees. But it wasn't enough. The union must have 30 per cent to get an NLRB "show of interest" hearing. As a matter of policy the union won't even ask for such a hearing unless it gets 65 per cent. There can be too many changes of opinion, resignations, transfers, and firings between card-signing time and "election day." That ended the last major attempt to organize Cannon.

Mr. Cannon was fair with the organizers. They passed out literature at the mill gate, and there weren't any discharges for union activity. Nobody was drenched with fire hoses, bopped with pop bottles, or manhandled by deputies.

While Charles Cannon does not exercise complete political control over the area, he exercises enough to satisfy his needs.

When the liberal Frank P. Graham was running for the Senate against the conservative Willis Smith, Graham's county manager sent a few of his workers into Kannapolis to distribute circulars. These Graham workers stationed themselves at the mill gate to distribute the campaign literature at the end of the work day. As fast as they appeared at their positions, the mill guards had them arrested on the charge of "littering the streets." The Graham manager finally lost his patience: "I'll bet there is one thing Cannon Mills has not thought of—anti-aircraft batteries," and so he hired an airplane to circle over Kannapolis and drop the Graham circulars.

There is a constant vigilance. A young reporter on the Kannapolis *Independent* was fired the day after he told a PTA meeting that children of textile workers were not getting adequate education. The principal stockholder of the *Independent* is Robert G. Hayes, son-in-law of Charlie Cannon, a member of the towel city hierarchy. (According to the 1960 census, 23.9 per cent of the population of Kannapolis completed four years of high school. The census figure of 8.3 for median school years is the lowest of all urban communities in North Carolina.)

Nevertheless the power of this last American feudal barony is exercised with considerable restraint and much benevolence. But Mr. Cannon can recognize a threat even before it has had an opportunity to materialize. In June 1954, the Raleigh *News & Observer*, edited by Jonathan Daniels, author and press assistant to Presidents Roosevelt and Truman, sent his star reporter, Jay Jenkins, after the story. Mr. Jenkins, now with the Charlotte *Observer*, called it "the story of a harnessed colossus." It has since become a cherished document in many of the mill colonies. It is also something of a collector's item because, hours before this Sunday edition of the *News & Observer* hit the street in Kannapolis, the newsstands were given to understand it would not be wise to sell or display the paper. There was a well-founded rumor that Cannon dealers around the State, truckers, and textile-machinery people were buying up every copy of the paper they could get their hands on.

Mr. Cannon and his fellow directors took the company off the "big board" recently because they did not want to comply with new regulations which would require them to solicit proxies for stockholders' meetings and reveal executive salaries and stockholdings. Cannon stock had been listed for thirty-three years.

The worker in a Cannon Mill house pays a rent of roughly ten dollars per room per month. He pays $2.40 a month for electricity. Cannon Mills buys the power from the Duke Power Company at a wholesale rate and sells it to its tenants. The charge for water is $1.50 a month. But to outsiders, those who have no connection with the mills, the charge for water is $3.15 a month.

The local golf club (Charles A. Cannon Memorial Golf Club) is managed by the superintendent of construction for Cannon Mills. For a long time Mr. Cannon resisted the idea of building lockers in the club, because he said, "Lockers hold beer and whisky." Recently lockers have been installed, but they are only large enough to hold a pair of shoes, according to one of the members.

But with all his precautions, Charlie Cannon grew a little careless a few years ago concerning a threat from within. This is the story of Kannapolis lawyer Bedford Worth Black, giant killer, junior grade.

Black was once considered quite friendly with Charles A. Cannon, but his strong support of Senator Graham in the Senate race of 1950 apparently drew a line between them.

Black didn't become a thorn in the side of the Seigneur until 1958, when he won a seat in the North Carolina House of Representatives from Eugene Bost, a Cannon attorney and one-time speaker of the House. Black definitely was not "Cannon's man." He did not campaign against the mill owner; he did not mention his name in public. But he left no doubt that he believed Representative Bost and Representative Dwight Quinn did a much better job of representing the Cannon Mills than they did Cabarrus County.

A House race is important in Cannon's county. In the absence of a chartered government, the State Legislature is really the town council, once removed, for Kannapolis. Kannapolis ordinances must be enacted as State laws.

Mr. Black and the conservative Bost deadlocked at 5,450 votes each in the first election. In the recount, Black wound up with 5,488 votes to ten-term veteran Bost's 5,457—a 31-vote margin.

From the floor of the State Legislature, Black said he was refused access to Kannapolis' books of record despite a ruling by Attorney General Malcolm Seawell that records are open to anyone. Black wanted to find out how much Cannon Mills contributed to the upkeep of the Kannapolis police department.

The Kannapolis *Independent* banned the name of Black from its news columns. The publisher says he ordered his staff to strike Black's name completely, even from wire-service dispatches from the State capital—because, he said, Black is a "controversial figure."

In the General Assembly, Mr. Black also sought to amend a bill calling for mandatory re-evaluation of property by county to have Cannon's county listed in a bracket calling for re-evaluation in 1962 instead of 1967. He charged that Kannapolis business property was taxed by the acre. He said property with a "gully on it big enough to hide a wing of the capitol" was taxed the same as downtown business property. Representative Quinn, a Cannon Mills executive, objected. The amendment was defeated 102 to 6.

On March 17, 1962, Black announced for Congress in the Ninth District. His opponent: Hugh Q. Alexander, a recognized "Cannon man" who lives in a Kannapolis house owned by Cannon Mills.

Black apparently is a realist. He said it would "be a miracle" if he won the nomination from Alexander. The miracle did not happen. Alexander breezed home with 39,047 to 10,394 for Black.

Thus ended the storybook political career of the Cannon giant killer, Bedford Worth Black.

But an associate of Black who wanted to open an office of his own has not been able to rent office space in downtown Kannapolis.

Do not think Kannapolis and its feudal lord are the last remnants of a time gone by. The mill towns which dotted the Southern landscape have disappeared bit by bit. But most of them were ugly ramshackle affairs with little if any realty values. The Cannon Mills do better than two hundred million dollars a year and the weekly pay roll in Kannapolis is almost one million dollars. Kannapolis is not about to go away. Kannapolis and the Cannon Mills are every bit as good as General Motors and Detroit except that Cannon Mills owns the town, too.

The new aristocracy

The boss he died one evening
And climbed up to the Pearly Gate.
He said, "Oh, Mr. Peter, one word I'd like to tell
I'd like to meet the Astorbilts and John D. Rockefell.

Old Pete said: "Is that so?
You'll meet them down below."

THE above was an old Wobbly (International Workers of the World) song. Listening to it now, one realizes the immense change that has come over the country in the last fifty years. The "Astorbilts" and "John D. Rockefell" will not be in hell but in heaven, as a reward for siring the saviors of America.

The American aristocracy is saving the cause of social progress. Our nobility, the Fords, the Harrimans, the Guggenheims, the Rockefellers, are champions of the liberal cause. They have been the greatest supporters of the United Nations, they have figured out the plans by which we exchange students with foreign countries and, above all, they have spearheaded the integration movement in the South ever since the Carnegie Foundation financed Gunnar Myrdal's monumental study, *An American Dilemma*. The rich kid has wound up on the side of all the people.

It is the chore boy who deplores the new social dispensation, and who would revoke social security, TVA, rural electrification, cheap postal rates, and thereby claim he is giving everybody back his freedom. The chore boy who worked for a living is always the ironclad conservative, the fellow with two feet on the ground crying about the money "down the drain" that goes into foreign aid. The fellow who milked the cow at 4:00 A.M. and took care of the younger children while his mother was at the jute mill is our conservative, and the boy born with a silver spoon in his mouth is our liberal.

The chore boy got nothing free and he wants to make sure no one less privileged in natural talents gets anything free either.

But I suspect his is a losing cause. The American aristocracy is far more noble. A friend of mine wrote me some years ago, "The Rockefellers have just given me a five-thousand-dollar grant so I can write my book on socialism." Only in America.

The genius

IN A RECENT article, "Are Writers Born?" I said that while geniuses may be born, they are few and far between. Writing requires hard work. After reading this, a charming housewife in Brooklyn wrote to say that her little boy, age nine, was normal, although he did show flashes of being pretty smart. On "Parents Day" she visited his class. All the kids were singing or reading but her little boy was going around picking up a piece of paper, scrutinizing the bottom of a chair, dusting erasers, cleaning a table, and the mother immediately wondered how such genius went unnoticed.

She was barely able to conceal her excitement when she approached the teacher after the session. The mother wildly tried to think of words to inform the teacher tactfully about the hidden jewel, her son, who was picked to do the scrutinizing. The mother said, "Miss Clark, does Robert always wander about the classroom while you teach?" The teacher replied, "Only when he's janitor for the day."

Another park commissioner loses a battle

THE city council in Sacramento, California, decided that the century-old Plaza Park in the heart of downtown Sacramento should make way for a parking lot. "The first step," said one of the city fathers, "is to get rid of the bums." So the tables and benches where old men played pinochle and argued with their friends were to be removed. The city council was promptly stunned by the outraged protests of citizens.

It seems the citizens obtained rest and recreation in their own busy lives by watching the old gentlemen enjoy themselves without the steaming pressure of modern life. The tables stay. Good for Sacramento.

The giant boiler

TWICE in this century the enemy miscalculated. The Kaiser and Hitler miscalculated.

But one man in Europe understood. Sir Edward Grey, the British Foreign Minister. Sir Edward looked out the window one day in August 1914, and said: "The lamps are going out all over Europe; we shall see them lit again in our lifetime." You would think that any man capable of such great wisdom would have been listened to. He said something else, in 1916: "The power of the United States is deceptive. She is like a giant boiler; once you light a fire under her there is no limit to the power she can generate."

Let us hope, for the sake of mankind, that Khrushchev does not miscalculate; that he does not let his "space" achievement obscure his vision; that he is not deceived by our annual purchase of one billion dollars' worth of cosmetics and deodorants; that he does not "light a fire" under this giant boiler.

It would be a great sorrow for millions and millions of decent, warmhearted Russian people if Khrushchev did not take to heart the words of Sir Edward Grey in the year 1916.

The boxing announcer

HARRY BALOGH, the boxing announcer, died recently. He brought to the prize ring a better command of malapropisms than Dizzy Dean brought to baseball. Once, indeed, he beseeched a crowd to watch the fight without "anchor or prejudism." He also introduced the stiff white shirt and the dinner jacket to the squared circle. He went to the top rank in his profession in 1933 when he succeeded Joe Humphreys, and Balogh's first innovation was to change Humphreys' famous injunction, "And may the best man win," to "And may the better boxer emerge victorious."

I remember Joe Humphreys better than Balogh.

Humphreys was intensely Irish. If an Irishman fought an Italian, a Jew, or a Negro, Humphreys always introduced the Hibernian first, even if the other man was the champion. On the many occasions when two Irishmen fought, Joe Humphreys always looked sad because he knew one of them had to lose, and he would take off his green fedora and kiss it reverently after the introduction.

Brendan Behan

BRENDAN BEHAN writes drunk or sober, in jail or out. He writes and writes and people read and read. Nobody ever seems to get enough of the Irish (except the Irish).

Behan can be coarse, insulting, reckless, frightening, lovable, wistful, and outrageous. You can't run out of adjectives and he can't run out of things to write about, and people say "terrible," and keep on reading. Under it all it is Behan's deep boiling hatred and four-dimensional love that is serene, self-sacrificing, and natural—all of it held together by good Irish whisky.

Eighteen mistresses

RICHARD LLOYD GEORGE, second Earl of Dwyfor, has written a book about his late father, David Lloyd George, British prime minister during World War I. The information George, Jr., offers us is that his father had eighteen mistresses, four of whom bore him illegitimate children.

I do not doubt the story. Anyone who has read the history of the Fabian Society in England or has read about the colonial sport of adultery in Empire outposts knows that the British, for all their reserve, are the champion mischief-makers of Europe.

But is this all that Richard Lloyd George, a man of seventy, can remember about his father? Very frankly, is this proper? Surely it wasn't the eighteen adulteries which led the British to build an eighteen-foot statue of David Lloyd George at Cardiff.

And how is Richard Lloyd George so sure eighteen is the right number?

5.

THE PARTISAN
FOR GOD

A Senate confirmation

NEVER think an appointment to the Federal bench is a cut-and-dried affair.

Some years ago, United States Solicitor General Simon E. Soboloff was named by President Eisenhower to one of the vacancies on the Federal Court of Appeals of the Fourth Circuit. The late Judge John J. Parker was the chief judge of this bench and had urged the President to consider Soboloff.

Senator Olin D. Johnston of South Carolina blocked confirmation.

Now why was the South Carolina Senator holding back the nomination in the Senate Judiciary Committee? Judge Soboloff's record was spotless—"a lawyer's lawyer," they called him.

Simon Soboloff had been the U. S. Solicitor General who argued the case which resulted in the Supreme Court decision of 1954 which declared illegal the segregation of the races in the public schools. Senator Johnston knew, of course, that any solicitor general would have had to defend the decision. But the Senator's constituents back in South Carolina did not know this and they were strong for racial segregation. Senator Johnston was doing his best to represent their views.

Let me say in all sincerity that Senator Johnston is a good man. If you met him socially, even though you were against racial segregation, you would get to like him and he would get to like you.

Many professional politicians like to boast of their humble beginnings. In the South this is particularly effective, even to nicknames, Pitchfork Ben or Cotton-Ed, and to articles of clothing, such as unpressed pants, string neckties, red galluses, and wool hats. But in the case of Olin Johnston it was real. The Senator had been a mill hand. In any other part of the country, such a

background, from mill hand to governor to Senator, would be
unbeatable. But in South Carolina, the politician needs something
more—he needs to "holler nigger," and if the other fellow should
get the jump on him and "holler nigger" first, then he must
"holler nigger" louder.

It is this factor which made the race between Strom Thurmond
and Olin Johnston so interesting. Olin was up against the champ
himself, Thurmond having run for President two years before on
the Dixiecrat ticket. But Olin Johnston won a remarkable victory.
The business of being for the maintenance of racial segregation
is something you must declare over and over. It is not like stating
a political philosophy once and being known forevermore as a
"high tariff man" or an "isolationist." You must keep asserting
and reasserting your position. Thurmond forgot this for the
moment. Having led the forces of segregation, he thought he
could rest on his laurels and go on to more statesmanlike matters.
Old Olin came right out "hollering nigger," and before the campaign was two weeks old, Thurmond's restraint in the matter of
race was interpreted as softness on the "nigger" question.

And so, holding up the appointment of Simon Sobeloff was
merely another way of "hollering nigger."

At this moment, Judge Parker was deeply concerned lest the
President or Sobeloff, himself, decide to withdraw the nomination.

Judge Parker and I were close friends. We took walks together
and we met occasionally for the sole purpose of talking. When
we arranged an appointment, the judge would send me a note
establishing the agenda, "Let's discuss the Book of Job tomorrow
at lunch . . ." or "Give me the Zionist viewpoint . . ."

At this time the judge was saying, "I need Simon on my bench
. . . I must have Simon."

And he offered a suggestion. "Harry," he said, "you are close
to Kerr Scott [then junior Senator from North Carolina], why
don't you see him about Simon; he may be able to help get the
appointment out of committee and onto the floor."

I went to Washington to see Kerr Scott and outlined a plan.
A constituent would soon write him a letter urging his support
of Simon Sobeloff and the Senator would reply, "While I am not
a member of the Judiciary Committee, from all I know of Judge

Simon E. Sobeloff, I'd be inclined to vote for confirmation if and when the appointment reaches the floor of the Senate."

Scott thought about all of this but was noncommittal. He said, "Harry, I'm a Southerner, and I'll never go against the interests of the South." But, added my good friend, "Stay overnight; let me see you again tomorrow," and it did not sound like a mere bit of politeness.

Along about 11:30 A.M. I took my seat in the appointment room outside the Senate chamber. A Senate page already had my slip, on which was written that Harry Golden was in the waiting room to see Senator W. Kerr Scott at the Senator's pleasure and convenience. And within a few minutes the handsome tobacco-chewing North Carolina Senator was extending his hand to me with a smile from ear to ear. He motioned for me to sit down and, without further preliminaries, he said, "Harry, I spoke to Lyndon Johnson about this Sobeloff affair and Lyndon said, 'Kerr, all of us Southern boys are going to stick together and vote against Sobeloff, but you tell your friends that he'll be confirmed.'"

I reported all of this to Judge Parker who said, "Thank God for Lyndon Johnson."

Billy Graham–partisan for God

I CONSIDER Billy Graham a great Christian and an eminent gentleman. He is an evangelical minister of the Gospel who never tries to evangelize me. Billy Graham merely says to me, "The world needs God," and to this I say, "Amen." I know Billy Graham means it because I can remember when he accepted the invitation to dedicate Charlotte's new stadium, provided the audience was desegregated.

For a large part of 1960, Billy Graham was abroad. He had been in West Berlin and had traveled around Europe, and, upon his return, he had a message from Henry Luce, the publisher of *Time*, *Life*, and *Fortune*.

Mr. Luce told Billy he wanted him to contribute a nonpolitical article to *Life* about Dick Nixon.

Said Mr. Luce to the Reverend Billy Graham, "You are a friend of Mr. Nixon's. You have played golf together and you admire his wife Pat, and you love his children. I would like a human-interest story about Nixon from you without relation to the present campaign."

Billy went home to North Carolina and wrote the article and mailed it off. It was scheduled to appear in one of the first two issues of October 1960.

Let me presume now that when Mr. Luce read the article, he realized he had a gold mine. Mr. Luce made no mystery of his political sympathies. And before him he had a beautifully written story about this young American politician, Richard Nixon, and his family, written by a universally respected Christian leader who did not engage in partisan politics.

Then the Democrats got wind of Billy's article. A good Democrat in the Luce organization told Governor Abe Ribicoff, who told party leaders, who immediately got in touch with George Smathers, Senator from the State of Florida, close friend of both Billy Graham and Senator John F. Kennedy. Said Senator Smathers over the phone to Graham, "Billy, you have written an article for Nixon and we are deeply concerned about it."

Billy said he hadn't intended to urge Nixon's election, he had simply intended to tell a human-interest story about a good American family.

A day later Billy Graham received a call from another close friend, his own governor, Luther H. Hodges. Governor Hodges was even more worried than Senator Smathers. So worried were the Democrats, said Hodges, that they had asked Dr. Reinhold Niebuhr of the Union Theological Seminary to "answer" Billy's *Life* article on behalf of John F. Kennedy.

Billy now realized he was embroiled in a political controversy.

That night Billy and his wife prayed. They said, "God, if You think this article should appear in *Life* magazine, we will abide by your judgment. But if You think it shouldn't appear, take it out of the magazine."

Right at the moment that Billy and Ruth Graham were asking the Lord for advice, Henry Luce was deciding that the article would have a much greater effect if it ran in *Life* later in the campaign, preferably on the *last* Friday before the first Tuesday of November. Accordingly, he rescheduled it for five days before the election.

I cannot say whether He, meaning the Lord, had acted. But when Billy did not see the article on its scheduled date, he wired Henry Luce that he was glad the article had not appeared.

Mr. Luce was quick to explain. But Billy told him simply, "No, Mr. Luce, the Lord does not want that article to appear at all, and I am in agreement with the Lord on this issue."

Mr. Luce tried to argue with Billy, but Billy told him the matter was entirely out of their hands. He agreed to write a different article which would urge his fellow Americans to vote.

He sat down and wrote it and Mr. Luce called to congratulate him, but said, "I still like the other article better, Billy, the one on the Richard Nixon family, so I think maybe we ought to reconsider running it."

But Billy Graham is not one to ignore the Lord.

History, pro and con

THE Hebrews put into their religious writings, "And thou shalt tell it to thy son."

They meant a man and a people must be true to history, to an accurate account of what happened. Until the twentieth century, if history had some inconvenient or disgraceful consequences, people forgot it. But with the advent of Fascism, Nazism, and communism, people began to rewrite it.

When Khrushchev decided to discredit Stalin, the Communists not only tossed his bones out of Red Square, but began to tear down the statues and rename the cities. They have rewritten all the history books to minimize his influence. It is an impressive job, to erase from modern history a name as powerful and fearful as that of Joseph Stalin.

The basic idea of democracy is the notion that the past must be tied to the present. Take the case of James Rivington, who was the publisher of the *Royal Gazette*, a Loyalist newspaper in New

York City which, from 1760 to 1780, espoused the cause of the British. Rivington was the leading spokesman for the Tories.

During the Revolutionary War, there were several times when the patriots annoyed Rivington by smashing his presses. But he kept the paper going, and, whenever things looked black for the British, Rivington would get up a headline to encourage them.

When the British surrendered and withdrew from the new continent, however, there was no thought of wiping out Rivington's name. As a matter of fact, the street on which Mr. Rivington had his press was named Rivington Place, and this was later changed to Rivington Street. No one in the new United States Government suggested discrediting the name of the Tory publisher.

A democracy, based on the ideals of human dignity, has no fears of the past.

It is interesting, too, that the number one American Tory gave his name to the street where millions of immigrants eventually settled.

There is something appropriate about this. James Rivington, the printer, was a contestant in one of the first crucial tests democracy faced. He guessed wrong, but the whole idea behind the emerging democracy was that every man is entitled to his opinions and to stand up for what he believes right, and that history will remember him—one way or another.

The amazing fluoridation story

Four years ago, the health authorities and the medical and dental associations jointly announced that beginning, say, April 1, the city water of Charlotte, North Carolina, would contain fluoride.

These good societies, as well as the newspapers, the district attorney, and the mayor were inundated with telephone calls on that date. For one solid week, more spines stiffened, more cancer grew, more thirst was intense, and more goldfish died than ever before in Southern history. Of course, these phone callers all claimed the "poison" in the water was responsible. Then on April 7 the health authorities, the medical and dental associations, joined by the district attorney, the mayor, and the newspapers, announced they had not added fluoride to the water as planned. They had simply waited a week to test the reaction of the anti-fluoridation-niks, and since everything that had happened was in the mind, they were going ahead on April 7 and save the teeth of the children.

Nearby Gastonia, a famous city of textile spindles, was not so lucky. Absolute hysteria raged over a referendum about adding fluorides, and in the end the anti-fluoridation-niks won and thereby arrested cancer, kept spines loose, and saved the goldfish.

Nothing strikes me so sad as the controversy over fluoridation. The opposition is no different from the fierce antagonism of the witch doctor in darkest Africa to the first British scientist who attempted to treat the sick in the jungle. Every competent medical and dental association in the country has approved fluoridation. In addition, much of the country's drinking water naturally contains sodium fluoride.

Why, then, such agitation from the "right wing" about it? I think the answer is this: the "right wing" has been perpetually upset because their politics is not a viable politics. They hate change. They argue that the natural way is the best way. They resent the intrusion of do-gooders who say they are trying to save the teeth of the young and therefore add something to the water. Imagine that! This arouses them. Don't fuss with nature; meaning, don't disturb the nineteenth century.

Since our food is already sprayed with God-knows-what chemicals to keep its color and adjust its flavor, as well as being lightly sprinkled with strontium 90, one can understand the anti-fluorides' desperation.

So they not only invent the sudden departure of goldfish but probably invent the goldfish as well.

Genuine Australian imports

H. L. MENCKEN once wrote that the discovery of the Australian continent was "justified" because it gave the world one superb word—"wowser"—meaning a universal kill-joy.

If he had lived longer, Mencken would have undoubtedly got "the drum" (the low-down) on other choice Australian words. "Urger," for instance. There is no precise American equivalent for this noun.

An "urger" does "press with importunity," says an Australian dictionary, but that is only one tenth of it. Australians usually smile when they call a man an "urger."

We now have two "fair dinkum" (genuine) urgers in our midst. Harry Bridges and Dr. Fred Schwarz. Both these blokes are home-grown Australian exports to the United States.

Dr. Fred leads (you should pardon the expression) the Christian Anti-Communism Crusade. Harry Bridges is the longshoreman's boss of the West Coast. One is extreme right wing, the other extreme left wing.

No "digger" (Australian) would fall for Fred Schwarz or Harry Bridges. He would know that Fred could just as easily be leading the "wharfies" (longshoremen) and Harry whipping up the root-out-the-Reds brigade. An urger by any name is the same—full of passionate conviction—and is always what our own Eric Hoffer has called, "a hitchhiker of mankind."

In Australia there is also an apt description of urgers—"bloody fool."

"Bloody fool" must be said carelessly and without venom—with a laugh, if you like. It must convey a measure of beneath-consideration.

The threat is abroad

ROY M. COHN, one-time counsel for the McCarthy investigating committee, and George E. Sokolsky, syndicated columnist, and some others are all speaking out, as the phrase goes, against the Communist menace. They have formed the American Jewish League Against Communism. Fascinating.

It is my opinion that the fight against communism is not the special business of any particular group. The most effective weapon against communism is the wholehearted support of the United Nations and the Administration, particularly as its foreign policy concerns foreign aid, the Peace Corps, NATO, our encouragement for continued success of the Common Market, and the cultural-exchange program.

The American Jewish League Against Communism is based on the assumption that the threat to freedom is *here*, in America. It isn't here at all. It was never *here*.

Even when there were some fifty thousand Nazi sympathizers in and out of Madison Square Garden shouting, "Heil Hitler," the threat wasn't *here*. At no time since 1939 has the American Communist Party mustered the strength and influence the Hitlerites mustered before Pearl Harbor. Yet no one ever called these fifty thousand sympathizers to account for their ideas and actions before World War II. I do not imply that there are no Communists and subversive agents here now. Indeed, I am quite sure there are. There are also some Americans who would be disloyal. But we have responsible agencies of government to check up on these matters, agencies with the power of arrest and records of competence.

The American Jewish League Against Communism wants us to direct our attention to the villains among us. The trouble is there are not enough villains to go around. For the feeling of accomplishment we must substitute hysteria.

What brings communism? Poverty and hunger! Wherever there are humans whose lives are miserable, there you find the easy victims of the promise, "bread and land."

Where is the great threat? In Asia, Africa, and Latin America, where millions scratch out a bare living from day to day and political leaders have enriched themselves selfishly and cruelly. Where is the threat the least? In those countries which have programs of social legislation: in the United States, Great Britain, Scandinavia, and Western Europe.

The best way for the United States of America to perpetuate the American Dream is to encourage the Dream throughout the world.

The swivel chair

THOMAS JEFFERSON was our greatest liberal and do-gooder. The Federalists used to mount rages against him. They called him a "philosopher" and they meant by it what the conservatives meant when they called Adlai Stevenson an "egghead."

Jefferson expected these attacks. He was in no way unprepared for them, but they did cause him pain. When a man is accused of being a "philosopher" or an "egghead," it is hard to defend himself. It is not like being called a Communist. After all, you can always say, "I am not a Communist," but it is quite hard to say, "I do not think."

Jefferson, said his critics, "had impaled butterflies." They meant he was a lepidopterist. They thought his drawing up a report on weights and measures was scandalous and a waste of time, and for a President to wonder about the differences between a white man and black man was simply muddle-headedness.

The thing that really enraged them was his invention of the swivel chair. This proved he didn't have both feet on the ground. "Ability to contrive turnabout chairs may entitle one to a college professorship, but it no more constitutes a claim to the Presidency than the genius of Cox, the great bridge builder," one of Jefferson's critics wrote, as reported by David Cushman Coyle in his book *Ordeal of the Presidency*.

The curious thing about this whole business is that the conservatives who deride the modern-day "eggheads" do it from the swivel chair. In fact, if the conservatives were to choose a symbol, it would be the swivel chair. No one who was scorning Jefferson as a "philosopher" realized that he would be the inventor of the very seat of Tory power.

Of course, today, the intellectual John F. Kennedy does in the blockheads from the vantage point of a rocking chair, an earlier invention.

Politics of old New York

TAMMANY HALL Boss Dick Croker once told Lincoln Steffens: "Our people could not stand the rotten police corruption. But they'll be back at the next election. They can't stand reforms, either."

Croker was right. The voters of New York can get mad as hell over police corruption or scandal. They proceed then to throw the rascals out—but after a little while they become remorseful and vote the machine back with a vengeance. Once Tom Foley, a big Tammany district leader, was exposed as having banked a half-million dollars within four years on an aggregate salary of sixty thousand dollars. A year later he ran for district leader and was elected, bigger than ever. In the old days the machine did a wonderful job for itself on election day. The joke went all over town, "Vote early and often," and it was much more than a jest. In the various flophouses on the Bowery, they would gather hundreds of the bums and hangers-on, and, as the vote was being counted in the various districts, those in charge of the bums would receive phone calls to the effect that such-and-such district needed two hundred votes and such-and-such district forty votes. The phony voters would then be taken to the designated polling place, each armed with "credentials," usually the name of someone who, up to an hour before the poll was scheduled to close, had not shown up to vote. Sometimes whole ballot boxes just disappeared. When the vote was going heavily against Tammany, the lights would suddenly go out and the ballot box was gone. The vote tabulators, too, were sometimes provided with various devices, such as a ring in which a piece of charcoal had been mounted. They palmed the ring and defaced the ballot, making it "void." In other instances, the "X" mark in the box had to be absolutely perfect, touching each of the four corners of the square—if it was for the opposition, of course. If it overlapped a millionth of an inch, it was marked "void."

When Dick Croker became boss of Tammany he was a poor man. Six years later, according to M. R. Werner's fine book, *Tammany Hall*, Mr. Croker had an eighty-thousand-dollar mansion and three hundred and fifty thousand dollars invested in race horses. It was a different kind of corruption. Mr. Croker improved on Boss Tweed's crude stealing and embezzlement. Instead, Mr. Croker engaged in what one New York police commissioner once called "honest graft." He merely padded the bills. In one year the city paid two hundred and eighty-five thousand dollars for letterheads and envelopes, and the cost of the courthouse rose to twelve million. Mr. Werner suggests that it was four times more than the cost of constructing the British Houses of Parliament.

Charles F. Murphy, probably the greatest of all Tammany bosses, was interested in a company distributing a product known as "Rochester Cement." The city building inspectors would inspect all new construction. No Rochester Cement and you got a violation. So naturally you bought Rochester Cement.

Most of this sordid business, which occurs in each generation, was revealed first by the Lexow Committee in 1894 and again by the Seabury Investigation in 1932. But essentially Boss Croker was right. After a siege of reform the public voted Tammany Hall back again, time after time. After one reform administration, Tammany Hall ran on this cute and original platform—"To Hell with Reform."

During the Seabury Investigation that brilliant old lawyer, Samuel Seabury, had Mayor Jimmy Walker on the stand for three days, and what Mr. Seabury was revealing, piece by piece, was a terrible story of graft, cynicism, and callous contempt for New Yorkers. Yet every question by Mr. Seabury was greeted with boos from the audience and Jimmy was cheered after each answer. But Mr. Seabury was patient. It was in the Magistrates Court that Mr. Seabury really hit pay dirt. It seems that some magistrates had paid for the job by putting up in cash an amout equal to one year's salary. In one Night Court where they tried prostitution cases, they had an established filing system. They arrested a girl, and she paid her fine. Then they put her card in a follow-up file, maybe for two months later, in order to give her a chance to earn sufficient money to "stand a pinch." It was revealed that, in putting in the "defense," a lawyer would say, "*Your honor, there are one hundred reasons why this girl should be put on probation.*" The magistrate was thus tipped off how much was to be paid—one hundred dollars. If the papers in front of him showed that the woman had a long record and it was worth more, he would shake his head slightly—and the lawyer would bend down to his client and whisper, "*Can you raise another fifty?*" Then the lawyer would amend his plea and say, "*There are a hundred and fifty reasons why ...*"

Boss Murphy started in life as a streetcar conductor, then he ran a saloon and quickly worked his way up to district leader. When he died he was worth a cool five million. Another big source of revenue, of course, came from selling legislation in the form of "contributions" from those who wanted a bill passed or defeated. When he was defied by a Tammany governor, William Sulzer, Boss Murphy was so powerful that he simply proceeded to have the governor impeached. The "charges" against Governor Sulzer were meager, and he was being destroyed only because he tried to put over the direct primary in New York, which, of course, would have sawed the bosses in half. The amazing thing about Charles F. Murphy was that he could command the loyalty of good men, and I am sure, wherever they are, neither the late Alfred E. Smith nor the late Senator Robert F. Wagner are particularly proud of the fact that, as members of the New York Legislature, they helped impeach Sulzer. Sulzer was a dynamic speaker of the old school. I remember him well, traveling in an open car and waving a big black hat. He drank whisky all the time and he developed a good system. He drank corn liquor, an unusual thing for a New Yorker, but this enabled him to take his quota in public. At a public meeting there's always a pitcher of water on the dais, but a thing that looks very much like water is corn liquor, with which Mr. Sulzer was refreshing himself.

Tammany Hall, of course, was the most realistic organization in the world. It developed the knack of rolling with the punch. Thus, after a very bad scandal, it retired from the field for the moment by picking candidates "unspotted from the world." There was a calculated risk involved, but it was better than losing out entirely. Tammany took a chance that a high-minded, honorable candidate would eventually show his gratitude. But sometimes, as in the case of Mayor William J. Gaynor, he would sock Tammany on the head every chance he got. Occasionally, too, Tammany had to pay a political debt, such as allowing Mr. Hearst to pick himself a mayor. This Hearst mayor was quite a card. His name was John F. Hylan.

Hylan was an honest mayor, however, and there does not appear to have been much serious graft in his administrations, but let us not get any wrong ideas. Boss Murphy was taking it easy. He was preparing to achieve his greatest ambition—to put a man in the White House—and during those years of grooming Alfred E. Smith, the rough stuff was suspended.

In one of the hot campaigns for mayor of New York in the old days, both sides used some interesting campaign posters. Tammany had refused to renominate Mayor Gaynor and instead Boss Murphy picked one of his henchmen, a man by the name of McCall, to run for this great office. The anti-Tammany forces nominated a Fusion candidate, John Purroy Mitchel. Both sides were very eager to get the Jewish vote down on the Lower East Side and the Fusion people used a poster with a big headline, VOTE FOR MECHEL. (Mechel is a Yiddish name usually Westernized into "Max" or "Manny.") Tammany, not to be outdone, printed a photo-poster of Mr. McCall with the same headline, VOTE FOR MECHEL.

On unions

WHEN I was a boy, my older sister worked in a sewing shop nine hours a day, six days a week, and earned an average weekly wage of twelve dollars. I visited her shop on errands, such as that occasioned by the need for an umbrella in an afternoon rainstorm.

I saw the hundreds of her fellow workers performing various operations in the manufacture of ladies' petticoats and other undergarments. It was a time when the employer had not yet learned that his best customers were sitting right there in his shop.

Today the girls in the organized sewing shops spend more on lipstick alone than my sister and her co-workers of 1915 were able to spend on their entire wardrobes.

In those days when the teacher asked a boy what his father did for a living, the boy answered without humor or guile, "My father is a striker." Everybody's father was a striker, which brings me down to the present time in the South. When I see the millworkers in my State of North Carolina driving to work in automobiles from homes with refrigerators, TV sets, and electric washing machines . . . when I see their wives going to garden clubs and beauty parlors, I always say to myself, "Little do you know how much of this you owe to those pioneer strikers of forty-five years ago."

And the most amazing development of all is the fact that some of the important advantages of belonging to a union trickle down to the hundreds of thousands of unorganized workers who pay no dues.

The whole business of understanding unions is complicated by a whole mess of fixed ideas that twist reality into knots.

For instance, this perilous American decade attempts to measure patriotism by the degree of hatred a man can mount against the Communists or the extent to which the Communists have claimed they hate him. But that this "test" involves the complete renunciation of logic is clearly evident by the fact that trade unionism has been denied its advantages. For there is no established institution in our Western culture which the Communists hate more than organized labor.

The Communists do not let generals or admirals or schoolteachers or novelists or millionaires excite them, but they cannot abide trade unionists. This hatred reaches as far back as Karl Marx, who did not expect that trade unions would help at all in the revolution. Lenin actively worked *against* and inveighed *against* all unions in his pamphlets. He warned that they were the supreme danger.

The Communists have always been kinder to the proprietors. If you want a revolution, you've got to have proprietors to revolt against; and organized labor fills the vacuum between them and their target.

When the Russian argicultural experts came over here, they talked to prosperous Iowa farmers and to the manufacturers of farm implements and to granary operators. Anastas Mikoyan got along with millionaires and managers. The cocktail hour was highly civilized.

But no Communists ever want to talk to a shop deputy. When Communists go backstage, the last person they want to talk to is the Equity representative. They don't want to banter and trade jokes with George Meany or David Dubinsky. The proprietors and the managers are toys in their hands, but the union men are cobras. The unionists want to talk about political freedom, and the right of workers to organize, strike, vote, change jobs as they see fit, and go where they please.

Of course we hear things about unions today which would indicate that many people long for the days when the governor could call out the militia and chase strikers off into the hills. But even the most medieval manager doesn't really want that day again.

We forget too often that organized labor increased the profits for free enterprise in the same proportion that they raised the wages of the workers. But unions could not do what mankind itself has not yet been able to achieve: to remove from the hearts of men a misdirected drive for power for the sake of power itself.

And what is obvious is that we do not always understand mankind, and that unions are among the things we understand least.

The conscience of Mr. Goldwater

THE English conservatives recently won an election with promises to expand the program of the Socialists. Like his British cousin, the American conservative whose *own* programs remain *in vacuo* finds his only strength in the existence of such liberal programs as the New Deal, the Tennessee Valley Authority, and social security. His strength is a strength by nostalgia. Senator Goldwater opens his book, *The Conscience of a Conservative,* with the statement, "The ancient and tested truths that guided our Republic through its early days will do equally well for us." But the conservative has no intention of abandoning or repealing the Securities Exchange Commission, the Tennessee Valley Authority, or social security, which are certainly no ancient and tested truths. Thus they speak of the great "conservative" South, but let us see a minute. In my State there are one hundred and seventy-five thousand conservative Southerners who would not have electricity, telephones, refrigerators, washing machines, or television sets were it not for the "radicals" who instituted the rural electrification program. Rural homes and farmhouses light up today for the simple reason that privately owned power companies could not possibly have stretched their lines to them without doing grave injustice to their stockholders. For electricity and power stations these conservative Southerners were perfectly willing to let the Federal Government encroach upon their States' rights. The conscience of a conservative is no more than a dream, the same sort of dream that nourishes the segregationist, a dream of a past that cannot, and should not, be recalled.

Let's call the whole thing off

THE one deal we must make with the Russians concerns the dropping of the bomb. The Russians must guarantee to drop the first bomb during prime television hours, when the whole family is gathered around *Father Knows Best*. Any other time is intolerable. If the Russians don't accede to this deal the whole fallout-shelter program goes down the drain. The folks are torn now between building community shelters and building home shelters, but neither of these is enough.

If the bomb drops at noon, the kid will take refuge in the school shelter, where he will plot with other kids more mischief to inflict on the teacher when he gets out. The husband will be in his office shelter with his secretary and receptionist and the new clerk with the big breasts. For him, it will be much like being on a desert island. And the wife—she will have to run to the community shelter where she will be locked up with her neighbor whom she hates and their two Negro housemaids.

It won't work. If the Russians won't guarantee to drop the bomb at night, then maybe we just shouldn't have the war.

Ben-Gurion

THERE are many reasons why David Ben-Gurion remains the leader of his country, but I like to think of it in terms of the one big reason. Ben-Gurion, along with such men as Winston Churchil, Harry Truman, and John F. Kennedy, understands politics. He is probably the most astute politician in the democratic world today.

When his party lost five seats in a recent election, there was all sorts of maneuvering by the rival parties. The conservatives, the religious parties, and the far left (the *Mapam*) formed a club to prevent forming a cabinet with Ben-Gurion and his party. Some even spoke of inviting the *Herut* (the ultra-right) to join the club in this one attempt to get rid of Ben-Gurion.

At that moment, Ben-Gurion's stock was at an all-time low and his retirement was widely discussed.

The old man bided his time. He understood that the only thing that united his opponents was their opposition to him.

So he let time work for him. It took nearly three months, but the new government that was formed included two religious parties and another group only slightly to the left of Ben-Gurion. Thus, the conservatives, the far right, and the left were left out again.

On Presidents

WOODROW WILSON proved a college teacher could be President and Harding proved that a "good-time Charlie" could be President. Calvin Coolidge proved you don't have to say much and Herbert Hoover proved you don't have to do much. Roosevelt proved a man could be President as long as he lives and Truman proved that just about anyone could be President. Eisenhower proved that you don't even have to have a President and John F. Kennedy seems intent on proving that you had damn well better be the President.

The message

A DEAF-MUTE walked into an office in Charlotte and presented his card:

STOP COMMUNISM!
GIVE
GENEROUSLY!
(I am a deaf-mute)

International bankers

THE professional anti-Semites in California issue a circular in which they talk about the "international bankers." It always seems to me that most of these crackpots have been abject failures in life and as a consequence they seethe with resentment over anyone who is not. When they focused this spite on the Irish forty years ago, they learned that they got a healthy busted nose in no time. So they figured it would be easier to pick on Mr. Katz. Mr. Katz is not the "international banker." He only runs a secondhand bookstore. It is his son who works nights to go to school who is the "international banker."

6.

FROM MADISON AVENUE TO GUAVA JELLY

Madison Avenue

MADISON AVENUE not only has manners but a slang all
its own. People up there use the suffix "-ish." They say, "I'll meet
you ten o'clockish," or, "Be there eleven thirty-ish."

They also use the suffix "-wise." He's pretty good afternoon-wise,"
they say, or, "He's knowledgeable car-wise."

The fellow that confuses "-wise" and "-ish" is an outlander.
For instance, it is bad form to say, "I'll be there ten o'clock-wise,"
or, "His wife is a good hostess, martini-ish." No siree, those are
dead giveaways.

The other great accomplishment of Madison Avenue is the
way the fellows tie their neckties. I have tried it a dozen times
but I cannot make it work. They manage a very tight knot which
they squeeze tightly against their necks, but at the same time I
notice that the Adam's apple has complete mobility and keeps
bouncing up and down all the time. They talk to me, but all I
do is watch the Adam's apple and that tight little knot.

I have a good friend who for many years has been successfully
employed by a firm which had its offices on Fifty-seventh Street.
Largely through my friend's efforts, the firm expanded to a point
where it had to find more spacious quarters. They moved from
Fifty-seventh Street to Madison Avenue. It would seem that such
an event would give a man a more secure feeling about his job
as well as make his chest swell with pride.

But not my friend. He won't even confess that he works on
Madison Avenue. He is afraid of the social criticism and scorn
that may be directed toward him. He is very secretive about his
address and even about his office phone number.

Madison Avenue is in bad graces right now. When anyone
wants to complain about bad taste or bad spending habits, it is
always the result of Madison Avenue.

If Madison Avenue is taking the brunt of all our troubles, there is a silver lining to the situation. Madison Avenue has taken Wall Street off the hook. Years ago it was thought Wall Street was the source of all the ills that afflicted Americans. The Populist Movement, which numbered adherents in the hundreds of thousands, would never have gained any impetus had it not been for the existence of Wall Street.

Wall Street was always responsible for the bad crops, the low prices, the threat of war, and the interest rates. No doubt Wall Street had something to do with all of these but it wasn't the only villain. People never said Pennsylvania Avenue put us in the war, it was always Wall Street.

The truth is that for some reason Americans tend to blame most of their troubles on streets.

On the Lower East Side years ago, we used to blame our troubles on Hester Street. Hester Street was very narrow and the pushcarts permitted no space for egress or ingress. It was a dirty street, too, so dirty that the street cleaners wouldn't work it. But all our poverty and dirt and hard work we imagined were caused by Hester Street.

Let me cheer up Madison Avenue. Every street has its day of blame and this, too, will pass. People will find a newer street with more activity and center their complaints there and my friend can invite us up to his office for a bit of fellowship and a little bourbon without shame.

The car salesman

CAR salesmen are the last true believers in the powers of hocus-pocus.

They are men loaded with secrets and they keep these secrets under their blotters on their desks. There is no mystery about how much a brand-new car costs since such statistics are prominently displayed. It's what the agency will offer you for your old car that's the great secret. It's the trade-in value that sets the gears of secret signs and signals grinding.

The salesman and the agency appraiser look over your old car with a more careful scrutiny than you give the new one. You think they are trying to evaluate the old wreck. But you are wrong. They are indulging in mental telepathy. They are trying to communicate with each other on how much they think you intend to spend.

You walk back into the office with the salesman, who adds the cost of white-wall tires, radio, and sun visors, and then he takes a deep breath, lifts up that blotter, and says, "We can give you eighty dollars on the old car." He watches your face. If your expression doesn't change, he lifts the blotter up higher, looks around to see that no one is listening, and whispers, "Make it one hundred dollars." If you say something to the effect that the dealer on the other side of town offered more, he peeps once again under the blotter, this time with a flashlight, expels his breath like a high diver, and says, "One hundred and thirty dollars!"

If you peek under the blotter while his back is turned, all you'll find is a picture of his wife and kids and a two-year-old shopping list.

On TV

You didn't need to be a worldly sophisticate in the old days of vaudeville to realize that those acts that went into the finale waving an American flag and the musicians playing "The Stars and Stripes Forever" were usually terrible. The fellow who closed his act with a rendition of "Mother is Your Friend," you knew, was trying to immobilize the audience with sentimentality so that he could get off stage. These acts made you wince.

But it's nothing like the wincing you do today when the entire cast of a TV spectacular comes out with bowed heads singing, "The Man Upstairs."

The very blandness of some of these television shows makes me hope something desperate and new will happen. I like to imagine Robert Young coming home from his insurance office to see his son (a big galoot who looks to me like he's at least twenty-three years old) and finds the boy reading a book. In his best *Father Knows Best* voice, Robert Young asks, "Son, what are you reading?" And son answers: "Pop, I picked up an interesting book —good stuff—it's called *The Life and Times of Eugene V. Debs*."

Hoo-ha! Can you imagine what would happen! Television executives would pack up their bindles and take to the rails, and the whole structure would begin to crumble.

I cherish one other dream of irrigating television's wasteland. As yet, television has done nothing to improve upon the greatest continuing series ever invented. The myths about the gods never die and reappear in age after age. You could take all those family-type series off the air and substitute Mount Olympus. Now that's a real family. That's *Father Knows Best* with a difference. There is Zeus, with his interminable lecheries, and Juno, with her interminable jealousies. Isis, Osiris—there's an infinite number of mythologies from which the stories can be culled.

The worst crimes

THE major cities of the South are bursting at the seams. Urbanization is in full swing as the great agrarian civilization is becoming industrialized. Like all other metropolitan centers, the Southern cities now have an occasional big-city murder. The difference between a big-city murder and a small-town murder is not that anybody is less dead, but that the newspapers make drama out of it as though people weren't killed every day in every imaginable way.

In the matter of crime, the South is very tough on a man accused of beating a woman. The South prides itself as the last outpost of chivalry.

Following is the list of the worst crimes you can commit in the South in order of the indignation they evoke in the community:

1. Rape or attempted rape by a Negro on a white woman.

2. Winking at, waving at, or familiarly addressing a strange white woman in public by a Negro.

3. Murder or attempted murder of a white man by a Negro.
4. The beating of a white woman by a white man.
5. The burglary of a white home by a Negro during the night (in many Southern States, the law provides capital punishment for this).

Juries are never too severe on a white woman who kills her husband or lover. She nearly always gets off with a reprimand.

One of the less serious capital crimes is a Negro killing another Negro. Two years in the pen is the average penalty.

Even less important than this is a white woman killing another white woman because of the victim's alleged fooling around with the husband of the accused. The arrest and the trial are mere formalities to make certain the lady will not be unnecessarily annoyed in the future, while the husband heaves a sigh of relief.

As you can see, there is not too much action for the newspapers, so they are always glad when a big-city murder comes along and the folks can get their minds off the capricious stock market and the miserable fortunes of the local minor-league team.

Ah, what a book!

THE current craze for ladies' wigs was, of course, bolstered by press reports that both Mrs. John F. Kennedy and Mrs. Robert F. Kennedy wore them so that they'd always appear well groomed during their recent trips abroad.

Passing through a large department store in one of our big cities, I got mixed up in a surging crowd of women pushing against a counter where the clerks were selling false hair. As I tried to extricate myself from the crush, an elderly woman standing beside me said, half to herself and half to the assemblage, "In my day I wouldn't have been caught dead in a patrol wagon with my hair looking like mattress stuffing."

I looked at this elderly woman with diamonds on her fingers and said to myself, "Ah, could you write a book!"

The barefoot tourists

WE AMERICANS are the most efficient people in the world. Except, on occasion, when it comes to the little human principles.

We have begun a large tourist program to attract Europeans here. By and large, it is enjoying some success and, given another two or three years, may prove both a boom and a boon. But we will have to save the Europeans their shoes. For the touring Europeans are losing their shoes left and right.

Wherever you go in Europe, when you retire for the night, you may deposit your shoes outside your hotel-room door.

During the night a bootblack makes his way through the hotel, collects all the shoes, shines them, and before morning redeposits them outside the guests' doors. If you are the recipient of this gesture you cannot find this bootblack to tip him. You don't even know who he is; he is performing one of the traditional services of any European hotel.

Perhaps mistakenly, Europeans have the idea that perforce what goes on in Europe goes on even better in America. Such a mistaken assumption leaves them barefoot.

They check into an American hotel and when they retire for the night, they put their shoes outside the door.

Spying them, the chambermaid thinks, "Ah! Here is a good pair of shoes for my husband. These good, rich Europeans don't want them any more and they have kindly called my attention to them."

Secretary of Commerce Luther H. Hodges needs to commission some alert public relations writer to redo the travel catalogue we issue European tourists. We have to insert a black headline in bold type: DON'T PUT YOUR SHOES OUTSIDE THE DOOR!

The paragraph will go on to explain that in America you get your shoes shined during the day at a shoeshine stand and the customary price is about a quarter. We might even add that the shoeshine boy won't look at you for less than a quarter.

We must always remember, international good will is built in little ways.

The source of the Nile

NEXT to discovering the source of the Nile, the hardest search is to discover who first wrote the joke that is currently making the circuit.

I invented a joke. At least, I believe I invented it, but then you never know. Maybe I did hear it some place first. At any rate, I was in serious discussion with my agent who is housed in the largest and most famous agency in the world—on Madison Avenue. The place runs rampant with wall-to-wall carpeting and wood paneling and even the elevators are air-conditioned.

All the men who work at this huge agency are crisply perfect in their dress. No one can tie a necktie knot like a member of this agency. It is the smallest knot in the world.

Looking around at the ostentatious good taste of the room, I told my agent, apropos of nothing, that each office in the agency ought to have a sign similar to the famous THINK sign invented by Thomas Watson of IBM. Only the agency sign should read:

DRESS BRITISH
THINK YIDDISH

Visiting in Detroit three days later, I met a press agent for Twentieth Century-Fox who asked, "Have you heard the latest? Dress British, Think Yiddish . . ."

The next night I was on a midnight radio program in New York. A good friend of mine who handles press relations for a famous motion-picture producer was there. He got us all in a huddle and said, "Have you heard the latest?" And here it was again.

I think I invented this joke but in a matter of days I heard it from all parts of the country. This leads me to conclude that jokes are concocted by some sort of spontaneous combustion, like

folk songs, or that my agent indeed followed my advice and had
the sign hung that said:

DRESS BRITISH

THINK YIDDISH

"Personality" speeches

I was one of the panel of seven judges who decided on
Miss U.S.A. in Miami Beach. Right from the start it was apparent
that Miss New York, Miss California, and Miss Louisiana would
be the front runners. Miss New York was *too* good which sounds
like a paradox. But after all, these contests are supposed to involve nonprofessionals—students or secretaries or car hops—and
it was felt that Miss New York was either a great genius or had
considerable experience as a model or entertainer. Quite frankly,
we might have done her an injustice, but all the judges agreed
on this point. Miss California, my own choice for first place,
knocked herself out of the running with her "personality" speech.

The "personality" speeches by each of the girls were horrible.
"Horrible" is not only the apt word, but the only accurate word
possible. We all felt that if any one of us had written a speech for
any girl in that outfit, she would have swept the audience off its
feet. These "personality" speeches sounded as though Mayor Bob
Wagner of New York had written all of them. Whoever wrote
Miss California's speech, however, wanted to get her knocked off.

Forgive me for even trying to remember a few of her lines,
but the poor girl was sabotaged:

"I'm from California, and I want to invite all you people to
California where we have many sandy beaches, lots of fishing,
and wonderful, wonderful, wonderful people. I want to tell all
you people in this audience that if you did come to California
you would never want to leave and you would all become California citizens in no time, that's how wonderful California is."

And so we decided on Miss Louisiana, with that you-all accent
and her little speech and the charm about her, and make no
mistake, she is beautiful.

The bookstore raid

THE New York City police one summer night raided several bookstores which were selling books to customers after midnight on Saturday.

I wonder if the raid was like the old raids on the speak-easies during the twenties. The cops used to bust in with drawn guns, the jazz band would stop tooting, the women would giggle, and the bartender would stuff in his pockets as much money from the cash register as he could before marching off to the pokey with one of the officers. There was always a police sergeant, however, who winked at the patrons and announced: "Anyone who wants another drink can go down to Louie's which we won't be raiding until next Wednesday."

Did the cops tell those hardened book buyers where they could buy a book in the early hours of Sunday morning?

In the same week, every elected, prestigious, and appointed official of New York City was lending his name to the committee for the Lincoln Center of Performing Arts. They were asking for contributions to build one of the theaters—for one thousand dollars any citizen can endow a seat with his name on it or off it, as he chooses.

All anyone had to do, really, was arm these cops with applications and send them out to the bookstores, because anyone who is browsing after midnight Saturday is obviously for culture.

My advice to the State and the cops is to stay away from books. You always come out second best when you tangle with them.

One of the signals of corruption and decadence is when civic officials get terribly busy about trivial things, like banning folk singers, or abolishing free Shakespeare lest the crowds trample the grass, or instituting an antijaywalking campaign, or raiding bookstores, while one million tons a week is mysteriously stolen from the docks, juvenile gangs roam the city streets, and motorists kill each other by the thousand.

Why Tom Waring is mad at me

TOM WARING, a Southern gentleman of the old school, is the editor of the Charleston *News and Courier*. Every so often he runs a piece about me which he headlines, "Golden Fights Dixie," or "Golden, Go Back to the Garment District." Tom Waring is a die-hard segregationist and he wants to fight me because I am a die-hard integrationist. Up until a few weeks ago, I thought this political difference was the root of our disagreement.

But I have changed my mind. I doubt seriously that the integration issue is what bothers Tom Waring about me. My intuition about our real differences is a little tortuous to describe but I shall attempt it anyway.

One of the local tycoons recently returned from a trip around Europe. This man is a world traveler and he told me that in former years when he told government officials or foreign businessmen that he was from Charlotte, one of them was sure to say, "That Charleston is a delightful city," or, "My wife has relatives in South Carolina." Whereupon this world traveler wearily but without fail had to go into a long explanation that Charlotte is in North Carolina and has nothing to do with Charleston, which is in South Carolina.

But now, says this world traveler, the shoe is on the other foot. In Madrid, Berlin, Minneapolis, or Tokyo, when someone says he's from Charleston, someone is sure to volunteer, "Charleston? Isn't that where Harry Golden lives?"

This sad state of affairs has been filtering back to Tom Waring and has inspired his vituperation. He has nightmares that perhaps I really do live in Charleston and he wants me back in the garment district of Charlotte.

Tom: Stop worrying. I am home.

The children take over

THE children have taken over. Books that are banned are invariably banned for their sake. Modern architecture has developed to a point where the schools look like Babylonian palaces so the kids should not even object to staying after class when some sharp-eyed teacher spies them stealing hub caps. Slowly but surely children are approaching the status of monsters more devastating than any invading army.

The television show that walked off with many of the awards in recent years as well as the honor among the highest ratings was Robert Young's *Father Knows Best*. Father is an insurance man who comes home to listen to the son say, "Dad, I waited for you to get the keys to the car." The interesting thing about this scene is that the son is easily of voting age and the whole relationship he bears to the family is his need to borrow cars or go fishing or indulge in innocent escapades with the girl next door. (Some fifty years ago on the Lower East Side of New York, at the age of twenty-two you were a veteran of at least ten years of productive work and earnings.) So this program wins a prize and I suspect it is true to life.

Like successful armies, the children have succeeded in taking over all lines of communication, particularly the telephone, on which they talk back and forth about how unreasonable their parents are in forbidding them to call friends at 11:30 P.M.

Most of the teen-age conversation via telephone is in code:
She didn't!
She didn't?
She didn't!!!
I know a kind mother who had earned a Master's Degree at the University of Chicago and then generously surrendered her own career to take care of her children as they came along. She told me she overheard her fifteen-year-old daughter complaining to the boy friend about her. The daughter said: "My mother is

on her usual 'maturity' kick. She insists I must be mature and I could scream every time I hear that word."

"Yeah," replied the boy friend, "my mother's the same way. The squares are all born mature."

The housewife's loss

ONE of the reasons for the growing boredom of the American housewife is that society has taken away her natural enemies. For many years the housewife had a daily tilt with the butcher, for instance. And a most welcome bit of warfare it was and every housewife looked forward to it.

The housewife agreed that the butcher generally got the best of her. Nevertheless she welcomed this daily bit of drama and felt a rare fulfillment when she went home with a package of exactly the cut and weight of meat she wanted.

Now the meat is wrapped in cellophane and weighed and priced, and at the supermarkets there isn't even a butcher in evidence.

She played the same high-spirited game with the grocer and the fruit peddler. There was a time when she held each egg up to the light. And she was followed around by the merchant who kept repeating sorrowfully, "Please don't squeeze each of those apples."

Now there is no one to complain to, unless it's the clerk who didn't count out the appropriate number of trading stamps.

And no housewife has yet figured out how to complain to a laundromat or an automatic vending machine.

The guest speaker

THERE are several large concentric circles in the American scheme of things. Television is the focus of home life; from it radiates happiness and security. Credit is the center of economic life; nowadays it is unpatriotic not to buy a new car. And the guest speaker is the center of all our charitable impulses. Sometimes it seems there can be no charity unless a guest speaker is present at the kickoff dinner.

But Americans have always been suckers for the hard sell. They have managed in their time to buy more bad bills of goods than any other society. Take the guest speaker and the fund-raising dinner, for instance. It's just no fun for the big givers.

The husband and the wife get dressed for the reception, he in his black tie, she in her new cocktail dress. He feels very good. He has found the cuff links, the shirt is starched, and the shoes don't pinch. And she looks pretty good. She looks nicer tonight than she's looked in twenty-one years of marriage. After the cocktails, they march to the dining room for the main event. The dais is aglow and aglitter, and it seems to him all eyes follow his pretty wife.

There are a few preliminaries which are not too bad—only two of the leaders address remarks to the assemblage. The dinner is good. He holds her hand during the coffee. Then it all evaporates.

After five speeches the chairman introduces the guest speaker, and our big giver is a little tired, and the shoes pinch after all. By the time the guest speaker has finished, the wife doesn't look so pretty either. By the time the eleventh leader rises to thank the guest speaker, the big giver is toying with the idea of chucking the whole thing and becoming a Baptist.

Southern short story

THIS is a true story of a charming Southern town. The town has the old Southern charm in the old Southern tradition. Its people are kind and hospitable. For many years the town prided itself on being a bit above the storm and strife of modern commercialism. Everyone was getting along fine in a charming, hospitable, and traditional sort of way.

Then came this "bring new industry to the South" program,

the "balance agriculture with industry" business. And this charming little Southern town, with timidity, albeit with hope and optimism in its heart, joined in. The officials of the charming town opened negotations with a firm in New York—a firm with a potential of five hundred employees, manufacturing housedresses and aprons. Ah, a fellow who not only meets a pay roll, but a pay roll of five hundred! That was a fine pay roll to look forward to, and the conservative Southerners sat down and weighed every possibility. They offered this pay-roll-meeter a large mill which had been closed for some time. But the manufacturer pointed out that the mill needed major repairs, and anyway there was no way to get to the mill without new roads and other improvements.

And so the town began to figure once more. With a bond issue they raised five hundred thousand dollars which they used to build the fellow new roads, sewers, and public utility facilities, in addition to making the necessary repairs and improvements on the mill itself.

Everything was all set. But what the manufacturer did not tell his Southern friends was that David Dubinsky had been after him for the longest time; and that all this time he was stalling Mr. D. and the International Ladies' Garment Workers' Union.

Finally the guy moved. In the first place it wasn't a pay roll of five hundred, but a pay roll of only two hundred and fifty. Second, Dubinsky followed the guy down there, and the quiet little town finally saw its first picket line, its first strike, its first settlement, and its first union. And so as we take our leave of this charming little Southern town, we hear above the murmuring palmettos and through the soft strains of the music for the quadrille, the bewildered whisper: "We spent a half-million dollars to buy ourselves a labor union!"

"The wretched refuse"

At new york's International Airport at Idlewild, the folks dedicated a plaque in honor of Emma Lazarus' famous sonnet which appears on the base of the Statue of Liberty. The mayor cut the ribbon. The New York press wrote a sentimental story, and all the Jewish papers expressed pride and appreciation.

The plaque at Idlewild Airport is as follows:

"Give me your tired, your poor,
 Your huddled masses yearning to breathe free . . .
Send these, the homeless, tempest-tost to me.
 I lift my lamp beside the golden door!"

In place of "The wretched refuse of your teeming shore," they put . . . three dots.

When Emma Lazarus wrote that line, "the wretched refuse of your teeming shore," she thought in terms of Czarist Russia, and of the third-class citizenship imposed upon people everywhere in Europe. In addition to their political disabilities, the people of Italy, Ireland, and the Balkan countries were plain hungry. They were indeed "refuse." But when this "refuse" entered the "golden door" it took on new hope, and eventually the vast majority became valuable citizens. This was the whole point of Emma Lazarus' sonnet. There was no need to fear a line of poetry.

The laundry

THE number one activity of the American home must be laundry. One look at the sales' charts of washing machines and dryers, of clothespins and clotheslines, is enough to convince any sane American that most women are washing most of the time.

If that in itself is not convincing, one has only to count the proliferating laundromats and cleaning establishments in any city.

Just a cursory survey of laundry and cleaning and ironing would give you a good picture of the American society. When the modern steam irons were introduced on the market at around twenty dollars, sales were negligible. Then the manufacturers started to display the irons in the credit jewelry stores and sales boomed. The ordinary woman with an extra twenty dollars obviously didn't do her own ironing while the woman who needed credit did.

The constant laundering and cleaning of clothes is a boon to the American economy. The more you clean and wash clothes, the faster they wear out, which necessitates replacements. It also helps keep the soap manufacturers in business and where would hundreds of thousands of housewives be without the daily installment of *The Guiding Light?*

We live in a society in constant turmoil. We tread over ashes beneath which glow the coals.

My campus research

At the University of Wisconsin and the University of Missouri, on campuses all over the country, I have noticed that sartorial splendor for the pedal extremities consists of tattered sneakers over athletic socks which must have a colored band. These sneakers are called "gyms" and are *de rigeur* for all occasions save the annual prom. If the "gyms" are clean and neat, you are a square. A pair of shoes makes you a foreigner.

As far as raincoats go, I've been told when the boys buy a new one, they soak it in dirty bathwater for three or four days to make it look worn and baggy, as though the owner had just escaped from Barcelona.

Thus the folly of youth.

I am reminded now of the girl who telephoned home to mother, telling her, "I weigh one hundred and fourteen pounds, stripped for gym," to which her mother replied, "Who the hell is Jim?"

Georgia incident

Two Jewish salesmen were sitting around the lobby of the motel. Said one, "Today I have yahrzeit [annual memorial prayer for a departed parent], and the closest Temple is in Macon twenty-six miles away and even if I went there I am not sure I can make the necessary arrangements this late; what can I do for the sacred memory of my father—may he rest in peace?" After careful thought the other salesman said, "Why don't we go to that new kosher-style delicatessen on the highway and get a couple of Jewish corned beef sandwiches?"

The dry run

IF MOONSHINING is North Carolina's third biggest industry, then catching the moonshiners must be the fourth. Well over a thousand stills were raided and destroyed last year in my state. You can imagine the number that are operating. Four years ago revenuers seized a small model of a still from a high school boy who had entered it in a science fair. It was a precautionary measure. Last year the boy, now a graduate and a man, was seized with a real still.

The "think board"

I HOPE that a lot of the office managers in the large advertising agencies read this piece, because it will help them decide to make wholesale changes in their office layouts. Recently one of the biggest of all advertising agencies installed a huge bulletin board across the conference room wall. They called it, I believe, a "think board." On it they pasted and pinned new ideas for slogans, layouts, artwork, media research, and consumer impulses. Whenever the executives were in the conference room they would sit and ponder these creative scraps laid out for them. Whenever they had a meeting, preparing for some new account which would run into millions of dollars, they devoted the entire "think board" to the competitive ideas and layouts for their final presentation to the new client.

Another agency got wind of this "think" program. They rented a room on the fourteenth floor, directly across the street, with a window that let onto the conference room window. Just like the FBI after a most-wanted, they posted two or three executives with high-powered binoculars and telescopes and long-range cameras to record everything their competitors put up on that "think board."

So successful was their spying that they recently landed a huge account, not only by their own presentation but by pointing out the pitfalls of the presentation of the competing agency with the "think board." Of course an agency might deceive competitors with false layouts on that bulletin board, but the risk is too great. They might also confuse their own executives.

The departing drummer

THE farmer's daughter is now perfectly safe, for within another decade the traveling salesman, the fellow with a shoeshine and a smile who solved the problems of the world in the smoking car of the sleeper, the old-time drummer, will be a thing of the past. Slowly he is being eased out of the commercial world of America.

Along with the salesman, the departmental buyer, who alone was the efficient cause of the expense account, is also disappearing.

All the large stores today have "buying offices" in New York or Chicago or the cities which supply them. The buyer who once made the crucial decisions as to what people would buy six months from now is in reality a clerk with little authority. The buyer takes his orders from the merchandise manager, a man who deals in figures and statistics and who rents the IBM computers which always print the profitable price, the quotas, and the future.

There is more than the buying office involved in the decline of the salesman. Today the large manufacturers spend their money for national advertising. And once a product builds up an identifiable "national" name, the salesman no longer needs to make contacts and take the buyer out to lunch. The salesmen still linger with the small manufacturer who does not advertise "nationally" but it is a dying profession. Few salesmen work any more on commission: most are paid salaries and they get their salaries as often as they meet their quotas. Arthur Miller's great play *The Death of a Salesman* told more than the story of Willie Loman. It recounted the demise of the old-time drummer, a noble man who was the most interesting conversationalist in the smoking car.

Worry is the telltale giveaway

BOOKER T. WASHINGTON wrote that if you were curious about what race a man of dubious shade and color belonged to, all you had to do was give him something to worry about. A white man will walk around like a fool while the colored man will sit down and go to sleep.

In the same vein a wise subscriber of mine tells a Jewish story:

Troubles will drive an American or an Englishman to dissect himself with psychoanalytic bosh while the same troubles will impel an Irishman or a Spaniard to the nearest church where he will light all the candles. Troubles will drive a Norwegian, a Dane, a Swede, a German, or a Swiss to drink, with the good probability that the German or the Swede will commit suicide. Of troubles a Dutchman will think, "Even this I may perhaps turn into a fast guilder." A Frenchman or an Italian will look for a woman. But the one thing about which I am positive is that trouble will drive a Scotsman or a Jew to eat good before divulging it.

Hi ya, Tar Heel

SOME time ago I lent my car for a couple of days to a fund-raiser from Brooklyn. He represents (while studying for the Orthodox rabbinate) a famous Jewish orphan asylum, and he had to make a few stops between Charlotte and Chattanooga. I have known the fellow for some years—a charming, cultured man. He speaks English haltingly, and I enjoy his annual visits because it is an opportunity for me to speak Yiddish for hours and hours. When he returned my car he told me that on the highways of Tennessee he had three or four experiences which puzzled him. Every once in a while a passing motorist would lean out of the window of his car and yell, "Hi ya, Tar Heel!" The third time it happened, the young rabbinical student pulled over to one side to see if anything was wrong with the car. He asked me in Yiddish, "Mr. Golden, what's this *Tar Heel* business, is it good or bad?"

So goes the West

IF YOU go into that wonderful "Appetizing Store" run by Mr. Saperstein on the corner of Rivington and Essex Streets on the Lower East Side of New York, the first thing Saperstein will say, is, "Khrushchev should drop dead." Naturally you ask what's the matter now. And Saperstein will tell you, "Do you see a barrel of schmaltz herring standing on the floor? No. Why not? Because Khrushchev has become very friendly with Iceland. Iceland is in K's orbit now and we don't get schmaltz herring any more and for that Khrushchev should drop dead."

This is indeed a very serious matter of which the newspapers didn't print much. People would regard it even more seriously if they knew the wonders of schmaltz herring. I have become convinced that as schmaltz herring goes, so goes the West, and let's hope our Secretary of State discusses this matter with Mr. Saperstein.

Foreign affair

IN A California city there is an Immigration Service inspector whose job is to round up Mexicans who have entered the country illegally. With several guards, the inspector takes the Mexicans by bus back across the border. Once back in Mexico a crew of these wetbacks chartered a plane and were back in California long before the bus returned. By a strange coincidence one of the Mexicans rented a room in the same rooming house where lives the immigration inspector, and—this is absolutely true—the Mexican took a bath, had a refreshing sleep, and was coming down the stairs, fresh as a daisy, just as the weary immigration inspector was coming upstairs after deporting him.

Six-word epic

THE kids and adults who use soap to decorate empty store-front windows compose at best a subliterate message. Sometimes these scrawled legends reveal a flair for advertising: "Call Lois, a red hot mama, Graceland 8600." Never literature.

Except once. A six-word short story was on a window in Charlotte last week. It said something. It said:

> Shorty Allen
> Local boy
> Chicago bound.

Guava jelly

A GENTLE lady—a stranger to me—pressed six jars of home-made guava jelly upon me with the explanation, "I know how much you like guava jelly." For the life of me, I can't imagine how that nice lady could even suspect that a fellow from the Lower East Side of New York would like guava jelly. I never heard of guava jelly on bagels, onion rolls, or rye bread. I would like to find that lady again. I would like to know whether you serve guava jelly cold or do you heat it up, like broth?

7.
THE INVISIBLE
NEGRO

The story of Fred Beal

FRED BEAL was unlucky. Whatever he did was wrong, and when he did do the right thing it was at the wrong time. I liked him very much. We had a long correspondence during his imprisonment. He died recently of tuberculosis. Now he can make no more mistakes. He was involved in that Gastonia strike trouble in the early 1930s. The chief of police was killed and Beal and a group of Communists were tried for the killing. Beal had nothing to do with the killing of Chief Aderholt, but when you cannot come into court with clean hands you are in bad shape.

Beal was unlucky. He went to work in a cotton mill in Lawrence, Massachusetts, at the age of twelve or thirteen—and he was obsessed with the idea of doing something to improve the working conditions and the pay of the textile worker. He let himself get involved with a union which was dominated by Communists. They weren't interested in improving anyone's conditions. They thrived only on trouble. Beal told me an amazing thing—hard to believe, but there was no reason to doubt it—he wasn't saying it for publicity or in any way to exploit his anti-Communism. He told me that William Z. Foster, the Communist leader, directed the whole Gastonia show, and the people in the Kremlin insisted on getting weekly reports on the doings in Gastonia. How do you like that? He marks the sparrow's fall. Anyway, Beal, after conviction with the others involved, forfeited the bail and escaped to Russia. After two years in Russia, he was ready to come back and go to jail. I met him when he returned from prison. He told me that during those two years when he watched the Russian workers line up for their black bread every morning he kept saying to himself: "I'm in trouble because I was fighting for people (in Gastonia) who are eating flapjacks and bacon this

197

morning." But when he came back with his eyewitness story
that the whole Communist setup was a tragic fake, *no one would
listen to him*, except a few true Liberals—the Social Democrats,
who then as now are the rocks upon which Communism will
eventually be broken.

Beal was unlucky. He became a Communist at the wrong
time, and he became an anti-Communist at the wrong time.
In 1937 when he came back with his story he couldn't get a
publisher to print a pamphlet against the Soviet Union. He found
himself cut off from friends and jobs, not because he had once
been a Communist but because he was now an anti-Communist.
He finally wound up getting his story published in the *Jewish
Daily Forward*, the old stalwart Socialist paper, one of the
few publications in America which never once took a single
backward step in its opposition to Communism from the day
after the Russian Revolution to the present time. He came back
to North Carolina to serve his prison sentence. When he came
out of jail, the climate was just right for him—everybody was an
anti-Communist. But Beal, as I said before, was born unlucky.
Again he was wrong. He was an anti-Communist all right, a
man who chose four years in an American jail rather than a
Commissar's job in the Soviet Union, but Beal found out that
now the anti-Communists were popular only if they became
Republicans to the right of Senator Bricker of Ohio, as part of
the redemption process. Beal couldn't do that, and turned down
many offers to lecture on the subject. He went back to Lawrence,
Massachusetts, to write for an A.F. of L. newspaper. He had
tuberculosis which he contracted in the Soviet heaven, and the
labor union sent him to a sanitarium. He is dead now at the
age of fifty-two.

He was unlucky. He became a Communist at the wrong time
and it resulted in his downfall. He became an anti-Communist
at the wrong time, when no one would believe his stories of
the tragedy of Bolshevism. Finally when everybody went all-out
in their feeling against Communism, Beal couldn't take advantage
of it and give them anti-Communism in the terms that were
demanded. The man who summed it up best was Judge Wilson
Warlick of the Superior Court (now a Federal judge). When

Beal applied for the restoration of his citizenship, Judge Warlick said: "Mr. Beal, I've read a lot about you, and I give you credit for speaking out about Communism in the 1930s when you came back, and I feel you'll make a good American citizen. I wish you luck."

Fred Beal the unlucky is at rest now. I hope he has peace and quiet.

Twenty blocks away

MR. JAMES BALDWIN is an important American writer.

He spent a day with me in Charlotte; then I had to leave on a lecture tour and we agreed to meet again in Atlanta, since our schedules called for us both to be there the same evening.

I called Mr. Baldwin at the telephone number he gave me but my host for the lecture that night had invited me to dinner with the committee. In nearly every city I have a friend whom I bring along to such functions. The host always says, "Of course." I could not invite Mr. Baldwin to the dinner. I did not even ask the host. Mr. Baldwin would not have been permitted to enter the restaurant. Mr. Baldwin is a Negro. And I could not invite him to the lecture, either, because it was being held in the auditorium of a private club.

Sometimes I visit with a local friend after the lecture at my hotel but I could not do even that. Mr. Baldwin would not have been allowed to come into the lobby of the hotel.

All these thoughts flashed through my mind as I kept talking to James Baldwin on a telephone. There was no place I could get together with him, except perhaps the airport, but mine was an 8:00 A.M. flight and it would have been impolite to ask Baldwin to get up that early. I looked around helplessly at my hosts and the committee. One of America's best novelists was just twenty blocks away, I had made a "date" with him, I wanted to talk with him some more, but all I could say over and over again was: "How's everything, Jim?" "How are you, Jim?" and I felt like such a damn fool.

No more hong shew gai

(A true story that grew out of the 1962 demonstrations against segregation in restaurants along major highways leading from Baltimore.)

Two young ferrows walk in Woo Lin's Chinese Restaurant on Washington-Baltimore Parkway.

Walking softly over, as the gold of dawn steals over the rice paddies, is Woo Lin, proprietor.

"Mushroom egg foo yung?" asks Woo Lin. "Gai kew? Harr kow? Hong shew gai?"

But, before young ferrows can answer, Woo Lin notices something. Young ferrows not corored pale white. Not corored yerrow. Corored blown.

Ah, thinks Woo Lin, these must be the sit-ins.

So, as Amelican lawyer for restaurant association advise, Woo Lin takes out bulky papers and reads Maryland Trespass Law. Many difficurt words. Takes rong time.

Finarry, young ferrows get bored. They walk out.

Immediatery, two more young ferrows come in. Also corored blown.

Too much, thinks Woo Lin. He pulls shutters and locks door of restaurant.

No more hong shew gai today.

The turban plan

You are, perhaps, familiar with my Vertical Negro Plan to end segregation (based on the observation that segregation persists only in a seated situation, and not in the South's supermarkets, banks, department stores, or at the cashiers' desks of big utility offices). This plan, which entails removing all the seats from classrooms and permitting white and Negro children to stand amicably together, has been put into effect successfully by a number of lunch counters at Southern dime stores.

Since removal of the stools at these establishments, Negro and white kids munch hotdogs without the slightest show of emotion.

The stools, of course, will come back, gradually. Maybe at first the Negroes can just lean against the seat in a sort of half-standing position; and by such easy stages finally get to a sitting position without stirring up anything.

But now it's time to review several other Golden Plans.

My Potemkin Toilet Plan was suggested by my observation at a recent concert in the civic auditorium of a large Southern city. At this concert there were few Negroes in the segregated audience. During the intermission I counted no fewer than twenty-eight white ladies waiting to get into the "white" powder room (at least half of them hadn't gained admittance at the sound of the intermission buzzer). Less than twenty yards away, behind a post, was the "Negro Women" powder room, empty and silent, a complete waste.

I suggest that we build a dummy door marked "white" and attach to it a sign, "Temporarily out of order, use 'Negro Women' door," a system that would work very well in the upper South—Virginia, North Carolina, and Tennessee—but which might be a bit too drastic for the Deep South.

My SRO Plan actually is an adaptation of the Golden Vertical Negro Plan.

But it is simplicity itself:

In all America there isn't a movie owner who doesn't dream of the day when he can again hang out an SRO sign—standing room only.

The Negro audience has segregated movie houses stuck in some out-of-the-way alley. Yet here are millions of people hungry for a first-run movie.

Let the motion-picture distributors hang out the SRO sign. This is justified because they are also going to take the seats out of the theater. While it is never comfortable to stand through a two-hour movie, certain sacrifices are necessary in order to do this thing gradually. The inconvenience of standing can be somewhat alleviated by installing vertical hassocks, which need not be elaborate, modeled along the lines of the hassocks Englishwomen use at the races. This would allow folks to lean during the movie.

Finally, I present to the world my Turban Plan:

You have all heard of the Negro reporter who, a few years ago, visited a half-dozen Southern cities wearing a turban, and how well he was received in fancy hotels and on a basis of fellowship with leading citizens, and how in one city a ladies' society actually sent flowers and an invitation to make a speech.

Well, I have seen this work. A Negro social worker I know often visits a white colleague for two or three days at a time.

"I felt guilty about disrupting their family routine," he reports. They want to go to the movies and I see them looking at each other in embarrassment, because they know I can't go, and so I carry a turban and use it when necessary; we are all more comfortable."

The Golden Turban Plan has many facets. It will relieve the depression in the textile industry (caused by Japanese imports), which Secretary of the Interior Luther Hodges fights so hard to control and balance. If the textile industry were to start grinding out eight million turbans for the men and eight million saris for the women, the mills would hum morning, noon, and night, and the officials of the Kennedy Administration could turn their attention to the problems of Africa, Berlin, and South America.

Already Negro students at the University of Texas have adopted my plan with modifications. They do not wear turbans, they simply swear to movie ushers they are Egyptians.

Keeping a straight face, three college students raise their hands and swear they are respectively Egyptian, Hawaiian, and Hong Kongese.

The supreme test, however, is yet to come.

There is now a Negro literary club, numbering eighty-odd, which has adopted my suggestion to wear turbans once a week wherever they go. The turbans are expected to arrive early next fall and these four-score-and-some-odd fellows will venture forth on a Saturday night in the near future to various cafés, movies, and the like. It will be very interesting. The Angles, Picts, Scots, Celts, and Saxons always roll out the red carpet for one guy with a turban. Let's see if it works for eighty guys with turbans.

A liberal's creed

AN IMPRESSION persists that perhaps we liberals are trying to help "our little brown brothers." This is an attitude no different from that of the paternalistic segregationists who put up the bail for their favorite Negroes.

I'm reminded here of a story about Captain Alfred Dreyfus, the Jewish officer on the French general staff, who was framed by a military clique but who found some noble defenders.

Captain Dreyfus was not a particularly pleasant fellow. During a moment of frustrating conversation with Captain Dreyfus, Emile Zola said, "You are mistaken, Captain Dreyfus; we are not doing this *for you*—we are doing this *for France*."

Excommunication and integration

NOTHING explodes the myth about the monolithic Roman Catholic Church like the integration issue. Many of us who are not Catholics naively presume that whatever the priest says, the Catholic congregation has to obey. It simply isn't true and probably never was.

When the Archbishop of New Orleans, His Eminence Joseph F. Rummell ordered the integration of his parochial schools, some of his Catholic parishioners fought him. Now by any standards in the world, it is an archbishop's prerogative to run the parochial schools in his bishopric as he sees fit. Archbishop Rummel promptly excommunicated the leaders of that group which had opposed his fiat: the excommunicants were Leander Perez, Jackson G. Ricau, and Mrs. B. J. Gaillot, Jr.

The Archbishop very firmly made it clear he would not retract his excommunication decree until the excommunicants repented. What was surprising to some, however, was that none of the ex-

communicants hastened to seek the Archbishop's pardon by re-
pentance. Those of us who live in the South and have interested
ourselves in this issue of integration, however, knew that Catholics
were not in accord on this issue.

Bishop Vincent S. Waters of the North Carolina diocese immediately integrated his churches and parochial schools after the
United States Supreme Court ruled segregated schools unconsti-
tutional. Belmont Abbey College and Sacred Heart College for
girls, run by the Benedictines and Sisters of Mercy, respectively, at
Belmont, North Carolina, integrated not only classrooms but dor-
mitories. Most of the North Carolina Catholics accepted this. In
the town of Laurinburg, when the young priest there started his
Mass that first "integrated" Sunday, he found only three parishioners in the pews—all Negroes. The "white" Catholics waited outside the church. The priest went on with the Mass and on the next
Sunday, he found five Catholics, again all Negroes, waiting for the
sacrament of the Mass. But on the third "integrated" Sunday, the
"white" Catholics realized Bishop Waters was not going to change
his order and the church at Laurinburg filled up with its usual com-
plement. That ended the matter.

But in Atlanta, Georgia, in Charleston, South Carolina, in Mobile, Alabama, the Catholic schools were segregated and remained
segregated; and in Charleston and Mobile they will probably continue to be segregated in the foreseeable future. The integration
issue cuts across class lines, to be sure, but it cuts across religious
lines, too. Our society is essentially a secular society and its issues
and values are secular issues and values. Our religions become secular. This secularization is more evident in the South than elsewhere
because the South was presumably the "Bible Belt." It no longer
is. The clergyman, the Protestant minister (and the rabbi), has
lost his classic function as moral leader in the community. He has
lost this function because the laymen have taken over the affairs of
the church and have made the church a social rather than a
spiritual community institution. Thus a few Roman Catholics
could actually denounce their archbishop because he had ordered
desegregation, just as some Jews in the South and the overwhelming majority of Protestants paid not the slightest attention to the
resolutions and decrees against racial segregation proposed by their

clergy at synods, and at the many conferences and conventions since 1954.

Even the Unitarians! Who would have thought it? But the point I make, that we tend to reflect the attitudes of the society in which we live, affects this liberal sect, too. The Reverend Paul H. Osborne of Charleston, South Carolina, was the only open pro-integration minister in that seaport city. He expected trouble with the press and with Charlestonians, but not from his fellow Unitarians. But that is where the trouble came from and the Reverend Osborne's ministry was terminated.

The Southern tragedy

THE United States Census Bureau reports the continuing movement of Negro migration to the North. The State of Mississippi showed a loss in Negro population of 323,000 from 1950 to 1960, and the States that lost 175,000 or more Negroes included Alabama, South Carolina, North Carolina, Georgia, and Arkansas. I have seen segregationists smile at these figures, but they are smiling at a Southern tragedy. They should know that the more Negro college graduates there are, the greater the movement of Negroes from the South to other parts of the country.

I would like to submit my own survey in one corner of the South to the Census Bureau. Early in 1960 we were able to track down one hundred and sixty-two of the graduates of three North Carolina Negro colleges of the two previous years. We found that only forty-seven were still in my State and that most of those forty-seven were teachers and clergymen serving the Negro population. Only eighteen were following the professions for which they were trained. The other one hundred and fifteen college graduates were in twenty other States. Thus my State had spent a fortune in preparing a Negro engineer who is now working in Camden, New Jersey, and a Negro stenographer who is now in Washington, D. C.

Where is the intelligence behind this? And what does this do to the Negro of the South? Suppose the Scotch-Irish immigrants in my State had lost most of their high school and college graduates. Would they have been able to build fine cities such as Charlotte? What would have happened to more recent immigrants, the German, Irish, Jewish, Italian, and Polish groups, if year after year they lost two-thirds of their high school graduates and 95 per cent of their college boys and girls? Could they have helped build such cities as Chicago, Detroit, Milwaukee, Boston, and New York?

Yet there are Southern segregationists who misinterpret this migration. "We are losing our Nigras," they say, but they live in a dream world, because the Negro high school and college graduate leaves behind his semiliterate brother, his older sister who works as a domestic, and his father who has arthritis and lives on welfare.

Thus the costs of two separate systems of education mount higher and higher, as welfare costs parallel the mounting figures. It is a tragic loss not only of wasted millions but of human resources.

On Mark Twain

In *The Adventures of Huckleberry Finn* by Mark Twain, Huck arrives late and immediately starts lying to Aunt Sally. He tells her the boat ran aground. Aunt Sally asks him where. Huck thinks up another lie.

"It warn't the grounding—that didn't keep us back but a little. We blowed out a cylinder-head."

"Good gracious! anybody hurt?"

"No'm. Killed a nigger."

"Well, it's lucky; because sometimes people do get hurt. . . ."

This is the Mark Twain we hide from ourselves, the Mark Twain who understood the brutalizing effects of white supremacy. We refuse to admit Mark Twain was a flaming liberal. Nor do we admit that one of his central themes was the dehumanizing relationship between black and white and its divisive effect upon this culture we call America.

We deal with Twain as we deal with Lincoln. That part of their personalities which does not lend itself to the concept of "togetherness" we simply ignore.

Like Lincoln, Twain saw the dark side of life and was not terrified but rather awed by it. We are able to ignore his religious heresies by insisting Twain is a humorist—but we fail to understand it is a grim humor. Twain, for example, did not believe in the sanctity of the home nor in getting ahead. How else explain Huck Finn and one of the world's great novels? Every time Huck leaves the river and vagabonding and comes to shore he sees hate and cowardice and deceit. Twain's criticism of America is harsh.

Mark Twain is one of the great adversaries of racial segregation.

Neither Twain nor Dickens wrote to celebrate life, but to reform it.

No room at the landings

THE Detroit River is famous for its yachts. The steel, automobile, and small-parts executives float up and down the river in their fine craft, stopping occasionally for refreshments at luxurious yachting clubs.

So one of the most successful Jewish businessmen of Detroit bought himself a yacht. (I do not believe he'd object to the use of his name, but it is not really necessary.) He resolved to have a fine time sailing up and down the Detroit River. But, after two weeks, he was back at the boat company. "You'll have to take the yacht back, I can't use it," he said.

The builder couldn't understand it. "But you had looked forward to it with such joy," he said, "and it's the finest boat of its kind afloat."

"There's nothing wrong with the yacht, and my family and I love it," the Jewish businessman reported, "but there's no place to land—no one let's me land."

Across the river and into the trees

ACROSS the Catawba River in the famous textile city of Gastonia, the textile union fellows were trying to organize one of the industries, and they finally won the right to an election.

The union organizers arranged a pre-election fish fry in a public park, and among the one hundred and fifty employees who had signed cards there were about twenty Negroes. A few people suggested discreetly that it wouldn't do for the whites and the Negroes to sit together, so the Negroes set up their tables under the trees about one hundred yards from the center of things.

Then a very interesting thing happened. The people at the "white" tables began to dawdle over their food in silence and kept looking toward the Negroes under the trees.

No one gave the order. It was an instinctive action on the part of over one hundred men and women who suddenly stood up and carried their food-laden tables to join the Negroes under the trees.

Judith and Ruth

THERE was a street in the Auschwitz death camp known as "Twin Block." This block was set aside by the Nazi Doctor Mengele, to "investigate" into the causes of twins.

The boxcars crowded with Jews arrived at the camp and the people inside were immediately classified. Some were sent to the gas chambers forthwith; others were kept alive for slave labor; but twins were sent to Twin Block and were placed in hospital beds side by side to await experiments.

In October 1944 the boxcars from Budapest brought the Gagoda family—father, mother, and twin girls aged ten. The girls were uncommonly beautiful, and even the parents had trouble telling Judith from Ruth. Twin Block was also a break for the mother because she was incorporated into the experiment. That is why the mother and daughter Judith now live in Tel Aviv. The father was never seen again after the classification that first day, and Ruth died in the camp. The Nazis had not the time to get around to Judith, the second twin, after they had finished cutting up little Ruth.

Nazi doctors were particularly interested in the eyes and hair and the nerve centers of twins. They wanted to see whether pain inflicted on one twin would cause any psychical emotion in the other. They were also interested in the texture and color of the hair. Ruth lasted three months because the Nazis exercised particular care with her after each major experiment. They wanted to keep her alive as long as possible to continue their experiments. In February 1945 it began to look bad for the Nazis and there was a relaxation of the surgical experiments, even though the gas chambers continued their work.

After the Russians entered Auschwitz the few survivors of Twin Block were transferred to a field hospital and later returned to Budapest for further rehabilitation. Mrs. Gagoda and the remaining member of the family, Judith, migrated to Israel. Judith is married today. She is a handsome young woman who works in a government office helping her husband get his engineering degree from the Hebrew University and awaiting their first child. They hope it will be a girl so they can call her Ruth.

The triumph of shame

"Go NOT to the Senate," said the Emperor Vespasian to the Senator Elvidius Priscus, and the latter answered, "While I am a senator I must go to the debates."

"Thou mayest go, but say not a word."

"Ask not for my consent, and I shall keep silent."

"But if thou speakest I shall have thee killed."

"When did I tell thee that I was immortal?"

One moment after his birth man is already being dragged away like a bushel of beans. The bushel of beans, however, cannot think in terms of resistance, while man feels that he can resist and sometimes he even wins a skirmish on the way. The man who struggles against this current sometimes vanquishes it and sometimes is dragged under, but whether he wins or loses he has played his part with dignity.

There is not a single white supremacist in the North or the South who will happily pass along to his grandchildren the intelligence that he fought the good fight for the continued discrimination against people of different color, race, or creed.

Therefore he must needs find himself a device to tide him over the terrible struggle with himself, and he says that it is not a matter of discrimination and segregation, but that he stands instead for "States' rights," or "tradition," or "way of life," or that "real-estate values will go down," and by such a device he demonstrates the victory of the human spirit over the lower animals and over that bushel of beans. Only man feels a sense of shame and that shame is his crowning glory. Neither technological advances nor scientific victories can adequately explain this redeeming sense of shame, man's greatest gift.

If fifty million people say a foolish thing, said Anatole France, it still remains a foolish thing.

The Bond Issue Plan

THE population of Jackson, Mississippi, is 144,422.

A Southern city of 144,422 belongs in a special class. On the basis of population, banks determine the rating of a city's bonds, and prestige among investors. Chamber of Commerce people also use the population figure as an inducement to attract new industry and more distributorships to the city.

What's the population of Jackson, Mississippi? You say 144,422? But what about the 51,556 of that total who are Negroes? These Negroes are discriminated against in education, political activity, health facilities, employment, and entertainment facilities. They are segregated. But they are not segregated in the population figure.

Jackson is not the only city thus involved; all of the other Southern cities that boast of increased population are guilty of using figures to prove something which is not wholly true.

Cities may well be bursting at their seams, but they still want it both ways. They want to include the Negroes as part of their population but exclude their Negroes as people.

Therefore the new Golden Plan to end racial segregation: the next time a Southern city applies for a bond issue and boasts of its tremendously increased population, let the NAACP file a demurrer with the Chase-Manhattan Bank and say, No—the city does not have 144,422 population. It segregates 51,556 of its population and it should also segregate the population in its bond application.

Presbyterians and the Bible

THE essay on the Presbyterians in my book, *Only in America*, prompted a great display of good humor on both sides of the Atlantic.

When I was in London and appeared on a BBC television program the director asked me to read that essay, and as a result the great newspaper *The Scotsman* devoted a lengthy article to my views that the Presbyterians are indeed one of the Lost Tribes.

I have friends in Charlotte (the citadel of American Presbyterianism), who tell me their eighty-year-old mothers stamp their canes on the floor in anger at the divided chancel, the cross on the steeple, and the vestments on the minister.

One lady refused to read the Sunday papers even on Monday since she believed the paper was printed on the Sabbath, which is a desecration of the Lord's Day and a violation of the Commandments. Her son tried to prove to his old mother that the papers were really printed on Saturday. After a trip to the printing plant, she saw he was right. Thereafter she read the Sunday papers on Monday, but refused to read the Monday papers. She knew well enough a law had been violated.

Despite all the reading I have done in my lifetime, I was still surprised at the depth of knowledge these Presbyterians displayed about the Hebrew Bible, or what they call the Old Testament. These were laymen, agents, businessmen, doctors, and lawyers. More than surprised, too; a bit jealous that these Presbyterians knew more about the Jewish Bible than I.

I began to read the Bible about ten years ago and I gave it the same intensity of concentration I had given Shakespeare some years before. I often feel it would serve more if at the interfaith meeting, the Presbyterian ministers, instead of delivering the same old speeches year after year, gave a lecture on Judaism.

Don't think for a moment they couldn't.

I advance the theory because of the many parallels between Orthodox Judaism and Calvinism, particularly in the deep concern for the Sabbath which each religion considers the most important observance of their faith. But like Orthodox Judaism, Presbyterianism has seen many changes during the past fifty years. The adherents are about equally divided in both sects: those who call the recent developments "more conservative," and those who say their religion is now "more liberal."

Did Stanton murder Lincoln?

A NEW JERSEY attic recently disgorged a code which charged Edwin M. Stanton, Secretary of War in Lincoln's cabinet, with having helped, abetted, or encouraged the President's assassination. I suspect we will have more such, though none of it will be true.

Carl Sandburg's monumental six-volume *Lincoln* leaves me with a very clear impression that Stanton was probably the best Secretary of War the country ever had and that we could probably make use of him today. He was, to be sure, a stubborn, humorless, and harsh fellow, but Lincoln understood this and visited Stanton in his home and in many other ways deferred to his temperament. Lincoln wanted Stanton to supply the Union Army, and in this Stanton did not disappoint him. He had the men and materials where they were supposed to be, when they were needed, in sufficient amounts, and on time.

Considering the times, the lack of adequate rail facilities until the end of the war, the greed and corruption among war profiteers, and the colossal job of organization he had to handle, Stanton did a most remarkable job and to question his patriotism is bootless.

The man who killed Lincoln was not an ambitious Northern politician but a Southern, half-crazed actor who thought slavery a most noble invention of God and shot Lincoln for abolishing it.

"Little" Dr. Goldberger

OFTEN, when a white man is telling a story, he will say, ". . . and then along came this *big*, fat Negro woman," or ". . . here's this *big* colored fellow," or ". . . he was the *biggest* colored man you ever saw." To most whites Negroes are monumental. Never mind the statistics which show that the average American Negro is shorter than the average white. And never mind the tubercular Negroes of the South and that there are far more tubercular Negroes in the South than there are ". . . the *biggest* colored man you ever saw."

Calling all Negroes big or maintaining that all of them are in supreme health serves two ends: one, it justifies the false fears the whites have of the Negro appetite for food and sex; and two, it helps relieve their guilt over imposing a second-class citizenship upon a part of humankind.

But when folks talk of Jews it is always, ". . . here comes along this *little* Jew," or (even in kindness) ". . . she was the nicest *little* Jewish woman."

Some years ago, I heard a famous and truly great Virginia editor deliver a lecture on the contributions the Jews have made to America. As an example, he cited the work of Dr. Joseph Goldberger, who discovered the cause of pellagra in the South and devised its cure. The editor said, by way of preface, ". . . and here this wonderful *little* Jewish doctor . . ." and I smiled.

Dr. Joseph Goldberger was a lanky guy slightly over six feet tall.

The invisible Negro

IN A SMALL West Texas town the school board was faced with a unique problem: the town's oldest Negro boy had become eligible to enter high school, but the nearest school available to him was in a city about forty miles away. Since his family could not afford to pay for his transportation, they had asked the board to pay his way for the daily trip. And therein lay the problem. The State statutes could only provide a school bus. But again the board was stymied. There had to be a minimum of seven students before a bus could be furnished. The board took its problem to the town's lawyer.

The answer he finally gave them was fairly simple. He told them that there was nothing that kept the board from exercising its judgment and discretion in deciding who was and who was not a Negro. The board, being fairly smart, caught on fast. Quite hastily the members agreed that this colored boy (whose skin was very dark) was not a Negro.

On the boy's high school entrance paper the space for "race" was discreetly left blank, so that no questions from outside the town were ever asked. Apparently few, if any, were asked in town either. He went all the way through high school there, and graduated with the "other whites."

The boy is practicing law in Illinois today. Apparently he was not prepared to risk practicing his profession in Texas—as an invisible Negro.

What is a Jewess?

A MINORITY often begins to believe the propaganda used against it. It begins to absorb the phrases of its opponents.

One of these big deals is "Jewess."

Now what is a Jewess?

Strangely the suffix "-ess" is used only for the Negro and the Jew.

"Jewess" is actually an anti-Semitic term. It has been used for centuries, but gained popular usage with the genteel anti-Semites toward the end of the nineteenth century.

When one thinks of the promiscuous heroines of literature, they are either poor like Miss Forever Amber or rich like Miss Constant Nymph or sophisticated like Brett or soulful like Sophie or selfish like Emma Bovary. But the Jewish girl in the novel of promiscuity winds up playing the third act in a sadistic daydream. She is voluptuous and ripe and dark and electrically attractive, like poor Rebecca of Sir Walter Scott's *Ivanhoe*. People want to drag her through the streets by her hair. They'd love that, wouldn't they? And all because a high social status group has always stereotyped a low social status group as somehow being sexually primitive.

Thus "Jewess" and "Negress"—like lioness and tigress.

Anna Magnani says, "I am an Italian," and Vivien Leigh says, "I am English" and the chairman of the Woman's Guild at Christ and Holy Trinity says, "I am an Episcopalian." No one says, "I am an Italianess," "I am an Englishess" or "I am an Episcopalianess."

The unforgivable crime

AFTER a Federal court told the Danville, Virginia, library it would have to integrate or close, the City Fathers decided on segregation at any price. The library closed.

There were many good people in Danville who had not believed it would come to this. Many protested. In a public letter, Dr. Samuel Newman, a practicing physician in Danville for many years, wrote: "The closing of the Danville Public Library does violence to the American spirit. It is not too late for the City Council to listen to the voice of reason and in a spirit of contrition reopen the public library."

It is already too late even for contrition. Not that the library at Danville won't reopen—it will—but violence has been done to the spirit of reason.

The closing of this library is comparable to the burning of the Alexandrian Library. This was the greatest library of antiquity. It contained the Dialogues of Aristotle, the plays of all the Greek poets, the complete works of Sappho, and when it went up in flames from the torch of a Roman legionnaire, the world lost a part of itself.

But fire is, after all, only an impersonal force, and the legionnaire was perhaps only an ignorant soldier, half-drunk and careless. The world does not suffer from a lack of writers; the loss of the Alexandrian Library was momentous, but it was, in the long run, an impersonal loss.

This is not true of Danville. It is not impersonal. It is a vicious self-mutilation. Danville not only shut its library doors to Negroes, but this Christian community shut its doors on the Bible, the Church Fathers, the works of Luther, Calvin, John Fox, and Paul Tillich.

Hitler burned the books. The German children raced through the libraries cleaning the shelves of Thomas Mann, Albert Einstein, and Stefan Zweig. Their enthusiasm was so great that in their excitement they also consigned Goethe, Lessing, and Neitzsche to the flames. As the flames roared higher, up in smoke went the regency of German culture: up in smoke went the scholarship of a century and a half that had virtually re-created Greece; up in flames went the tradition of musical excellence; up in flames went the poetic inspiration. "He who destroys a book destroys life itself," wrote Milton.

The citizens of Danville may have closed their library doors by popular vote. But, along with the perpetrators of the Alexandrian fire and the burning of the books in Hitler's Germany, they have convicted themselves of a crime history does not forgive.

The colonel and the chauffeur

AN ATTEMPT was made to get a room for Faye Emerson's colored maid at one of our leading hotels in Charlotte. Faye Emerson was here with Eva Le Gallienne for a one-night performance of *Mary Stuart*. Miss Emerson's maid is also her hairdresser and companion, but she could not stay in any one of the leading hotels and a room had to be rented in a hotel in the Negro district.

In speaking with Mrs. Allen, who owns the Negro Hotel Alexander, I found out that quite a few white persons stop at her hotel.

"Why, the other night an Army car came up here with a colonel who wanted his chauffeur with him in the same hotel and rented a room for him."

"I suppose the colonel wanted his Negro chauffeur near him?"

Said Mrs. Allen, "No, the colonel was a colored man and he wanted his white chauffeur near him."

The Israeli flag

WHEN Golda Meir comes to New York City she stays at the Essex House. Because she is Israel's Foreign Minister, the Essex House hangs out the Israeli flag. They hang it to the right of the American Flag where it flutters toward the windows of the New York City Athletic Club. In all of its long history, the New York City Athletic Club, as "exclusive" as Idlewild Airport, has never allowed a Jewish member to desecrate its purity. But once, on a breezy day, when Golda Meir was in the Essex House, it looked for all the world as though the Israeli flag was flying from the Athletic Club itself. The taxi driver and I laughed like hell.

Gradual integration

IN THE emergency room of the Alachua General Hospital at Gainesville, Florida, there are three thermometers. They stand in a row on a small shelf with nothing else. The first is in an open container labeled: "WHITE—ORAL," the third is in an identical container labeled, "COLORED—ORAL," and the middle one, which protrudes through a cork, in its otherwise sameness, is labeled, "RECTAL."

This is what I call *gradual* integration.

This is progress

LAST year the Garinger High School in Charlotte had a lone Negro to satisfy the system of token integration. This year no Negro boy or girl applied for a transfer. The school board is tickled to death if no Negro makes formal application, for this saves lawyers, teachers, and parents all sorts of speeches.

But the interesting thing about it is that the faculty and the students at Garinger High School are lonesome without that one Negro boy, and they are going around the high school with long faces hoping that they will get themselves another Negro soon.

Breakfast in New Orleans

NEW ORLEANS is justly called the "Paris of America." It is the only city in America in which to eat breakfast. You should start with an absinthe frappé, go on to those very thin pancakes filled with ham and swiss cheese, and then eggs Benedict with sauce *Béarnaise* and hot French bread and marmalade along with a bottle of chilled rosé.

And a culture capable of such wonders stands now jeering at little Negro girls going to school. And the millionaires, the shippers, the oil men, the merchants, the Chamber of Commerce—the folks who go to the opera and who eat this breakfast—are strangely silent.

The smart policeman

IN A New Mexico town a polite young policeman told a Negro, "Fella, may I suggest you get rid of that ten-gallon hat you're wearing. If you keep it on, one dark night a Mexican or a Navajo will sticks a shiv in you."

The policeman understood that any attempt by the Negro to look like a Mexican or an Indian arouses great resentment. The same thing happened in North Carolina when the press of America applauded the Lumbee Indians who routed the Ku Klux Klan one night a few years ago.

The Indians prepared their ambush after the Klan had declared war on the Indians because of their "color," but what the press missed was that Indians did not attack because they despised the bigotry of the Klan, but because the Klan identified them with the Negroes.

The rhythm of equality

THE University of South Carolina has traditionally prohibited Negro bands and when the freshmen scheduled a colored band at a campus dance last December 3, the University officials revoked permission for the dance and explained they feared a racial incident.

But the student newspaper, the *Gamecock*, has a different version. The students want Negro bands at their parties for two reasons: their music is more enjoyable, their price is more reasonable. The students claim you can hire an excellent Negro band for sixty dollars to one hundred and fifty dollars while a comparable "white" band costs three hundred and fifty dollars.

A fine way to go about winning equality for our citizens. But then again, every little thing helps.

8.

DEEP SOUTH
KOSHER PICKLES

No more report cards

THE curriculum of the high school has been reduced to the lowest common denominator. In these beautiful ranch-type buildings, the most popular elective is called "Family Living." The kids figure it will be a little sexy and certainly more interesting than some of the other electives. The kids stand in line to register for this course. Then there are courses in Music Appreciation and Art Appreciation. There's also a course in Driving Education—learning how to drive a car and presumably bust someone else's head on Saturday nights. There is another course in Clothing. Clothing? In this class they put hems on dish towels, and the boys make Bermuda shorts and the girls make toreador pants. So much for Clothing.

General Office Practice is for the kids who cannot possibly make the grade as typists and so this course teaches them how to sharpen pencils and when to leave the office for the coffee break. This General Office Practice elective is not to be confused with the Secretarial Office Practice. That is a different course and set aside for the advanced students who might possibly learn to use a typewriter.

General Commercial Business Arithmetic is for the kids who have shown themselves to be hopeless as far as algebra is concerned.

Let us not forget the course in Ceramics. Now if they called this course "Making Ash Trays" there would be some purpose behind it because we all need ash trays, but they call it "Ceramics" because Sherlock Holmes and Philo Vance dabbled in this art between solving murder cases.

I have the evidence in my hands that in some freshman classes in a large State university, high school graduates turned up who could not write a single English sentence, and in fact had difficulty in writing their names.

The graduation day awards which I have studied confirm the terrible state of our high schools. One of the awards—perhaps the most important one—is for Distributive Education. This means retailing and salesmanship. Then comes what I call the Cherry Pie Award for baking. Next in importance is the athletic award. In several schools in North Carolina and South Carolina this award is called, "Athlete Showing Most Christlike Traits." The citizenship award goes to a girl and the DAR is the donor, which at least makes some sense. Last, of course, is the Beauty Queen Award and this award is known as Miss Hi Miss. Somewhere in this list they do indeed smuggle in an award for scholarship.

All of this is in preparation for Business Education Day, when the chamber of commerce fellows return to their old high schools and laugh like hell about how they cannot sit in their old seats, and the teachers who have spent a lifetime in preparation for their profession have been drilled for two weeks in on "How to Receive Guests." All of this, my friend, is the American High School in the Space Age.

The grade schools aren't much better.

What ever happened to the report card and "A," "B," "C," "D," and "F"? Why does a mathematics teacher write home that a student seems to be making a concentrated effort to adjust to the group? The question is: can he do long division? And whatever are these "peer" groups the educators keep talking about? A peer group! Peers sit in England's House of Lords, and the only time you ever hear of them is when some Baron gets arrested for passing bogus checks and wants to be tried by a jury of his peers. Then these Lords sit in trial and give him just as stiff a sentence as any collection of haberdashers, salesmen, or gentlemen mechanics would on an ordinary jury.

True, in my day there were not twenty-seven electric ranges on which the young girls could learn how to make fudge between their classes in Language Arts and the World We Live In. These classes used to be called English and Civics and we seemed better instructed for it.

School buses have become station wagons driven by trained

psychologists. I will make one compromise with the educators. I will give them sole rights to their jargon and the unrestricted use of "peer group," if they will promise to make out report cards once again.

Will Mortimer Adler replace TV?

DR. MORTIMER ADLER, who is one of the inventors of the "100 Great Books," has also compiled the *Syntopicon*, a two-volume index to the thinking of seventy-four great authors who have thought mankind's great thoughts. This project, which I suppose ought to be listed along with the other great thoughts, cost its sponsor, The Encyclopaedia Britannica, several million dollars.

Right now this good philosopher is about to take stock of the one hundred and two great ideas of Western mankind. Recently he completed a 689-page volume called *The Idea of Freedom*, and he will start work soon on "a follow-up" tome numbering nine hundred pages.

Dr. Adler has not always enjoyed universal acclaim, for the simple reason that Dr. Adler is not typically a philosopher, but a businessman. Philosophers never mention the number of pages in their books.

Do not mistake me, there is nothing wrong in being a business-man. The National Association of Manufacturers assures us it is businessmen who have made the country what it is. I suspect the NAM is right. But it is a little bewildering to have a businessman pose as a philosopher. The businessman-philosopher will not confuse philosophers, but he will confuse businessmen.

Nor is it presumptuous to call Dr. Adler a businessman. Business in America is a pretty omnivorous thing. Sinclair Lewis and the expatriate writers of the twenties and the muckrakers of the nineties rained in the body blows, but American business is nothing if not resilient. It recovered. Businessmen and their wives buy Picassos today and talk about his Blue Period; corporations are the financial mainstay of the smaller colleges; and for a while business executives even contemplated running the government.

How did business manage this? They simply hired everyone. Some of the hiring was obvious—they gave a man a job. They swallowed up hundreds of World War II generals like Lucius Clay and Douglas MacArthur. And while the rest of us were pitying the hard-working scientist and psychologist toiling away in the laboratory for the benefit of mankind, business hired them. We look up and here are these white-coated men on the pay roll, preparing for tomorrow by persuading us what and how to buy today.

This talent is not hard to muster if you have money. Business has the money and there are thousands of men who want to do business. And business, for instance, sends executives to Dr. Adler's Institute of Philosophical Research in San Francisco.

What makes Dr. Adler a fit subject for admiration in the business world is his cataloguing mind. There are one hundred great books, seventy-four great authors, one hundred and two great ideas. Businessmen are practical. They want to deal in finite and specific quantities. "Will we make this year's quota?" "What is the cost per issue per thousand?" "How profitable are our distributorships?" "Will it sell flour?" Business has expanded and it expands on a piecemeal basis. Businessmen know there is a point at which expansion and profits reach a certain delicate and wonderful balance. So they will embrace the one hundred and two great ideas, seventy-four great authors, and one hundred great books. If there is a balance point in profits, then there must also be a balance point for intelligence and knowledge.

The only real problem Dr. Adler may pose for business is if he happens to discover that there are really one hundred and nine great ideas and adds three more great authors and maybe finds two more great books. But businessmen do the same thing with improvements; as soon as they've saturated the market with black-and-white TV sets they discover color television, and when all the people are drinking martinis business suddenly makes it chic to drink bock beer.

Dr. Adler knows where he is going, but I wonder if we do. Is he the *American* philosopher? Surely no philosopher has more publicity—not C. I. Lewis of Harvard, or George Geiger of Antioch, or Sidney Hook of New York University, or Max Black of Cornell, or W. T. Stace of Princeton, or Horace Kallen of the New School. Only Jean-Paul Sartre rivals Dr. Adler in favorable notices and, after all, Sartre is French and drinks absinthe with Simone de Beauvoir, which explains everything.

On prayers

I HAVE come across some wonderful prayers in my life, and I know three of them that ought to stand anybody in good stead. The first of these was written by the Greek philosopher, Plato, for the instruction of his students:

> King Zeus, grant us the good whether we pray for it or not.
> But keep evil away from us whether we pray for it or not.

The second is one Sir Jacob Astley offered before he led the English troops to victory at the Battle of Edge Hill:

> Lord, I shall be very busy this day. I may forget Thee, but do Thou not forget me.

The third of these prayers is an old Gaelic one:

> May the road rise to meet you,
> May the wind be always at your back,
> May the sun shine warm upon your face,
> And the rains fall soft upon your fields,
> And, until we meet again,
> May God hold you in the palm of his hand.

I like the first prayer because it is one that asks for spiritual well-being; the second because it admits human frailty, and the third is my favorite because it is a prayer that offers total friendship.

The underwater landsman

How did the jewfish get its name? And after I conjured this question, I began wondering what is a jewfish and where is it found? While I am no fisherman, I admire fishermen and, if I had the time, fishing is an activity I would like.

I enlisted professional help. Mr. Stanley Meltzoff of the American Littoral Society and Dr. Lionel Walford of the Sandy Hook Marine Laboratory gave me their ideas freely.

Perhaps what caught my attention is that the name jewfish frequently appears in italics or is set apart by quotation marks. There are quite a few fish with national names for whom such grammatical isolation is not at all common. There is the Argentine, the French angelfish, the Bermuda chub, the doctor fish, the Cuban and Spanish heartfish, the Boston ling, the Spanish mackerel, the Louisiana piefish, the Irish pompano, the New York groundshark, and the West Indian shellfish.

I do know that the jewfish is the largest fish in our waters, except for sharks, which are not properly fish.

The jewfish is part of the family of giant sea basses which the French call *merou* and the Spanish *maro*. There are two species of jewfish, the Promicrops itaiara, which is spotted, and the Garrupa nigrita, black.

The jewfish feeds by opening its mouth and letting the current wash smaller fish into its gullet. Its meat is delicious but fishermen find managing all that bulk on the surface of the water a hard job.

It is true the jewfish goes by other names, like black snapper and guasa and black sea bass, but Mr. Meltzoff believes jewfish is the most common coin of acceptance and identifies the fish in any ordinary conversation.

Very probably the name is not intended as a slur. It came into common parlance, suggests Dr. Walford, as a part of dockside wit. In the Bahamas when a novice pulls in a purple fish and asks an old fisherman what kind of a fish it is, the sophisticate will tell him, "Well, we call that the big purple fish hereabouts." And when the novice asks what is the difference between this fish and a smaller purple fish, the old salt will say, "Why, man, can't you see? That other one is what we call the little purple fish."

Mr. Meltzoff has confided that he has some qualms about spearing the jewfish. It is as though he spears an underwater landsman. He often wonders whether he should make food of the fish or get food for it. He feels a little differently toward the jewfish but concludes this difference of feeling has made him feel more fellowship for fish generally and he is a better man for it.

Now I will see what I can find out about the jew's-harp.

Deep South kosher pickles

JEWISH food has made many inroads into the American dietary habits. The pastrami sandwich is a standard order and Jewish rye is relished all over the country. There is even a store in Charlotte which runs an advertisement for "Deep South kosher pickles."

Now what in Sam Hill are "Deep South kosher pickles"? I am all for cultural inroads, but I doubt that the Deep South kosher pickle is going to beat much of a path. First of all, it has no significance. Now, on the Lower East Side of New York City, the kosher pickle had a deep significance to the folks. If a young married woman came into the store one afternoon and asked for a pickle, everybody stopped and stared and said, "Ah ha, she must be pregnant." The kosher pickle was involved with our very life.

But it has gone, along with trolley cars, hobble skirts, and a pitcher of beer. All of the so-called kosher pickles that you buy now either North or South lack one basic ingredient. They lack the basic tomm (flavor). The modern folks all use vinegar to pickle the cucumber and, of course, the old-timers would have had none of that. Once you commit yourself to vinegar, it seems you can't get that real garlicky and spicy flavor into the cucumbers.

Despite the glowing attributes of the "Deep South kosher pickles" as set forth in the ad, you still have to go down to Delancey Street on New York's East Side, and put your hand in the barrel and pull out a pickle if you want the real kosher flavor.

The greatest kosher pickles in the world, I remember, were sold by an elderly woman forty years ago. She stood in a store on the corner of Clinton and Rivington Streets completely surrounded by barrels. She sold very sour pickles, pickled tomatoes, red peppers. Her real delicacy was sauerkraut. It cost a penny and she plowed into the barrel and brought out a fistful which she dropped on a piece of brown paper. I mentioned the store to an old-timer who told me that the woman had educated her three sons with her scanty profits. She was there in every sort of weather—rain, cold, or blazing heat wave. No one, to my knowledge, has ever duplicated her sauerkraut.

When everyone was labeling every bottle of pickles "kosher," and the Government made them stop, several pickle firms right here in the South went out and employed a rabbi so that they would indeed be kosher. They know full well the selling point of any pickle is its "kosher-ness." But it isn't the "kosher" that made that old-time pickle a wonderful memory. It was that woman who stood among the barrels, and the sad thing is you can't go out and hire her.

The woman at the window

GERTRUDE SCHLIER is a badly crippled woman who has been sitting at the window of a Lower East Side tenement and looking out upon America. She has written a good first novel, A Time for Living. It deserves more than the scant attention it has received.

This author and I have corresponded over the years, and now that her first book has been published the question arises: what does one do with a book?

Do you sell it as you sell potatoes or pencils? Do you retail it in a store? Peddle it on a street corner? How do you get the New York *Times* to review it?

And so Miss Schlier continues to sit at the window.

She sits in her wheelchair worried about her book, and she should know that the woman upstairs sitting at the window is worried about her husband squandering his paycheck in the saloon down the street, and that across the way there is a man sitting at his window worried about how to provide food for his children.

The radio and television bring us dire news about Berlin and the explosion of a fifty-megaton hydrogen bomb, but for people worried at the window, the world really stands still.

I like to watch the pitcher during a ball game. I never take my eyes off him. I love to watch him wind up and throw, and if the ball doesn't cut across the plate, he gets it back as quickly as possible and winds up again, and again he throws his best pitch.

Gertrude Schlier asks me what does one do with a book? And all I can tell her is about a baseball pitcher.

The Yiddish stage

No ONE has yet described the Yiddish stage in all its color and depth. It was one of the most productive of all theaters—and one of the most glamorous. There are people active now on Broadway, in Hollywood, and on television who received their early training on the Yiddish-speaking stage. Milton Weintraub, for instance, comes immediately to mind. Mr. Weintraub for many years has been the secretary and treasurer of the Association of Theatrical Managers and Press Agents, an organization which Victor Riesel once described as one of the best-managed organizations in the American labor movement.

The performers who made the jump from the Yiddish to the American stage would make a respectable Who's Who of the American theater. Paul Muni, Edward G. Robinson, Luther and Stella Adler, Jacob Ben-Ami, Menasha Skulnik, Joseph Schildkraut, and many others, including my friends, the Bernardis. Boris

Bernardi is now manager of the touring company of *Once Upon a Mattress*, and Hershel Bernardi plays Lieutenant Jacoby on the *Peter Gunn* show and is also "Harry Golden" in the West Coast production of *Only in America*, by Jerry Lawrence and Bob Lee.

The Yiddish theater was a world filled to overflowing with humor. The fractured English of those actors would leave you in stitches—"A steak, please, well-to-do."

And there must be many of my contemporaries who remember the famous Grossman poster announcing a new pyessa ("piece," a new show). "Samuel B. Grossman, Producer and Actor, Presents *The Sorrowing Father*, a new play in Three Acts by Samuel B. Grossman; with Irving Grossman, Joseph Grossman, Helen Grossman, Fanny Grossman, Miriam Grossman and Hal Grossman. Music by S. B. Grossman, Dances by Helen Grossman, Stage Designer, Miriam Grossman. For benefits write to Treasurer Joseph Grossman."

The noble cause

BETWEEN the outskirts of New York and Chicago, and from Chicago to San Francisco you cannot get a decent meal. The food would be absolutely terrible if it weren't for the Italians and Chinese.

I do not think there's a major town along any of the highways without a Chinese restaurant. Sometimes the Oriental in Charlotte or Foo Young's in Dayton or Ruby Lee's in Des Moines are the only places where you can buy food that is not fried or boiled.

The Chinese restaurateurs have great integrity. In city after city they are forced to advertise Chinese-American cuisine. Most of the townsfolk who drop in pass up the egg foo yung or the sweet-and-sour spareribs in favor of the American cheese sandwich. If the Chinese converted their kitchens to frying steaks and potatoes they could probably double their business, especially if they offered a piece of lemon meringue glue as dessert. But they hold fast to the good old fortune cookie.

It is the Italians, however, who have saved us from the boiled mediocrity. Where would we be without spaghetti and ravioli and tomato paste and lasagne? The Walter-McCarran Immigration Act is bad enough in the year 1962, but imagine if it had been passed in 1900. The boys and girls who go to the junior prom and then afterward drive off for a hot pizza would have to content themselves with a soggy beefburger and romance would fly out the window.

The gustatory genius of the Italians keeps making inroads. Little by little the Hero sandwich is taking over the position of the number one favorite. The Jews who did much to help the appetite of American luncheoneers with the corned beef sandwich will have to give way soon. The Hero sandwich, or grinder, is half a loaf of bread stuffed with olives, cheese, prosciutto, tomatoes, and mayonnaise or tomato sauce.

The Hero sandwich has easily outdistanced the hot dog and hamburger. It is not much more expensive and a more elaborate ritual is involved in preparing it.

I am told that the reason the new attaché cases all those Madison Avenue fellows carry are selling so well is that they are five inches longer with a special compartment in which they can carry their Hero sandwiches to work and eat them on park benches at noon.

Victory to the Chinese and Italians in this fight to win over our B-B-Que and Chicken-in-a-Basket drive-ins. It is a noble fight.

Gentlemen of the West

THE one thing that seems reasonable to me in the Western movie or its midget brother, the Western TV series, is that when the sheriff and the rustler confront each other, they aim for the knockout punch instead of a sudden quick kick to the groin. On the surface this looks like a silly and simple-headed decision. A knockout punch is a contingent thing. A good boxer will size up his opponent carefully, judging the thickness of his shoulders, the strength of his neck, and the resiliency of his jaw, before he tries to knock him out. It is often much more sensible to concentrate upon the stomach and blows to the heart. Neither the sheriff nor the rustler has this opportunity and they are not bound by the Marquis of Queensberry rules. Instead of a squared ring they have the whole prairie to rassle in. You'd think they'd try for the ultimate; that they'd aim a kick for the groin. Even the most poorly aimed blow, or one just barely successful, promptly ends the fight. But this never happens. The reason is men never try it. It may be they don't want to admit this weapon into the arsenal for fear of reciprocation, but I tend to believe it is because they don't think of it.

At any rate, it is rarely employed, even in street fighting. The curious thing is women think of it almost automatically when they tangle with a man. This is the weapon street walkers use to beat off a drunk. It's as though they planned it with the careful strategy of a military general. I think that's why they never have the dance-hall queens or the schoolteacher confront the rustler. Television has a soul and a certain integrity, after all.

Corn on the cob

THE one affectation that marks anyone born on the Lower East Side of New York City is an inordinate love for corn on the cob. Why did the immigrants love this corn on the cob with such passion? It was virtually a tradition among the immigrant people. It meant they could enjoy strictly American food, and yet it wasn't until people in the East along with the immigrants began eating corn on the cob that the rest of the country caught on.

During the summer on the Lower East Side you would see every kid coming out of the tenement with his buttered, salted ear of corn wrapped in a newspaper. At Coney Island for a nickel, you could buy corn on the cob from a vendor who would dip it in a vat of butter before he handed it to you. Along the streets —everywhere—you saw elderly women wheeling baby carriages in which were large vats of corn which they sold for two cents an ear—an extra large one for three cents. They speared it with a big fork and gave you a pat of butter and a bit of salt. Sometimes the poor woman had to spear a dozen ears before the customer decided to buy one.

A big treat was to wait till the woman was ready to turn in for the night when you could get two ears for a penny—the ears everybody else had turned down.

An interesting menu

IN BOLD red letters, the menu proclaims: "Every Wednesday night and every Saturday night is Chinese night at Bernstein's." Bernstein's is a Chinese restaurant at 135 Essex Street in New York City. This is the restaurant that makes it possible for Orthodox Jews to eat Chinese food. Every meal is prepared in a kosher kitchen. In fact, the menu goes on to say that Bernstein's is the best place to break the Sabbath fast: "This delicious Oriental food—made to order—is perfect for Saturday nights and is served from sundown to 3:00 A.M. The ingredients are the finest available and our chef, Pi-Ah-Hwn, guarantees the flavor is authentic."

The bill of fare includes moo goo gai pan, egg foo yung, pepper steak, and wonton soup, which a parenthesis explains is Chinese kreplach.

Moshe couldn't hold out

IN ONE of the most populated sections of the Bronx in New York there is a famous delicatessen known as Moshe's. Moshe used to do a tremendous business because he had most of the famous delicacies that reminded the young marrieds and the older marrieds of their grandmothers.

And so along with the smoked salmon, cream cheese, bagels, onion rolls, and halvah, Moshe also sold the general run of dairy products which you can find in any of the supermarkets. Moshe's was a very special enterprise in that his store was crowded with customers every afternoon, while the managers of the huge A & P supermarket in the neighborhood spent most of their time mapping all sorts of campaigns to get some of that Moshe business.

But the tide in recent weeks has turned against Moshe and the reason is something they call Plaid Trading Stamps. For a long time the giant A & P establishment held out against the use of trading stamps. But I suppose they became tired of watching Moshe packing in the customers. And so now A & P has Plaid Trading Stamps and the folks are flocking to the supermarket in droves.

Trading stamps, or premium stamps, of course, are not new. Fifty years ago when I was a boy on the Lower East Side, I remember, I stood in line with my mother at the premium store with her saved-up Octagon soap wrappers. After a while she sent me to get the premium because she knew exactly what she wanted: "Get a piece of cut glass, something we haven't got yet." I do not know what happened to all the cut glass. I remember plunking each piece to hear the sound it made. That was supposed to indicate that it was genuine cut glass.

But today the trading stamps are a tremendous business. I have checked into this and find that the Plaid trading-stamp people intend to sell about one hundred million dollars' worth (in merchandise sold) to the one big A & P chain alone.

And they have complete freedom to sign up any other store that may want to use the stamps. Several weeks ago in a test run in Springfield, Massachusetts, a city of nearly two hundred thousand, over one hundred independent stores immediately applied for the privilege of handling the Plaid trading stamps in dealing with their customers.

I was deeply interested in the margin of profit involved in all this and an authority advised me that at least 20 per cent of all the trading stamps—plaid, gold, green, and all others—are never redeemed. Husbands do not bring them home, people lose them, children soil them, housewives throw them out with the garbage, and others put them away safely and forget where they put them. But all I can say is, poor Moshe!

The mind can change, but the appetite never

JEZEBEL, who was popularly despised by Biblical Hebrew ladies, was known as "the painted woman." Cosmetics had an unsavory reputation among the devout, and despite the numerous references to them in The Song of Songs, they were always considered the tools of sin.

The twentieth century, however, has generally set new patterns and now in Migdal Haemek, on the road to Nazareth, the Israelis recently celebrated the opening of a branch factory of a large American cosmetic firm. And they opened the new establishment with the same fanfare the Americans reserve for the opening of a supermarket.

Israel finds it more and more easy to live with its age-old traditions and rituals. In Jaffa, there are about 100,000 Jews who have emigrated from Bulgaria and Romania. Most of these Jews arrived after the establishment of the state. Like other new Israelis they went through the process of learning the Hebrew language and sending their children off to the new schools.

For many years, these Jews still sang the old Romanian songs and went to movies with Bulgarian and Romanian subtitles. Then because of the stepped-up integration, all of the movies announced: no more Romanian and Bulgarian subtitles. Everything in Hebrew. And so it was. The songs were old Hebrew songs, the talk in the home was Hebrew, the movies Hebrew. But there is one exception: the restaurants are still Bulgarian and Romanian and their menus are printed in those languages.

The mind can change, but the appetite never.

Some years ago the Communists decided to let the Romanian Jews emigrate to Israel. Then the Reds suddenly clamped down. The real reason for it was that hundreds of Gentile Romanians were taking advantage of the offer and emigrating to Israel in the hope of later emigration to Argentina, Brazil, or America, and the free world generally. The Israeli government was accepting everyone on the reasoning that no one lies about being Jewish.

A Jewish girl becomes a nun

THE phone call came from Sister Michael of the Sisters of Mercy College for Girls in North Carolina: "Mr. Golden, we have a Jewish girl here who will be professed as a Sister next Tuesday and we would like you to come. She has been here for six years and none of her family will be in attendance and she was very happy when I told her I was going to invite you to the ceremony."

I was not thinking of this invitation in terms of a "story." I was interested, of course, to see the ceremony and flattered that this girl wanted me to be her guest, but it was with genuine trepidation that I asked Sister Michael if I could talk to the girl —alone—afterward.

Sister Michael laughed and said, "She would be thrilled."

The ceremony itself was brief but impressive; it took place during Mass. After the consecration of the Mass, each candidate, radiant with joy, carrying a scroll containing her vows in her right hand and a lighted candle in her left, proceeded to the altar rail. As the Bishop elevated the Blessed Sacrament, each Sister declared her vows of poverty, chastity, and obedience, dedicated herself "to the service of the poor, sick, and ignorant, and to persevere until death in the Congregation," then signed her vows and received her Lord in Holy Communion. After the Mass had been completed, each consecrated bride of Christ received a silver wedding ring. The Sisters then prostrated themselves before the altar as the choir sang a most beautiful hymn. The ceremony concluded with the choir chanting a psalm of David as each newly professed Sister expressed her obedience to her Mother Superior. I was startled for a moment when the choir closed the ceremony with the psalm we hear in the synagogue during every Sabbath service: "Behold how good and pleasant it is to see brethren dwell together in unity."

And now Sister Michael (with the assent of the Mother Superior) was as good as her word. She introduced me to Sister Mary Ann and we seated ourselves on the porch of the convent and talked together alone for a full hour. Sister Mary Ann is handsome, an effervescent thirty-one-year-old. After a year of postulancy, a Sister is received into the order and allowed to choose a new name in religion. She usually takes the name "Mary," and Sister Mary Ann chose "Ann" because it was close to her Jewish name, "Hannah." Her parents were immigrants from Russia and Sister Mary Ann told me her father was extremely orthodox. He gave each of his children a thorough Hebrew education. She told me she went to heder every afternoon for six years during her elementary school days.

Then came a decision which is part of the pattern observed in many immigrant households. The parents were struggling to eke out a living and could afford to send only one child to college. They picked the "smart" one, and Hannah was sent to Brooklyn College, where four years later she was graduated with honors, receiving her degree in education.

Sister Mary Ann told me, "I followed Judaism as a matter of habit and never missed a religious service or a Jewish event of any kind at the Hillel House at the college."

"When did you first consider becoming a Roman Catholic?"

"I was always searching, searching for something that I could not find in Judaism."

"Did anyone influence you or encourage you in this search?"

"No one in particular, Mr. Golden. I was intensely interested in religion and purely as a matter of course began to read Catholic literature and became interested."

"Did you decide upon conversion suddenly?" I asked, "and did you tell your family about it?"

"No," she replied, "it didn't happen that way at all. I became interested in Catholic theology—somehow I thought this might be what I was searching for, but I still was not sure."

"What made you sure, Sister Mary Ann?"

"I decided not to become a teacher but to become a nurse. I wanted to work in a Catholic hospital where I felt that a year or two would help me make up my mind."

"And is that how you came to the South?"

"Yes. I finished a course in nursing and when I requested a Catholic institution I was sent to a Catholic hospital in North Carolina where I decided not only to become a Catholic but to devote my entire life to the Church."

Hannah was admitted to the novitiate in 1954 and started on the required six years of study and preparation leading to the ceremony I had just witnessed.

"Did you notify your parents of your decision and what was their reaction?" I asked.

"They were sorry I had given up teaching, but since I was not yet sure about Catholicism when I came to North Carolina I did not tell them of my possible conversion until I formally entered the convent."

When her parents learned of her decision, Hannah's mother came to the convent. "She kept insisting I was held here against my will," said Sister Mary Ann. "I pleaded with her to understand that I could go home without so much as a goodbye if I chose, but I could not convince her. When I escorted her to the bus and we left the grounds, I said, 'Look, there is no one to stop me if I go.' But she has remained skeptical. I never saw nor heard from her again."

"What about the other members of your family?" I asked.

"I heard that my father never mentioned my name again, that he mourned me as dead, from that day until he died about two years ago. My sister told me this when she visited me here about a year ago. She stopped by when she was on her honeymoon."

"What did she say to you?"

"She asked me to give up my vocation for our mother's sake, but I told her this was my life and in no other place could I ever expect to be happy. She left and I never heard from her again. My brother also visited me once. He's a happy-go-lucky boy and did not question me at all, simply hoped I would be happy."

"Sister Mary Ann, what did you feel about this rejection of your family and the sorrow you inflicted upon them?"

"I knew exactly what a terrible thing it meant to turn my back upon my family, but this is a great joy and fulfillment to my life and for this great joy I know I must pay a price—this pain of rejection."

(My readers will understand why I kept discussing her family. It is a quite natural discussion for any Jew. Sister Mary Ann also understood it and talked easily and honestly about her mother and her late father and her family. She told me that her sister believed that if Hannah was not being held against her will, there was something wrong with her mentally. Her family has by now rationalized the whole process, she confided. They say that Hannah is "away" and mentally confused.)

"Sister Mary Ann, what about boys?" I asked. "You are a handsome young woman and I'm certain you must have had a flock of boys running after you while you were at college."

"Yes, Mr. Golden, I went out with boys and I liked one very much. While he had not proposed, we had an understanding we might eventually marry. But this was when I did not yet know what my destiny would be."

"Was it easy to surrender the joys of love, family, children?"

Sister Mary Ann responded to this presumptuous question by looking straight at me and then laughing. She was completely relaxed, and I couldn't help but admire her as she expanded on the answer to this question.

"Mr. Golden, I have fallen in love with my Lord, and have given myself to Him completely." To become a nun, she told me, she takes vows of poverty, chastity, and obedience. During the six years prior to her final vows, she receives instruction under her superiors, in the meanings and obligations of the vows and rules of the order. She is aware of the joys and ecstasies of married love and because she understands these pleasures and can turn her back upon them she intensifies her devotion. "We are not taught that these joys we are giving up are bad, we are taught that they are good, so that we are fully aware of what we are giving up." She continued, "Everything a nun does, Mr. Golden, is a joy from the moment she rises until the moment she falls asleep. She is a woman in love with her heavenly Spouse, and any sacrifice seems small in contrast to the immensity of its Object."

She went on to say, "I know of the joys of life shared by a man and a woman, but I feel mine is a greater joy. You must remember that now I wear a wedding dress"—she gestured toward her nun's habit—"and how many women wear their wedding dress all their lives? And I have a wedding ring"—here she showed me her silver wedding ring—"You see, I am espoused to Him whom the angels adore." When she dies, she explained, she will be buried in her "wedding dress" and in her hand will be placed the scroll of the vows she signed.

Sister Mary Ann reads the great classics. She is thoroughly conversant with recent developments in science, politics, and history. Her first assignment as a nun will be as a teacher of mathematics and biology. She told me she will probably teach in one school for a few years and then the course of her entire future is in the hands of the Church, which is what she wants and what she has vowed to obey. She can never call any material possessions her own. If her glasses break, she will report to the Mother Superior and say: "I need a new pair of glasses, Mother." From now on she will obey her Mother Superior in all matters.

She rises at five every morning and with the other sisters of the convent attends Mass and says her morning prayers. "Mr. Golden," she informed me, "you'd be surprised at what we say at five-thirty in the morning—the Psalms of King David."

I asked this young nun about anti-Semitism. "Did you encounter any of it among the Catholics in the convent in these years of studying?"

"Mr. Golden," she said, "I never heard any. I taught the sisters the Hebrew song 'Zum Galli Galli' and we sing it often. Most of the nuns are deeply interested in Judaism so I'm considered a sort of special person. They want to know all about the Jewish religion, and I'm qualified to tell them because I know the religion very well. When I told them that it was because of the Passover Feast that matzoh became part of the Eucharist they were intrigued and respectful. My sisters in religion are particularly interested in the holiday Simchath Torah because I have told them of the great happiness it brought me when I was a little girl . . . I find my Jewish background more dear to me in its fulfillment than I could ever have comprehended before. The beloved teachings, customs, and ceremonies

of Judaism have become more dear and meaningful to me as a
Catholic. I have found my Jewish heritage more alive and prac-
cal in the fulfillment of all its yearnings."

Sister Mary Ann later introduced me to the other nuns and
priests who had attended the ceremony and she kept referring
to me as the Jewish editor, the Jewish writer. I wondered about
this on the way home. Why was this young nun so glad to see
me, a perfect stranger? Why was she willing to tell me all her
secrets and many intimate details, and why did she describe to
me her pride when she was finally professed? Then it dawned
upon me. Of course! I was her father—a proxy father. My having
come made her feel not quite so neglected. She felt a certain
security in the fact that a Jew had come to see her take her vows,
and to wish her well. For, indeed, I wish Sister Mary Ann well.
I gave her one of my books, and wrote in it, "To Hannah—Sister
Mary Ann with esteem and good wishes." She said, "I am going
to read this book and then I will send it to my mother, because
I want her to see the inscription in it from a famous Jew to a
daughter she thinks lost forever."

When the private interview was over, Sister Michael, several
other nuns, and a priest joined us in a drink of Coca-Cola. Sister
Mary Ann raised her paper cup and said, "Let us say L'chaim."

9

HATCH, MATCH, AND DESPATCH

The Germans and the Jews—1962

On the Lower East Side of New York, where I grew up, the old men in the synagogue always complained about children underfoot. The little boys stepped on everyone's toes as they squeezed back and forth through the pews, they disturbed prayers as they ran up and down the aisles, and the shoulders of the elders hunched as the children slammed the doors.

The synagogues of Germany today are strangely quiet. The Jews of Germany now are mostly old people, a small, spiritless community, a dwindling remnant of the six hundred thousand who once were a vital force in the nation. They are reviled by a few, fiercely protected by some, ignored by most. Dozens of young students all across West Germany told me they had never even met a Jew.

If they are ever going to meet one, they may have to move fast. Before too many years pass, the newspapers may run a picture under the headline, "The Last Jew in Germany."

While there are seventy million Germans—former Nazis, anti-Nazis, and many in-betweens—there are fewer than thirty thousand Jews alive in Germany, and as they all are in one way or another victims of the Nazi massacres, it should be easier to formulate their point of view than that of the seventy million Germans.

But it only seems that way. You need be only a few days in Germany to find that the Jews there are not very articulate. The Jews in Germany today are a pathetic remnant of a once most articulate community of more than six hundred thousand that gave the world an astounding number of gifted writers, scholars, artists, actors, and patriots. Today it is a silent community. It has a few spokesmen, functionaries who are called upon to speak for their fellow Jews—they speak before American TV reporters—

but are they representative of contemporary German Jewry? To put a question mark here is not to question their sincerity or ability. But what of the others? They do not care to talk to strangers. It is not for lack of trust, it is not out of fear or intimidation—it is simply a great tiredness, a complete resignation. They want to live and to die in peace. Period. They have experienced more bitterly than any other people the cruelty of history. And so they want no further role. They want to live out their days, and they feel that these are numbered.

I was told that I was more fortunate than most American reporters in that many Jews did talk to me in their community centers, in the homes for the aged, in the hospitals, and in the privacy of their homes. I made three trips between 1959 and 1962.

Landesrabbiner (District Rabbi) Hans Isaac Gruenewald of Hamburg said:

"The Jewish community in Germany is not a living community, but a dying community. There is no younger generation. There is no one to take over. The handful of young people who are here don't want to stay. Years ago in Frankfurt or anywhere else in Germany if you asked young people where they wanted to study, they would say Frankfurt or Heidelberg or Berlin. Today they say London or Israel or New York. None of them wants to stay here.

"Of the approximate one thousand, four hundred Jews in the Hamburg congregation, some eight hundred or nine hundred make every effort not to be recognized as Jews. There is no pulsating Jewish life. A religious class should begin for children at the age of six, but there are no six-year-olds in my congregation so I couldn't start the class.

"In all West Germany there are only seven rabbis, and I am the only rabbi in all of northern Germany. There is no rabbi in Berlin or Bremen or Munich or Karlsruhe."

Rabbi Gruenewald was born in Frankfurt am Main in 1914, and went to study in Jerusalem in 1936. "I am an Israeli," says the Rabbi, and in that declaration we have the story. I thought back to my boyhood when "I am a German Jew" was spoken with such pride and conferred such great status upon an individual throughout the Jewish world. "I am an Israeli," says Rabbi Gruenewald, "and I am here because I am needed."

To be a Jew in Germany is to live in a curious and unreal world.

"When my wife and I come home from the movies and pass a German who looks thirty-eight years old or over," an elderly Jew told me, "either she whispers to me or I whisper to her, 'I wonder what he was doing in Hitler's time?'"

The question is asked in genuine curiosity, without real bitterness. There is even a desire to forget to ask it, but the time never comes when this is possible. The Jews in Germany are an estranged and isolated people.

I visited the jewelry store of a middle-aged Jewish couple in Berlin. When they learned what I wanted to talk about, both of them came from behind the counter and asked me to go outside. They nodded toward an elderly German hunched over a bench repairing watches and said, "We do not want to talk in front of him."

Later I invited the German watchmaker to lunch. "My employers and I say good morning and good night," he told me, "and that is all, because I know what is in their minds. How can I tell them that I did not know the Jews were being killed? It is true, but it sounds hollow, and so we work in silence."

The Jews are emotionally involved at many levels and at the extremes. There is a very small minority who, like Dr. Siegmund Weltlinger (member of the Berlin City Parliament), sincerely believes that the Nazi regime was a bad dream, and did not express the feelings of the true German. These are the old German Jews who still cling to the memories of the Kaiser, and "the good old days."

At the other extreme is another small minority which lives in constant fear, a sort of masochism, which causes them to think of every German they meet on the street in terms of "How many Jews did he kill?"

Then we have the intellectuals, like Jeannette Wolff (who was a member of the German Parliament from Berlin), who genuinely feel that the Jews can play an important part in the building of a democratic Germany, and point out that there are many true democrats in both major parties of West Germany who need help.

And then we have the main body of Jews who just go about their business, without too much thought about anything, waiting for two things: the pension check and the letter from their children in Israel, or the United States, or Canada, or South America.

And there is a paradox here. The few who live in fear are the first to tell you that they are perfectly safe in Germany today. And there is more to it than mere safety. There is favored treatment, on direct instructions of the Government. "Give returning Jews preference in the matter of housing," Dr. Adenauer told the officials of the several Länder (states) in 1953. When a Jew applies for a franchise or a license of some kind, all the red tape so dear to the heart of the German civil servant is automatically eliminated. The country's two major parties actually compete to see which is the more anti-anti-Semitic. A Jewish young man in Hamburg said that when he was called up for the Army draft, he merely wrote a letter to the authorities indicating his religion and that he did not care to serve. He heard nothing further.

The trouble with all of this is that the Jews don't want to be coddled. They want to be treated like everybody else, but that may never again be possible in Germany. The scars are too deep, and the Jews in Germany are acutely aware that they live under a sternly enforced tolerance. They wonder what would happen if the enforcement ever lapsed. They are afraid, and so they do what Jews have always done when they are afraid. They look for strength among the only people they feel they can really trust: themselves. They don't live in ghettos, but they depend entirely on the organized Jewish structure, and they stick to the big cities almost exclusively. To be sure, they might conceivably establish social contacts outside their own groups, but there is always the possibility of an incident, an insult, and they refuse to take the risk.

Even among those who were very close friends before the Hitler era there has been no attempt to renew old friendships. The Jew hesitates to call his Gentile friend because he has no way of knowing how many sons were lost to that family. And the Gentile does not call his old Jewish friend because he does not know how many of the Jew's family died in the concentration camps. A Jewish doctor in Munich said, "As a professional I am given every courtesy. I attend medical institutes and meetings and the medical society, but visit in the homes of Germans, no. I cannot feel at home. The memories are too sharp."

"Why do you stay in Germany?"

"I am old, over sixty. I have family in the United States. They urged me to come. Here I have a large busy practice. In your country I don't even know if I could get a license. Some day I'll go, perhaps." His voice lacked conviction.

The Jews have learned that incidents can occur and have occurred in the small towns which lack the organized security of the large cities. In the small town the Jew is conspicuous and the German is self-conscious. A Jewish couple now living in Frankfurt told me that they had to run away from Windsheim, the small town where their families had lived for several generations. The husband said, "It may have been my imagination, but even the postman seemed annoyed with us when he delivered the mail. It was all quite impossible." And then the wife said something which I had heard over and over again from Jews in Germany: "Thank God we have no young children."

In each of the three homes for the Jewish aged I visited, the elderly ladies scurried around their rooms to show me pictures of "my married daughter in San Francisco," or "my son who is a professor in Canada." No Jew thinks of Germany as a homeland now. Even Jewish officials of the organized community have caught themselves referring to *your* finance minister, and *your* Parliament in public speeches.

I visited a Jewish engineer who had returned from Israel in 1956. When I asked him about his future, he replied by leading me to the window and pointing to the flag atop the Amerika Haus, where the United States Information Service has its offices. He said, "The day the Americans leave Germany, I will leave with them."

Even in the large cities with the organized Jewish community the Jew remains ever on the alert. He constantly fears that something he does or says may fit into the Jewish stereotype created by his enemies. One Jew who has done pretty well in the job-printing business apologized to me for the condition of his automobile. "My wife says I must not buy a Mercedes, even though we can afford it and need it. She's worried about what the neighbors will say." The neighbors, of course, may say nothing. They may even be pleased. But for this Jew, the fear of their displeasure is very real. This caution lends itself to a bit of grim humor. Where once the German retired to his castle to inveigh against "Jewish wealth," he must now face up to his wealth alone. The money is rolling, but there are no Jews to blame.

The entire intellectual and social life of the Jews in Germany today revolves around the community center or synagogue, and in visiting one another. When they get together they compare their memories of the past and they exchange the latest wry humor. The jokes, more bitter than funny, are almost entirely at the expense of the Germans. One story that had wide circulation was that General Eisenhower had sent false communiqués back to America on D-Day in 1944, for actually not a single German was defending Normandy. Instead, they were all on the Russian front "fighting communism." And if you don't believe it, ask the German veterans themselves. The latest Jewish joke tells of two Germans coming out of the documentary movie, *Mein Kampf*, and one saying to the other, "I liked the book better."

Most Jewish leaders agree that German democracy is still on probation. The critical test, they feel, might very well lie in the final attitude of the German people toward the restitution payments the government is now making to the Jews. Germany has paid the State of Israel over two billion marks and the Germans generally seem to accept this as fitting punishment for the crimes of the Nazi regime. But there has been some criticism of the restitution to individuals. "If the Germans lose their prosperity," one Jewish leader said, "we may catch hell again. We must wait and see what happens."

There seems to have been a time when this cynicism was not shared by certain Germans. Some people sincerely felt that the wall between Jews and Gentile could be worn down. Then came the anti-Semitic outbreaks of December 1959 and January 1960, and responsible Germans and Jews realized that their hopes for a

reconciliation had received a serious setback. The swastika paintings on synagogues that started in Cologne on Christmas Eve of
1959 could not be brushed aside as the work of cranks or political
fanatics. The large majority of Jews and most of the non-Jewish
professors and officials I interviewed were convinced, many of
them reluctantly, that these acts of vandalism were organized by
neither Communist nor anti-Adenauer groups. They were spontaneous outbreaks of the old anti-Semitism that surrounds the
Jews in Germany all the time and that the Jews have come to
think of as a fact of life.

One of the most interesting aspects of those outbreaks was that
the Jews were not terribly shocked. Measured against the tragic
events of the past, the swastika paintings seemed a trivial matter.
The Jews were amused by the fact that the German government
and people are rapidly acquiring what had always been considered a Jewish characteristic. The Jews, in governing their conduct
as individuals and as a community, have always asked, "What
will the Gentiles say?" Now the Germans are wondering uneasily,
"What will the world say?"

It was the timing of the outbreaks which disturbed the Jews
more than anything else. They came at the height of a prosperity
so great that Germany was actually importing workers from Italy
and Greece to fill some of the five hundred thousand jobs which
were going begging.

One result was to strengthen the organized Jewish community.
The Jewish leaders had estimated that up to then at least four
thousand Jews in the Federal Republic had not committed themselves as community members. In the three months after the
swastika incidents nearly three hundred came forward officially to
establish their identity as Jews.

There is a nasty undercurrent of anti-Semitism in Germany
today that I did not detect in 1959 and 1960. Not only are the
Russians exerting ever more serious pressure, which does the
German morale no good, for this time the German businessman
is deserting Berlin, but the world does not trust Germany yet. A
reliable journalist on one of the largest newspapers told me the
editors are not printing the hundreds of letters with strong anti-
Semitic overtones sent to the "Open Forum." Philosophers have

claimed you hate those whom you have wronged and the word "Jew" to the German is a counter of the terrible German guilt.

"The last Jew" is not merely a figure of speech. There are not many young Jews. The Jewish population of West Germany at the end of 1960 showed that 21,755 were registered members of the Jewish communities. About four thousand other Jews have not registered for one reason or another. Some of the unregistered are desirous of losing themselves, if possible, within the German society. Others, particularly those who have returned from Israel, do not register because, "I am staying here only temporarily."

The birth rate is practically zero. Between 1955 and 1960, three hundred and one children were born. During this period, one thousand, six hundred and two Jews died. The average age is approximately forty-nine for males and forty-six for females.

The Federal Republic's law of restitution and indemnification are as equitable as human law can be. Considerable sums have been paid by the German Land (state) governments to trust funds of German Jewish Communities. Such trust funds exist now in West Germany and Northwest Germany. Payments cover losses by the Jewish community for the destruction of synagogues and other communal properties.

The process of payments to individuals has been slow because of the need to study each of the claims involving losses which are not as easily identifiable as property. For example, one of the claims sets forth, "I was studying for medicine (and here the man attached his medical school records) and my studies were interrupted . . ." This claimant said that his treatment had been very fair and this is the consensus among the Jews in Germany today.

Upon completion of the restitution program the Federal Republic (including both Federal Government and Länder) will have undertaken financial obligations of approximately twenty-five billion marks, according to a recent analysis by the Ministry of Finance.

Indicative of the determination of the West German authorities (no restitution payments are being made by the Soviet-occupied zone of Germany) to press on with the task is that deadlines have been set by law. For example, applications under the Federal Restitution Law must be settled by the end of 1962.

Meanwhile, some ten thousand Jews in Germany are in total retirement, spinning out their lives on pensions provided by the Bonn Government—either as payment for identified property which was confiscated, or as compensation for persecution they experienced because they were Jews.

The Jewish community in Germany is controlled by a Central Jewish Council with headquarters in Düsseldorf and presided over by a secretary general, Dr. Hendrik George van Dam.

A day with Dr. van Dam recalls the memory of the "Fancy Jews," as we Eastern European immigrants in New York used to refer to the German Jews who worshipped in the big temple on Fifth Avenue. You do not slap Dr. van Dam on the back nor banter with him, and you write him a letter before you call him on the telephone. Dr. van Dam, who formed the Central Council ten years ago, knows how to use both status and power, and he has accomplished several near-miracles in the matters of compensation for the Jews. But it is quite apparent that he is not above nourishing the fiction of "Jewish power," to the extent that many German officials, certainly those below the cabinet level, actually fear him.

At the other end of Germany lives the second most influential Jew, Heinz Galinski, director of the Jews in West Berlin. A day with Heinz Galinski is like a day back home with the program chairman for the "Man of the Year" dinner in Great Neck, Long Island. And Galinski's Jewish Community Center in West Berlin duplicates the Jewish Community Center in Hartford, Dallas, or San Diego. A bouncy little bureaucrat, Galinski has an American approach in all his activities, even to the photographs on the wall of his office, one of him with Dr. Konrad Adenauer, another with Mayor Willy Brandt. He is a kind of benevolent ward heeler who wins his annual election in the best tradition of punishing enemies and rewarding friends. Galinski expresses himself forcefully on all problems: "I never thought that as a Jew I'd worry about the Germans and their politics," he says with aggressive anxiety, "but if we lost West Berlin, the Communists would get all of Europe."

The third important leader of the Jewish community in Germany is Dr. Karl Marx, the editor of the *Allgemeine Wochen-zeitung der Juden in Deutschland,* the mouthpiece of German Jewry. It is not an official paper of the Jewish Council, but it is a highly respected newspaper and read by most of the influential people.

Dr. Marx does not think it beyond the bounds of possibility that a sudden change in the world political situation might send Jews streaming into Germany.

His view, like that of Jeannette Wolff, is that it is important for a Jewish community to exist in Germany, and that it be as strong and influential as possible, because:

(1) Allowing the Jewish community of Germany to perish would give the final victory to Hitler and his *Judenraus* campaign.

(2) Jews in Germany can help spot anti-Semitic and anti-democratic trends. Given the proper leadership, as well as liaison with Jewish organizations in other parts of the world, they can help stimulate vigorous counteractive measures.

It is true, of course, that both Van Dam and Galinski particularly are proud of their individual status as shtadtlan, a Jew-ish title in Central Europe going back to the sixteenth century. The shtadtlan was appointed the "official" representative of the Jewish community in its relations with the rest of society and in its individual or communal problems with the government. On the Lower East Side of New York we called him "the Jewish Ambassador to the Gentiles." The pride of Van Dam and Ga-linski in this title, however, should not obscure the truth: after fifteen hundred years in Germany, the Jews must have the shtadtlan again. For a long time to come, communication be-tween Jew and German must be handled by "ambassadors."

Below the surface of official government policy toward the Jews there are several interesting strata of German attitudes. The truth that impresses itself immediately is that those who assume the greatest burden of guilt for the crimes of the Nazis are the innocent—those Germans who themselves suffered indignities, exile, or imprisonment. Professor Carlo Schmid, vice president of the West German Parliament and Germany's leading philo-Semite, who himself experienced hardships under the Nazis, told me: "The swastika paintings had their purpose. It is good for these sleeping hounds of hell to rouse themselves every once in a while to remind us Germans how close we are to damnation." Again, addressing a Jewish audience, Erich Lueth, director of the City Press Office in Hamburg, said, "We Germans must do everything possible to help build up a permanent Jewish community, because we must have someone to repent to."

In Darmstadt, there is an order of nuns who take vows to spend their lives in atonement specifically for the sins against the Jews. The Ecumenical Marian Sisterhood in Darmstadt (Protestant-Evangelical) began its common life in 1947 with nine sisters. At present there are about sixty sisters. Mother Basilea Schlink, one of the founders of the congregation, which includes publishing, catechetical, and retreat work among its activities, has become famous well beyond the borders of Germany.

A Jew who visits Germany can hardly be expected to have complete objectivity. But if the Jew is also a reporter, he must catch a spirit of optimism, not only for these church activities, but also for the young Germans in the schools and colleges. I could not help but appreciate their sincerity and authentic urge for democracy. After I discussed the massacre of six million Jews by the Nazis with groups of boys and girls at the Free University at Berlin, I listened to them say, "But we have done nothing." They are right, of course.

The students refer to the whole Nazi period of war, gas chambers, and slave labor as "the bad times." I do not think this comes from a desire to gloss over the Nazi crimes. I think these students fear that their teachers and perhaps their parents were involved. Some students told me that between them and their parents there exists a tacit agreement not to discuss the crimes of the Nazis. The elders do not like to admit their implication. Their children are afraid of what they might hear.

The teachers, most of whom are over forty, do not detail the Nazi crimes beyond a mere recital of a few major facts. They omit as many details of the horror as possible and German youth does not press for more.

It must be a sad thing to be a young German today and not dare to ask questions. It must be even sadder to be a German father or teacher and know that the terrible gulf is always there.

Given the tremendous problem of education that still remains in Germany, I think wholehearted support and encouragement and assistance should be given the numerous local government, church, civic, and other organizations and groups which have, on the whole, done a splendid job. Above all, the German press, radio, and television should be commended for their consistent, professional, expert, and comprehensive achievements. Not a day passes without some program or article devoted to the problem of the heritage of Hitler ideology. The Federal Republic, too, has on the whole done a magnificent job in this respect.

Although I have found that of the few Jews living in Germany today most tend to isolate themselves from their German neighbors, there has been a sincere effort on the part of some Germans to seek them out and to assist them in numerous ways and to make friends with them.

Yet it is a sad thing to be one of the remnant Jews in Germany today, and no one should hold back the story.

A Hamburg reporter told me, "There are more anti-Semites in Indianapolis than in Hamburg." He had proof, he said. He had been an exchange student and had lived with two different families in Indianapolis in 1958. Both families had told him that no matter how bad Hitler was, he did do some good in his measures against the Jews.

Similar stories have come my way from other Germans. For a long time I dismissed them as a rationalization for German guilt. But this journalist is a man of integrity and I have no reason to doubt his story about those people in Indianapolis.

Yes, indeed, I thought, there are anti-Semites in Indianapolis and in New Orleans and in New York City and in Charlotte. I get letters and phone calls from them. But there is a difference. Anti-Semitism in America has never been sanctioned by law or public opinion. Anti-Semitism has never been respectable.

In the English-speaking world, the anti-Semite must express his hate privately and often guardedly.

Throughout Europe and often in America, too, one hears the statement that the Germans killed millions of non-Jews, too. This strikes me as a cowardly rationalization. I do not mean that the

murder of millions can be reduced to the status of a rationalization, but the difference is this: the Nazis killed Jews indiscrimi-
nately, the others had a little choice. It may have amounted to
no choice but they were either belligerents or anti-Nazis or
Communists or democrats or opponents of the Nazi regime. The
Jews had no choice.

It is much too late for justice. But let the story be told.

Christianity

My FIRST impressions of Christianity came in the home,
of course. My parents brought with them the burden of the Middle Ages from the blood-soaked continent of Europe. They had
come from the villages of Eastern Europe where Christians were
feared with legitimate reason.

When occasionally a Jewish drunk was seen in our neighborhood, our parents would say, "He's behaving like a Gentile."

For in truth, our parents had often witnessed the Polish,
Romanian, Hungarian, and Russian peasants gather around a barrel of whisky on Saturday night, drink themselves into ob-
livion, "and beat their wives." Once in a while the rumor would
spread through the tenements that a fellow had struck his wife,
and on all sides we heard the inevitable, "Just like a Gentile."

Oddly enough, too, our parents had us convinced that the
Gentiles were noisy, boisterous, and loud—unlike the Jews. It is
indeed strange how often stereotypes are exactly reversed.

If we raised our voices, we were told, "Jewish boys don't shout."
And this admonition covered every activity in and out of the
home: "Jewish boys don't fight." "Jewish boys don't get dirty."
"Jewish boys study hard."

It wasn't until I was in school and was subjected to the influence of Gentile teachers and met Gentile social workers and
classmates that I began to question these generalizations. Then I
began to read and I found myself finally dismissing all prejudice
from my mind. I still had a vague idea that the Jews were *very*

special with God, but I discarded the notion that He was dis-
interested in or hostile to the Gentiles.

However Christianity itself, as a philosophy, did not impress
me until I began to watch the Negroes of the South fight for
their right to enter the open society as first-class citizens. When
Martin Luther King's house was bombed, he told his congregation to pray for the fellows who did it. This phase of the
Southern story (1954–1964) will yet prove to be the most remarkable of all. Twelve million Negroes, many of them semiliterate,
have not made a single mistake, despite the many provocations.

I've seen them sitting for hours with their children with an
application to the school board. And the school board plays
games with them to make it as tough as possible—"Come back
Tuesday."

And through all of this the Negro has maintained his balance
and, amazingly, his sense of humor, too. And when I studied this
phenomenon, I came to the conclusion that they are using a
mighty weapon—their Christian faith.

The Southern white imposed many influences upon the Negro.
But the one thing he most impressed upon him was Christianity.
The Negro is using it for all it is worth. And he is forcing the
Southern white into a position where he must make a choice.
Either he begins to practice Christianity—or gives it up.

I never miss an auf probe

"AUF PROBE," literally, "on probation," refers specifically
to the trial sermon and congregational interview of a new candidate for the pulpit. "Let's go and look over the new rabbi."

If I hear of an auf probe anywhere within a radius of fifty
miles, I am off like a fireman. There is no event in our culture
which is so rich in human interest.

In the old days the rabbi had a cinch. If he could keep in the
good graces of the president of the congregation, he was in like
Flynn. For all I know this may still be true in some of the congregations of the metropolitan centers. But down South it is an

entirely different matter. In fact there was never a time when *one man* made the decisions in the congregations of Dixie, and the reason was economics rather than democracy. In the large cities you have many strata of society within a single organization. There are manufacturers, bankers, white-collar workers, workmen, and the few men at the top quite naturally step into their proper positions of leadership. But in the South we represent, in the main, a single proprietary class. What we really have here are congregations composed almost exclusively of Medicine Men and no Indians—with practically every member qualified to sit on the dais.

Just imagine what that means for a rabbi.

The interesting fact about all of this is that it parallels that religio-social life of the Gentile community, particularly the Baptists and Methodists, who enjoy autonomy in their individual churches. In fact, one of the outstanding Baptist clergymen told me that the best way to retain a pulpit is to make a simple statement at the first interview. "Gentlemen of the board, I am the 'transient' here and you are the permanents; tell me how you want it done, and I will do it."

Another parallel is concerned with the actual mechanics of asking a clergyman to resign his pulpit, when the "leaders" feel that he has not met their requirements. The leaders know they must act quickly—within a year or, at most, two years. Once the rabbi or Protestant minister occupies the pulpit for three or four years, the leaders have lost their initiative. They can only keep praying that the man gets a call from another congregation. The reason for this is that the majority of the congregation is not at all close to the internal management of the organization. Since they do not attend services regularly the rabbi or Protestant minister is that fine fellow who sends them an interesting bulletin every week, and they are all for him. Should the leaders call a congregational meeting for the purpose of replacing the clergyman, the majority will nearly always uphold him. Another factor of course is the natural tendency to vote "against the machine," irrespective of the issues involved. The leaders understand this. If they do not like a rabbi, they know they must act quickly.

The auf probe session therefore is full of tension and drama.

The leaders are under great pressure, especially if they have already decided to take the new fellow. In such cases they must be very careful in the conduct of the meeting. Being a leader is not all beer and skittles.

The new rabbi is under pressure, too. What to give them? He wonders why they let the other fellow go. Of course he could use the sermon he wrote for his graduation from the seminary. But that doesn't go any more. He tries to feel his way to see if he can find a clue. What to emphasize? Community chest activities? Rotary work? Adult education? Interfaith? Sunday school? Mr. and Mrs. Club? The auf probe rabbi usually takes the intelligent course and comes through with a sermon on the Biblical portion of the week. There is one thing however which he does know: in most of the Protestant churches and Jewish temples of the South today, the leaders are emphasizing one thing very strongly: "Stick to religion—*only*."

After the trial sermon there may be some questions from the floor, and this part of the auf probe session reflects, I think, our most interesting characteristic—ambivalence. It is natural that the folks would like to have a handsome rabbi. On this basis we are no different than all the other peoples of the world. The shaman of the primitive peoples was always the tallest member of the tribe. Eventually when we discovered the uses of intellect we learned how to make up for lack of physical beauty by dressing him in robes, white wigs, purple togas, ermine capes, and miters. Most of the folks in the South, reflecting the attitudes of the dominant society, would like to have a rabbi (you should pardon me) who does not look "too Jewish" (as it has been so often said), yet there is much more to it than that. There is also a terrible longing for the religious and communal culture of their parents and an inherent devotion to the "glories of the past." They want a tall, blue-eyed rabbi, but they also want "a Jewish word," which is a Yiddish colloquialism for "Jewishness" in its deepest sense. What they would really like to have, of course, is Robert Montgomery with "a Jewish word."

Part of this ambivalence is in the theology itself. The members of the Reform congregation, never quite sure that they have done the right thing, want a rabbi with just a smattering of the Orthodox values. The Conservatives, on the other hand, want a rabbi with at least a tinge of the reformer. This often leads to the ambiguity we know so well in our American political structure: Tories who are Democrats and radicals who are Republicans.

And all during the auf probe the ladies are just dying to find out something about the rabbi's wife. They love to have a rabbi's wife of whom they can say, "How sweet," "How self-sacrificing," "She's such a good worker." This means, of course, that the rabbi has a homely wife, which is the ideal situation. A handsome clergyman with a homely wife can practically write his own ticket. But in the early moments of the auf probe the ladies do not even know whether the rabbi is married, and so the smartest of them starts the ball rolling. "Rabbah, do you-all think your wife will like it down heah?" What a brain!

And there are always the people who had been particularly fond of the "resigned" rabbi. In an attempt to demonstrate this loyalty they will make it as hard as they can for the new fellow. On the other hand, the leaders will find it necessary to go all out in their praise. Between these two extremes the new clergyman dares not hope for a smooth inauguration of his ministry.

But after a while the congregation scatters again: the majority reads the weekly bulletin and slowly but surely transfers all past loyalties to the new man; but the leaders take up their vigil: "For the first year we want written committee reports, and please fill in the space under 'co-operation.'" Eventually the new rabbi may even ask for a raise and the leaders sitting around the country club will shake their heads in disbelief: "What does he need an extra five hundred dollars for?" The wives will be sitting at the edge of the swimming pool and will join in: "They have such a cute little house—so neat. It's such a charming little place especially since we had those leaks fixed."

And so we'll continue along our interesting path, a dynamic people with a wonderful ambivalence. But if a rabbi in the North is looking for peace and quiet, let him not look toward the Mason-Dixon line.

Door-to-door evangelists

LORD BEAVERBROOK, the British press magnate, wrote an open letter to his own newspaper, the *Sunday Express*. Lord Beaverbrook wrote: "Paragraphs and interviews denouncing Mormon missionaries should not be given publicity in the *Sunday Express*."

Lord Beaverbrook had been angered by stories in the newspaper which deplored the tactics of door-to-door canvassers for the two religious faiths, the Jehovah's Witnesses and the Church of Jesus Christ of Latter-day Saints (Mormons).

Lord Beaverbrook is correct.

I listen to all the canvassers who come to proselytize, and if I have the time I spend as much as an hour with them, respectfully following their message.

Some years ago when I wrote some kind words about the fellows of the Hebrew Christian Alliance—the converted Jews who work for various Christian missions—many of my colleagues became angry at me. "How dare you treat converts with such kindness?" they demanded. There's no reason why I shouldn't treat converts from Judaism as respectfully as I treat the people from the Jehovah's Witnesses and all the other evangelizing Christian sects.

The canvassers for converts to their particular sect are really strengthening their own religious faith, and if I can help the fellow along with a bit of kindness, I've made him happy and he'll talk about it for a couple of weeks.

When they leave I always make kiddush with a bourbon and water.

Once again—the butchers

HOUSEWIVES have waged a longer war with the butcher than man has waged with his several neighbors over the course of history. A soldier's war has an end but the war against the butcher, once assumed, goes on forever.

Thus it was no surprise when the Markets Commissioner of New York City, Albert Pacetta, asked for legislation from the City Council, charging the butchers were injecting water into the corned beef. This upped the weight of the meat by a third, said the Commissioner, all of which is boiled away in the home and the delicatessen.

Ten years ago, of course, there was a similar scandal and ten years from now there will be another. Butchers, it seems, are always one step ahead. They are all born with three thumbs.

My mother on the Lower East Side of New York City would sooner trust an Irish cop than she would a butcher. But this had nothing to do with watering the meat or with the weighing-in process. My mother and many of her colleagues were afraid the butcher was not too careful about observing all the laws of kosher meat and thus the butchers would have us all assimilated in no time.

When the prepackaged meat appeared in the refrigerated trays of the supermarkets, the women were sure they'd know exactly what they were getting. But they have since found there is a great difference between the lean meat they can see through the cellophane and the fat meat which is hidden by the cardboard.

Lest I call a murrain upon myself from the butchers' associations, let me caution that suspecting the butcher is endemic to Western civilization (not unlike the landlords). But despite this age-old suspicion of the butcher, the kids get bigger every generation and their bones get stronger and their passions course as hotly, and it can't all be due to fluoridation.

I miss the old shul

THE Orthodox shul gave you *participation*. You had an opportunity to beat the champ, the way they do in golf and bowling. A considerable handicap is assessed against the champ when hundreds of people are out trying to beat him. For centuries every Orthodox Jew indulged in this practice. If the *champ* was a great cantor, each Jew would try to sing ahead of him, anticipating every tonal phrase, even to the cantorial falsetto. Or they sang behind him like an echo, or a tone above or below, in an attempt to overwhelm him. This was the real *participation* which is absent in most of our temples today. Only one thing remains—they are still trying to second-guess the rabbi. For the rest you may just as well be attending the eleven o'clock Mass at St. Malachy's.

Then, what about making kiddush, that greatest of all expressions of good will and fellowship? In the Orthodox shul after services on the Sabbath, the old men would make kiddush with a bit of brandy or like my father with "Parrk und Tilfurrds rrye."

It was either the brandy or the "Parrk und Tilfurrds rrye" out of a small shot glass, followed by a nice piece of honey cake, and then the gleam of good fellowship and wisdom in the eyes of each of the men as they began their long discussions of The Law. Today in the temples they drink either sherry in fancy wineglasses or champagne in long-stemmed glasses by Steuben.

The serene Irish

To THE Irish, "clan na Gael" means everything, and, like the Jews, their family ties are very strong. They keep in touch with fourth and fifth cousins as well as old neighbors. The elderly

Irishwomen are the only ones I ever knew who kept returning to their old neighborhoods to shop after they had moved away. They rarely gave up on this, continuing to trade with the same tradesmen, including the family undertaker, until he finally became his own last customer.

The problem of logistics should have had them whipped, but the Irish pushed the two ends of our railroads together in days when mules had to haul drinking water over the desert.

California, of course, has thousands of their descendants. The serious Governor Pat Brown is one of them—but not a true representative, I am afraid, since he seems to lack that Irish magic of cajolery which Al Smith, Jim Farley, Charley Murphy (and the Kennedy brothers) were blessed with in such abundance. But the Irish are serene.

I have never seen any statistics on it, but I would be willing to wager that the psychiatrists would starve to death if they depended solely on Irishmen. From my own observation, I have never known one with a complex, although many of them do have a secret. The secret is that, somewhere, each one of them with money is helping to educate a poor boy for the priesthood.

Rabbis, incoming and outgoing

THE honeymoon between the new clergyman and the congregation lasts about six months. During this period all is sweetness and light. The folks are trying to make up their minds about him, and he is trying to see which way the wind blows. You cannot go strictly according to the names of the men on the committee who sponsored the call to the new man. There are many sleepers; an unfamiliar name may very well belong to a top man in the power structure. The utmost discretion is desirable at this stage of the relationship.

A good plan would be for the congregation to hire an assistant along with the new clergyman. The "antis" then could direct all their criticisms at the assistant and give the new clergyman a free hand. The high school principals are on to this idea. The assistant is always put in charge of discipline.

The problem comes about because, unlike the Protestant fellowships, we Jews seldom provide a cooling-off period.

When a Protestant clergyman answers a call to another pulpit, he takes his leave, and then it is often as much as three months later before we see the announcement of the new man who has come to fill the pulpit.

In the temples, the contract of the outgoing rabbi usually terminates at the end of the summer, with the High Holy Days practically around the corner. This calls for haste in the calling of a new rabbi, and it also leads to a complication which really should be avoided. This complication involves the incoming rabbi's arriving to get acquainted with the congregation while the outgoing man is still in town. This is very bad for both rabbis. And what are the balabatim (trustees) doing? It shouldn't happen! But it does. While two rabbis are within a few blocks of each other, the balabatim are as nervous as a dozen cats on a hot tin roof. The main thing, of course, is to keep them apart. After all, there is usually one faction (the majority of the moment) that has crossed swords with the outgoing man, and they do not want to expose the new man to an unnecessary "briefing." Who knows what he'll tell him? On the other hand, the new man is wise if he stays away on his own. Actually, if he's a wise man he will know that the group that wants a new rabbi now are the same fellows who will want a new rabbi later.

But worst of all is when the incoming rebbitzen (rabbi's wife) comes to inspect the dwelling while the outgoing rebbitzen is still ensconced. Hoo-ha. This is something; and the sisterhood prevents a face-to-face meeting between the two even if the girls have to make a wall of living flesh across the highway.

But the whole thing is unnecessary. The two rabbis are not only colleagues, but often they have been classmates, too, and now a relationship becomes strained for life, through no fault of theirs. It could be avoided if all contracts were terminated on May 1 instead of September 1. Everybody could take his time. The sisterhood could arrange another book review instead of worrying about the rebbitzens, and the balabatim, who think they are "half" rabbis anyway, could take turns conducting the services until, in good time, the new rabbi arrives, "unspotted from the world," as our Methodist friends would say.

But I'm afraid the temples will not heed my simple plans to avert all the trouble. So I would like now to apply for one of the most desirable jobs in the world.

It would be nice if the Rabbinical Council of America and the Union of American Hebrew Congregations got together and offered me the position of traffic manager, in charge of moving rabbis.

I would take the job without salary and pay my own expenses, too. I figure it is approximately a $50,000-a-year industry and I am sure that the Associated Transport Company would gladly give me a commission of $5,000 a year if I could swing them the business. The average move costs between one hundred and fifty dollars and four hundred and fifty dollars per rabbi, with some costs going much higher. The rabbi goes from Maine to Texas, then to Montana, and two years later he's in Georgia. All of this costs money. The congregations pay the expenses. All in all, this would be a dandy job and would not require too much time either: Traffic Manager for Moving Rabbis. I can handle it, too.

Of course, being a layman, I cannot aspire to an even more attractive position.

The best job in the world is the Holiday Rabbi. Ah, how wonderful! There are dozens of such jobs open each year. Small congregations without a full-time rabbi usually call on one of the seminaries to send them a rabbi for the High Holy Days. Other congregations may engage a Holiday Rabbi because they are "between rabbis," so to speak. Their rabbi may have resigned in May or June, and they thought they had plenty of time to engage a new rabbi. Let's take it easy, and get what we want this time; but they dillydallied, interviewed about four prospects, held receptions for the wives of three of the prospects, and first thing you know the holidays crept right up on them and there they were. So they send for the Holiday Rabbi, which is a tremendous pleasure all around. No trial sermons, no teas to look over the rebbitzen, no interviews.

The Holiday Rabbi, like Lochinvar, sweeps out of the West.

His coming, his stay, and his going are one complete dream of peace. The committee meets the Holiday Rabbi at the station, places an automobile at his disposal. Nothing is too good for him. He's invited all over the place. The worry that he may favor someone above someone else is completely absent since he'll be gone soon. And for the Holiday Rabbi himself—it's wonderful. He can say what he thinks. He's not afraid that he may be saying something that may offend one faction or one trustee; he can shoot the works. And the congregation is as happy as happy can be. They sit back and enjoy every single word of every sermon and enthusiastically follow the entire service, because they can keep saying to themselves, "Ah, no contract."

I do not know of any job anywhere in this world that is as thoroughly pleasant as that of a Holiday Rabbi.

The synthetic Cohens

THERE is a reason why more Jews around the country are named Cohen than bear any other surname. The Immigration inspectors on Ellis Island made every Jew whose name they could not pronounce a Cohen.

From 1890 to 1920 hundreds of thousands of immigrants poured into America. Usually an immigration inspector was a young fellow testing out the new civil service idea and convinced that this was a good job while he was studying a trade at the evening vocational school.

Like most men, he developed a few tricks to help him over busy days. The immigrants he had to question came from Lithuania, Romania, Galicia, Poland, and the Ukraine, most of them armed with names of formidable syllables. So the tired inspector called them all Cohen.

Cohen is the oldest Jewish name in existence, and one of the earliest family names in Western history. It indicates descent from the priestly family (kohanim) which descends from Aaron, the brother of Moses and the first high priest.

In an Orthodox Jewish shul, a Cohen has the priestly prerogative, and on the important Jewish holidays he is the first man to whom the honors are extended during the reading of the Torah.

But some years back there were literally hundreds of "Cohens" who had come by their family tradition by the caprice of the immigration inspector. They were synthetic and plastic Cohens, and they saw an opportunity to achieve status without the required history and tradition. In an old Allen Street shul several of these newly made Cohens succeeded in elbowing their way into the reading of the Torah while the legitimate Cohens were completely neglected. Finally, an authentic Cohen sued to have this matter clearly established, and wise judges at the famous Jewish Arbitration Court on the East Side accorded him his religious rights and urged rabbis to exercise greater care in granting priestly honors.

Hatch, Match, and Despatch

"HATCH, Match and Despatch" is the title of a column in a London newspaper which lists births, marriages, and deaths. Aside from the charm of the rollicking rhyme, the title has some significance for us in America. It describes pretty accurately the duties we expect of clergymen in this second half of the twentieth century.

In all of the American religions there has been an accelerating secularization. Since Judaism and many of the Protestant sects are autonomous religious bodies, the secularization is much more apparent there. The burgeoning middle class has changed many customs. There is a need for a new kind of expression in the suburban communities and in the housing developments. The classical function of the rabbi and the Protestant minister was that of spiritual leader, teacher, and scholar. But they are losing this function, if indeed they have not already lost it.

As far as the temple or the church goes, the congregations want a rabbi or a minister to preside over the hatch, match, and despatch functions. "Stick to religion," say the balabatim, the elders, the stewards, and the just plain ordinary "leaders."

Church and temple are not absorbing the middle classes; instead the middle classes are absorbing them. It is too early to say whether this is good for the Jews and Protestants or bad for the Jews and Protestants. But Judaism and Protestantism remind me of a play where the actors have decided they don't need the director. Sometimes it's a better play for this decision, and sometimes the actors trip all over themselves.

On the second coming

IN CHARLOTTE the radio station closes the day with prayer and a short question-and-answer period conducted by one of our leading clergymen, Dr. Lawrence Stell. The other night a lady phoned him: "Should we tell the Jews about Jesus?" Dr. Stell agreed that the Jews should indeed be told about Jesus.

A few years ago there was a Christmas editorial in one of our daily papers which quoted the prayer: "Thou shalt love the Lord thy God with all thy heart and with all thy might, and thou shalt love Him when thou risest up and when thou liest down . . ." And the editorial said how nice it would be if everybody repeated that prayer, not only Christians but the Jews, Moslems, etc.

What the editorial did not say is that Jesus repeated the prayer as a matter of course and because He was a Jew. As to the question: "Should we tell the Jews about Jesus?" the only proper answer is that the local synagogue would be the only establishment in this entire society which Jesus would at least recognize as an institution of His times and it would be the first place He would go, if He decided to include Charlotte in His itinerary at the Second Coming. And He would very likely come to my office to ask a few questions, such as: "What are Presbyterians, Episcopalians, Methodists, Baptists, Lutherans, Catholics, and Jehovah's Witnesses?" I could brief Him with both knowledge of these sects and genuine affection for them.

Is this not so?

The New English Bible

INTERESTING about the Bible. I was reading the *New English Bible* the other day and it struck me that across the centuries there have been revisions and interpretations and further revisions. But no one ever asks us Jews. We're only the authors, that's all.

No matter how many revisions of the Bible take place, one thing is sure: the Jews remain the Chosen People. This is good to know, because the interfaith movement and the chamber of commerce rituals which have taken place over the past twenty years often obscure this.

Even rabbis are telling their congregations that the Jews are not the Chosen People. The theory behind this is that if Jews deny their Chosen-ness they will cease to offend Christians and they will be like everybody else and, who knows, perhaps some may even get an invitation to join the Bonnie Brae Country Club.

This is all foolishness. If we are not the Chosen People the Bible is wrong. It is far better to offend Christians, if indeed we Chosen Jews do offend, than to do them a disservice and cast aspersions on a basic tenet of Revelation and Prophecy.

Not being called the Chosen People is the reason Jews leave their temples half-deserted week after week. The rabbi's only recourse is to promise that the assistant to the Methodist clergyman will speak to the congregation during Brotherhood Week. While this is no doubt a tempting offer, it is not enough.

Can we possibly mean that the centuries of harassment, proscription, exclusion, and massacre were perpetrated on plain, ordinary, everyday folk? Intolerable!

Ireland's treasure

WHEN *The Playboy of the Western World* first opened in New York there were hundreds of Irishmen in the city who took offense at the play. How dare someone portray an Irish girl as a prostitute, they demanded.

For all I know, these Irishmen may well have been right. But Mr. Synge wasn't writing a play to prove that there are Irish prostitutes. He was writing in part about the tragic plight of Ireland where the men refuse to marry—if they marry at all—until they are over forty. In the small green country of Ireland there are two million unwed girls. It would be interesting to learn why this is so.

Irish girls certainly do not lack charm. Siobhan McKenna, that gifted actress from Belfast, has all the Irish gifts—humor, beauty, and intelligence. Admittedly, Ireland is a poor country, but there are parts of our South just as poor and the marriage rate is high —so high that girls are usually married by the age of fifteen. There must be a certain blindness in Irish men. They do not see their real treasure—Irish women.

Viva l'Italia

THE testimony at the Eichmann trial was not all a grim, savage indictment of twentieth-century inhumanity. Some of the testimony redeemed the era.

The Ukrainians, Poles, Hungarians, Croats, and Slovaks jumped at the opportunity to kill Jews. Eichmann needed only a skeleton crew of German Nazis. He set up a branch office in each of these areas and the next morning he had thousands of local applicants.

Yet, mystery of mysteries: the Serbs living right next to the Croats and Slovaks could not be budged. They refused to join in the slaughter. In fact they went out of their way to hide their Jewish neighbors. And surprise of surprises: the Romanians stalled and stalled until most of their Jews were saved. Romania had a bad record as far as Jews were concerned, and they had some pretty violent anti-Semites playing the Hitler-Eichmann game, but there were certain forces there which imperceptibly kept a staying hand; they gave all sorts of excuses about not rounding up the Jews until the Nazis were beaten. My poor mother used to love Queen Carmen Sylva of Romania and maybe she had an instinct about Romanians after all.

Eichmann complained bitterly about the Dutch and the Danes. The Danes, of course, actually risked their own necks to save 95 per cent of their Jewish population. But the palm goes to the Italians. They were right under the gun. Mussolini enacted the anti-Semitic laws of Nazi Germany, but the Italian people laughed at him. Even when their own country was overrun by the Nazi armies you couldn't make an anti-Semite out of an Italian if you stood on your head. *Viva l'Italia.* May her name be blessed forever.

The Southern background

A YOUNG rabbi, born and raised in East New York (Brooklyn), secured his first pulpit in a small Southern town. His wife didn't like the South, so at the end of the first year the rabbi began to look around for another pulpit, in the North. Up in New York there was a new Reform congregation composed of folks who had just moved from East New York (Brooklyn) to a new housing development on Long Island. They were looking for a rabbi, but they politely turned down some local applicants. The folks decided that they wanted a rabbi more in keeping with their new fancy surroundings. They didn't want a Yeshiva or even a Jewish Institute of Religion boy. They had made up their minds; the new rabbi should be from the Cincinnati seminary, and, if possible, he should be one "with a real Southern background." Do I have to tell you what happened? Of course! Our

East New York (Brooklyn) friend from the little town in the Deep South got the job, and after he was signed up the first thing he said was: "This is a real break for me, now I can visit my father in East New York (Brooklyn) every week."

10

AMERICA IS STILL
AMERICA

Music everywhere

When you walked along the Lower East Side of New York, you heard music coming out of most of the open windows: "one, two, three, four," of little girls practicing the piano; the monotonous wail of the boys on the violin. More often, of course, the Victrola was going full blast. You heard opera, Neapolitan folk songs, cantorial chants, Chauncey Olcott singing, "Ireland Must Be Heaven" or Maggie Cline's recording of "Throw Him Down McCloskey," depending upon the neighborhood you were in.

Music was one of the great joys among the immigrant families.

For all these people of perhaps five or six different nationalities, music was not only the common language but also a common love. And there were many occasions when people who did not speak the same language became friends because they could hum the same tune.

Men made sacrifices for music. In many homes the purchase of a violin for the son was included in the budget along with food, rent, and clothing. And thousands of little girls boasted, "I am taking piano lessons."

In my own home my mother had figured out a good system. She ordered me to hang around the house while my sister Matilda was getting her piano lesson, "and listen to everything the teacher says." One day after my sister's lesson, the teacher called me. "Come here," she said, "let me see what you can do." My mother was embarrassed and offered both an apology and that second fifty cents, but the teacher would have none of it. She said that she had this same two-for-one experience in many other homes, and she seemed happy about the whole thing.

In the midst of poverty along came the settlement house, which

279

not only tried to help the newcomer become a citizen, but also offered free music lessons. Thousands of children learned to play and to love music. It did not matter that they didn't play well; to hear a student play the scales gave many an immigrant father a sense of dignity. Nor did it matter that the talent was meager, as it was in my case. What did matter was that we were cultivating a taste for one of the basic values of our existence.

The New York settlement houses still stand, but their role is perhaps different than what it once was. The neighborhoods are different and so are the people. But music has not changed. The love for it is constant. Free music lessons, perhaps not the greatest gift America gave to the immigrant, certainly was one of the kindest.

Memories of an errand boy

WHAT I remember best about those years just before the Great World War are the sights and sounds of East Broadway. I can remember whistling "Waitin' for the Robert E. Lee," as I walked to pick up my copies of the *Jewish Daily Forward* to sell. Everybody was whistling "Waitin' for the Robert E. Lee."

On my way was Max's Busy Bee, which was nicknamed "Little Coney Island," where an ice-cream cone cost two cents and was "The Big! Big! Big!" There was a thrill in watching the elevated trains pull in at the station on Second Avenue. Two blocks over was Loew's Theatre on Avenue B, where you paid fifteen cents for a balcony seat to see Lola Blaisdell—"Vision La Flame." The orchestra played "Meet Me in the Shadows" and colored slides flashed on a screen to accompany the singer. Lola sang the famous:

> I lost the sunshine and roses,
> I lost the heaven so blue.
> I lost the gladness
> That turned into sadness
> When I lost you.

She sang this standing on a pedestal illumined by a blue spot. Eddie Cantor and George Jessel entertained there and when I sit with these two friends in California, the fact that we are contemporaries surprises me because when I was a kid sitting in the balcony they were on stage, professional performers.

There was another theater we frequented called the Broadway which had a second balcony, and I heard an all-time great song from a seat high up in it:

> You've got your mother's big blue eyes,
> You've got your mother's teeth like pearls,
> And the way you ask for pennies shows
> You know just what your mother knows.

There were no telephones in those days on the Lower East Side and electric lights had just made their appearance. Most of the people who sat in the balcony with me were immigrants too. They came from the far-off corners of the world. Sometimes they had been sent by parents who scrimped and saved in the ghettos of Europe just so these children could have the chance America promised. They had cut all the ties behind them; there would be no yearly get-together at Grandma's nor phone calls to parents. There were no phones. The parting had been forever.

"Saving" the ice

IN THE summer the Lower East Side of New York was filled with ice carts. The icemen were the same fellows who sold kerosene in the winter. During the winter there was no call for ice. Then, the housewives, like my mother, used to put perishable foods on the window sills. Every once in a while as you walk along the Lower East Side today you can see one of the old wooden milk boxes for the refrigeration of milk still hanging outside a tenement window.

The icemen were either men without conscience or very bad mathematical computers. The huge blocks of ice were divided into five slices or four. But their nomenclature was wholly arbitrary. People bought either a third of a block or a quarter of a block. The slice from the block of "four thirds" was more expensive than the slice from the block of "five quarters." The mothers would tell the children, "Run downstairs and get me a big quarter-ice," or, "Today you will buy for the icebox a small third."

If the iceman carried the slab of ice upstairs to the wooden icebox the price was correspondingly more. Few women paid this extra premium, but, when one did, we kids who trailed the ice carts would take advantage of the iceman's absence to swipe a few chunks and retire to an alleyway where we sat happily licking the ice.

Mothers were chary about what they put in the icebox, which somewhat resembled today's refrigerator, except it was made of wood and was appreciably smaller.

The theory was that the more food you put on the ice, the quicker it would melt. I have checked this with a scientist at Duke University and he says—no. I wish the immigrant women on the Lower East Side of New York had known this. To "save" the ice, as they believed they were doing, they rarely refrigerated butter, jams, or pastries.

And the most important duty in the house was emptying that drip pan into which the melted ice trickled. To forget this duty and to let water run all over the floor was disastrous, not only to the family but to the folks living below you.

Mr. Hines called me

ONE of these days I shall have to take pen in hand and write a thousand stories about my adventures when I was the clerk and day manager of the Hotel Markwell on West Forty-ninth Street and Broadway during the Depression years.

Mr. Hines, the night clerk, refused all and any responsibility other than the renting of rooms. At three o'clock in the morning he would ring my room to ask, "Is so-and-so good for a room? He says he'll pay the two dollars next week." If someone wanted to borrow a dollar, or if someone fell or claimed luggage had been stolen, Mr. Hines called me, no matter the hour.

Once in a while he would have a serious matter, and one night when I answered the telephone he was absolutely frantic. "There's lots of trouble in Room 804," he said.

I dressed quickly and went up to Room 804. Room 804 housed a permanent resident, an actress employed on the WPA Federal Theater Project. She had locked herself in the bathroom and this fellow, dressed only in his shorts, was banging at the locked door and screaming at her to come out or he'd knock the door down. Everything I heard and saw convinced me both had been drinking heavily.

But I approached the fellow and tried to quiet him down, because I recognized him as a mounted cop who often patrolled the theater district. All I said was "Come on, Jim, I'll not tell La Guardia about this."

At the name "La Guardia," the fellow became as sober as a judge, dressed quickly, and left.

A little later the girl came down to the desk fully dressed and began to apologize. I chatted with her for a few minutes, and she said she was from North Carolina and showed that she was a pretty nice girl trying to get a start in the theater. She explained that the cop had been her friend for a few months, but that he drank so heavily she realized she would have to give him up. And that was that. For the next year she was the perfect guest, paying her eight dollars a week regularly with one of those green WPA checks for $23.86.

Twenty-five years later one of the charming matrons of a leading North Carolina city, a woman with obvious prestige earned not only by her money but her civic works, stepped up to the book counter at J. B. Ivey & Company while I was autographing copies of *Only In America*. It was the actress. Every time I have an autographing session at Ivey's she comes, and I autograph a book for her, and she smiles. And I smile back.

Notes for an autobiography

For us, it all began in the year 1905, around Passover time, when my mother, born Anna Klein, my two older sisters, Clara and Matilda, and I arrived at Ellis Island on the Hamburg-American liner, the S.S. *Graf Waldersee* out of Hamburg. Clara was nine, Matilda was seven, I was two, and my mother was thirty-eight. We had journeyed overland from the most eastern corner of the Austro-Hungarian Empire, the town of Mikulinz on the river Sereth in the province of Galicia.

Thousands of Jews from Russia, Poland, Romania, and Hungary embarked at Hamburg. But at Hamburg there was always a wait—inspections, documents, examinations, and the posting of the ship's schedule. While these immigrants waited, the German Jews took over. They had established a free clinic and a hostel, and provided gifts of money if a family did not have enough, or had been robbed, as frequently happened.

The radicals on the Lower East Side always said the German Jews were so kind because they wanted to keep us moving and not cause them embarrassment in their Fatherland. But it is much easier to argue that they did all of these things because they were innately generous and because they were Jews—a most fantastic and interesting fraternity to belong to.

My family lived in the heart of the Lower East Side of New York, where three and a half million immigrants settled between 1880 and 1920. We lived in the "Times Square" of this voluntary ghetto—at 171 Eldridge Street, between Rivington and Delancey. In those days, one tenement fronted another. The two tenements were separated by a back yard about twenty feet wide. The rent "in the back" was considerably less than the twenty-two dollars we paid for four rooms in the front on the top floor.

My father, Leib Goldhirsch (born 1860), and my brother Jacob (born 1888) had preceded us to America a year earlier. This was the normal pattern, and that is why 90 per cent of all the Jewish immigrants from Eastern Europe between 1890 and 1920 were males, married or single, who came to America and began to save enough money from their earnings to send for fiancées, wives, children, parents, and other relatives.

My father became a Hebrew teacher and my brother Jacob took to peddling. Jacob, when he was eighteen years old, registered in night school and attended it for the next ten years, completing both the grammar and high school courses. The immigrants did not call it evening grammar school, which it was. It was more dignified for grown men (some of them with beards) to say they were going to "night school."

My father became a citizen in 1910.

How long does it take to become an American? Not as long as you might think. Arrive from Mikulinz in 1905 and four years later you are the "king" in a school pageant parading down Fifth Avenue, a participant in the Hudson-Fulton celebration of 1909 —how much more American can you be? My "queen" was the little Cohen girl whose parents ran the hand laundry in the basement of 171 Eldridge Street.

We played many street games, the most important of which was "puss and cat." "Puss" was a sawed-off broom handle about four inches long; "cat" was about fifteen inches of the broomstick. You put the "puss" on a "tee," usually a manhole corner, and hit it with the "cat," and from there played regular baseball rules.

Another game was Johnny-on-the-Pony. I have no idea of its origin. One team was "it" and bent over against a wall and the other team jumped on your back one on top of the other, and the idea was to repeat "Johnny-on-the-Pony" three times without falling off. If the "it" team caved in under the weight of eight guys or so, they remained "it."

The East Side was a singing society. We sang Yiddish songs, patriotic American songs, and the latest popular tunes.

My brother Jacob took me to school the first day at P. S. No. 20 at Rivington and Eldridge. He also took me to the De Milt Dispensary on West Twenty-third Street to be vaccinated, and not long afterward took me back for my first pair of eyeglasses, because my teacher had dispatched me with the written notation that I must have my eyes examined. I wore eyeglasses at so young an age it has always seemed to me I was born with them.

My sister Matilda got a job in a necktie factory at five dollars a week, and she immediately enrolled in night school to learn office work. My older sister Clara got a job that paid twelve dollars for a sixty-hour week in a sample-card factory on Green Street, and she went to school at night to learn office work.

My father didn't make much money. I doubt that he ever handled as much as fifty dollars at one time. But everyone listened to him. He had a license to marry people and he tied the knot for hundreds of couples, usually in the front room of our flat on the Lower East Side of New York.

I always made out the certificate for the county clerk and retained the stub in a little book as a record for my father. I wrote down the names of the bride and groom and all other pertinent data.

Many of these couples, I recall, had children, and many a bride was heavy with one child and carrying another as she took her place beside the husband for the official ceremony.

These children were "legitimate." The couples had been married in Europe by rabbis whose authority was never recognized by the state, and in their small Jewish villages they would have gone about their lives forever. In the United States they soon learned that a civil marriage was necessary; that without it, complications follow a family with respect to property rights, wills, and the rights of children. So what my father and others like him really did for many of these people was merely confirm a civil marriage. My own father and mother went through this civil marriage after at least four children had been born. Even then my mother was reluctant. She was not impressed with secular functions.

My mother was very pious, and I have already told of her piety. The essay "My Mother and God" in my book, *Only in America*, brought the most mail I have received for anything I have ever written.

With such a high male population it was not surprising that the East Side had its share of brothels. There were four or five houses of prostitution on Allen Street, a block from where we lived. Allen Street was "the street where the sun never shines."

The El tracks almost touched the tenements on both sides. In the summertime the prostitutes would stand in the hallway or on the stoop, and as a man passed they opened their wrappers and called to him in various languages. Most of them were young girls. The men didn't ask the girls to tell them any stories or make them relate how they got started. The men went to the brothel and from there to the union hall or to the settlement house. When we twelve- and thirteen-year-olds passed these houses we had a vague idea that when our time came for a sex experience it would probably be with one of these girls. That's precisely how it was, but that belongs in another chapter.

There was a clean line of demarcation about sex. The brothels were on Allen Street and further uptown, on Fourteenth Street, and no one ever thought of the average girl indulging in unmarried sex. When a fellow took a walk with your sister everybody surmised that they would probably get married, and if he had the Sabbath dinner at your home twice in succession, it was a deal.

I was graduated from P. S. 20 in June 1917, and enrolled immediately in the East Side Evening High School (in the same building) where I completed the regular high school course in three years. Eventually I went on to the College of the City of New York at the old Twenty-third Street Annex for three more years, making a total of six uninterrupted years of night school five nights a week.

Studying in the old Rivington Street Library, I read whole shelves of Jules Verne, G. A. Henty, the Dick Hazard series, as well as Dumas, Victor Hugo, and Bulwer-Lytton. I always carried a book with me to read on the trolley car and at lunch. Some of us actually developed an ability to read a book as we walked along the street, just as some soldiers learn how to sleep as they march. During all of those years of going to night school and the libraries I tried hard to maintain my status as "one of the gang" with my friends on the block. I made certain that I wouldn't be called "Sissy," and I managed this by concealing my books, keeping my necktie folded in my pocket, and tucking my clean white collar inside my sweater until I was clear of the neighborhood.

Selling newspapers between the years 1912 and 1917 taught me history, because we were living in a generation of headlines.

I was outside the Little Hungary Restaurant selling newspapers and shouting, "Austrian Archduke assassinated." Those who were born before June 28, 1914, and those who were born after, were born into two different worlds. When that shouting nationalist charged into the crowd and fired into Archduke Francis Ferdihand's coach, his bullet changed all expectations of what we thought this world would be like.

Yet, at the time, it seemed to me it was just a better headline to sell more papers.

In those days Chuck Connors was the "mayor" of Chinatown. Its big industry was the phony opium den and the phony joss house. A joss house was a place where they were supposed to burn opium as incense rather than smoke it. I say the joss house and the opium dens were phonies because tourists paid fifty cents and were shown through them. After the tourists had been properly shocked, the Chinese would put down their long opium pipes, brush themselves off, and go back to the store to sell their produce and earn a decent livelihood, all of them laughing like hell.

My brother Jacob spent these years as the night clerk at the Hotel Normandie on Broadway and Thirty-eighth Street. Every Friday I took the Sixth Avenue streetcar and brought him his Sabbath meal. My mother had made arrangements with Offer's Restaurant ("No one offers what Offer offers") to have the food kept warm until he was ready to eat. It was a great treat for me because I spent the night in the hotel.

During this period, I developed a great love for the opera and every Monday after school I took my place in line for the standing room admissions.

Movies were never called then, as they are now, an escape mechanism. We East Side immigrant boys didn't troop to see Bronco Billy Anderson because we couldn't stand our home life. We went to see Bronco Billy because he taught us the attitudes we admired in this New World. He was heroic. That is what we wanted to be, heroic—and a cowboy, too, if that was possible. The early Westerns conferred upon us the first ideals of American manhood: speak truth, shoot straight, and save the wagon train.

When I entered the East Side Evening High School I knew

the time had come to get a regular job and I found one in a factory manufacturing ladies' straw hats, Arnold Rosenbaum and Company, on Mercer Street. I worked nine hours every weekday and four hours on Saturday for ten dollars a week. I was a sizer. Let me tell you about a sizer. Twenty girls sat at machines sewing raw hemp into straw hats, and the sizer dipped these straw hats into a tank of hot glue. The boss warned me not to leave one dry spot. But this was a little difficult because of the great heat, and I am afraid I left many an Achilles' heel on the hats where my fingers held them. When I took the hats out of the glue I put each one on a rubber block, shaped it, and hung it on a rack to dry.

I worked for Arnold Rosenbaum and Company for about a year when suddenly a union organizer made contact with me at my home. I joined my fellow workers and signed up. This was a lucky thing for me because one of the provisions of the two-day strike, which we won, was that we were to receive "back pay," and that next Saturday afternoon I went home with nearly fifty dollars. The following week I was fired. The boss figured that, since he now had to pay me twenty-six dollars a week, he might just as well get an experienced sizer, a family man.

After I had unionized myself out of the hat factory I got the most important job of my life. I became a stock clerk for a manufacturing furrier, Oscar H. Geiger and Company, at 6 West Thirty-seventh Street, across the street from the fashionable Brick Presbyterian Church on Fifth Avenue. But Mr. Geiger wasn't an ordinary furrier. He was an amazing man to whom I remain indebted to this day, as do nine other men around the country.

It seemed that I was working for a boss who was just as bored with "business" as I was. When he saw me in his stockroom with that inevitable book in my pants pocket (this time Shakespeare), his eyes lighted up. He asked me to join his club.

Oscar H. Geiger had studied for the rabbinate and eventually became the director of the Hebrew Asylum in New York. He gave all of this up, however, when he became interested in Henry George and the single-tax movement. He organized a club of boys who met in his home at One Hundred Sixteenth and Lenox Avenue every Sunday morning. It was called the Round Table

Literary Club and it included his son, George, and eight other boys. Two of my particular friends in the club were an Irishman, John Duff, whose father was a fireman; and Murray de Leeuw, a Jew whose parents had come to America a hundred years before from Holland. I told my mother of the wonders in Murray's home—tomato juice, for instance, which I had never seen before —and when I said that Murray's mother spoke only English and could not speak Yiddish, my mother was skeptical and said, "I can't believe that she's a real Jewish mother."

Mr. Geiger, whom we called "the Governor" (he once ran for Governor of New York on the Single-Tax ticket), had a giant brain. I believe he was the most profound student Henry George ever had.

Mr. Geiger ran the club much as a college teacher might run a seminar. He gave us books to read, he delivered lectures, and he assigned subjects to us on which we ourselves spoke. Sometimes it was a play from Shakespeare, at other times a preface from a George Bernard Shaw play, and of course, every meeting had a lesson from Henry George.

When the decade closed I was still going to the East Side Evening High School five nights a week without interruption, except on the Jewish holidays. We left a decade where decisions seemed easy to make and everlasting.

To be truthful, these things are felt and understood only in retrospect, and in retrospect I can say that I am happy to have grown up between 1903 and 1918. I believe it was a better period than the one in which my three sons grew into manhood. It was more vigorous; it contained a higher sense of involvement and a wider feeling of hope.

If the boys of Mr. Geiger's club looked upon me with curiosity and interest, my friends on the Lower East Side now regarded me as an odd fish. I was not only consorting with Christians but also with assimilated Jews. We had always known of these assimilated Jews and on the East Side we called them "fancy Jews," because of the rumors that these people sat in temples without hats and listened to organ music, just like Christians.

But I never lost my contacts with the East Side. In fact I asked Mr. Geiger to give me a leave of absence during the summer of 1918 so that I could go to a farm in Connecticut as a participant in a settlement-house project. The settlement house gave you an entire summer on a farm as an individual. The settlement-house people conducted a vast correspondence with hundreds of farmers in Connecticut and New Jersey.

During that summer I received board and room and, at the end of the season, fifteen dollars in cash. The farm I was sent to was in Connecticut, a few miles from the Massachusetts border, and for the first time in my life I saw cows milked and vegetables grown, and I drove the horse and buggy into town every morning to get the mail. The farm was managed by three women, an elderly widow, a spinster sister who went off every morning to a civil service job at Hartford, and a spinster niece. The real farm work was done by hired men; my job was to take care of a small truck garden and do other chores around the house.

I also learned something about sex. One afternoon, I entered the barn and extended a hand to help one of those spinster ladies, and she tugged me on top of her. I squirmed from her caress and ran, red-faced, to the house. A few months later, back in New York it dawned upon me what embarrassment she must have suffered. I felt terribly ashamed, but I knew that now boyhood was over.

Moving the piano to the top floor

ON THE Lower East Side of New York it seemed that everybody you knew lived on the top floor of a six-story tenement, and a common sight was to see the new family piano being hoisted up. I haven't seen men hoisting a piano from the street to the top floor in forty years. In those days it must have been some profession, but I guess the architects have taken the meat out of it.

Those pianos not only broke the backs of the moving men but the backs of the factory workers who bought them on the installment plan and paid for them for years and years. No one ever paid the piano off. It was just like the sewing machine, which no one ever paid off either. My mother said of the sewing machine collector, "We grew old together."

To move the piano in those days cost a fortune because it not only meant hoisting it several hundred feet into the air, but also removing the window frames. Manipulating huge contraptions from the roof, three men would try to swing that piano through the window, and inside another three would wait to grab it and pull it in and finally put it in its place in the tenement flat.

When you moved away, you usually had to leave the piano behind. The cost of lowering it back down was staggering. At first, a family could count on receiving thirty-five dollars for a secondhand piano that had cost two hundred dollars on the installment plan, but there came a day when they couldn't even get that. However it did raise your prestige. If the landlord saw a piano in the house he came for the rent once a month instead of every week.

But what a great sight and great fascination it was to stand on the street and watch the moving men hoist up the piano. How many dreams went upstairs with that piano!

Election fires

ONE of the great memories of old New York was the bonfire the neighborhood lit on election night. It was a ritual. If the police and fire departments did not sanction it, certainly they did nothing to discourage it. I suspect they liked the bonfire as well as anyone.

The wood was collected early election morning. Boys roamed the streets and the waterfront for crates, boxes, discarded furniture, and loose fence boards. Tenants cleaned out the basements and many of the immigrant folks donated a chair that was beyond repair. Sofas and tables and old furniture were piled. To this day, I'm sure that folks saved stuff for the bonfire all year long rather than throw it out.

In my own district the bonfire blazed on Delancey Street,

possibly because this was the widest street in the whole neighborhood. The houses were sixty feet apart and the danger of the fire spreading was negligible. And what a tremendous fire it was! Folks came from blocks and blocks around to stand and watch it roar.

Of course, the folks may not have known it, but they were participating in one of the oldest rituals known to man. Since the beginning of time, fire has served as a symbol of tyranny, a symbol of horror, and a symbol of purity.

God usually manifests Himself to man, according to ancient tradition, through fire. In the Holy Writings He compared Himself to an ardent flame to display holiness and purity. And the Vestal Virgins of Rome were copying the Hebrews when they tended the everlasting and majestic flame.

And one should not confuse the election-night bonfire with the burning cross of the Ku Klux Klan. The burning cross derives from the burning wheel of the ancient pagans. When they were sore at God and felt they could not propitiate Him, they burned a symbol to get rid of Him. In the Middle Ages, when areas were afflicted with a blight or a famine or a plague, they burned a symbol of Jesus, and church authorities had to step in and brand the process pagan. The burning cross of the Ku Klux Klan is a symbol of displeasure at Jesus and the message of brotherhood.

The election-night bonfire has a different origin. The custom was imported to America by Englishmen who always celebrated the coronation of a new monarch with a bonfire.

From the bonfire that celebrated the crowning of Elizabeth I to the bonfire that celebrated the election of Moshe Graubard as a New York Assemblyman, we have a continuous tradition.

I remember, I remember

THE name Joe Bernstein meant a lot to the immigrants on the Lower East Side in the beginning of the century. Joe Bernstein was probably the first American Jew who gained popularity and prominence as a prize fighter. I know that Joe Choynski, the heavyweight who battled Bob Fitzsimmons, was a Jew, but he had no "identity" with the immigrants.

The New York *World* was the status symbol then. If you were reading the *World*, it meant you were looking for a job. Only the Los Angeles *Times* today has the number of classified advertisements the *World* had then. There were pages and pages of classifieds.

The *World* was a great paper and its editor, Frank Cobb, was probably one of the greatest editors America ever had. He was also one of Woodrow Wilson's closest friends.

In 1904, the Populists nominated Thomas E. Watson for President. The nomination of Watson was a protest against the Democratic nominee, Judge Alton B. Parker, a solid conservative.

William Randolph Hearst supported Watson, and then again he didn't. He printed all of Watson's speeches in toto, but nevertheless still urged on his editorial page, "Vote the straight Democratic ticket."

When Watson spoke on the East Side, at Cooper Union on Eighth Street, the hall was filled with hundreds of enthusiastic Jews. "Populism" to them meant socialism or liberalism with some measure of hope for better housing and better working conditions and all the other promises that were finally realized with the New Deal of Franklin D. Roosevelt.

A few years later, however, Watson turned into one of the most bitter anti-Semites ever to disgrace American history.

In 1906, when Hearst ran for mayor of New York, an election which he won but which was snatched from him by a fraudulent count, the famous publisher had dozens of workers canvassing the Lower East Side. Hearst knew that Tammany Hall was giving a dollar or two to each voter, so he countered this by having his canvassers tell each family, "If Hearst is elected, he will take over the gas company and you will save five dollars every month on your gas bill."

Dr. Will Durant, who has executed a philosophic magnum opus of this century, was a high school principal down on the Lower East Side. How old is this wonderful man? I remember that he was one of the fine Socialist speakers at the Labor Temple on

Second Avenue and Fourteenth Street. There are few boys who grew up on the Lower East Side in those years who did not hear Will Durant speak at least once or twice.

The Irish immigrant boys who preceded us Jews by a couple of decades held down all the clerk, messenger, and grocery jobs. We did not begin to infiltrate these positions until the Irish themselves grew tired of them or abandoned them for better positions vacated by the Germans (who had preceded them).

When these jobs first opened to Jews I became a messenger boy for the Postal Telegraph Company in the Longacre Building, Broadway and Forty-second. In those days, we received two cents for every telegram we delivered, a method of payment the telegraph companies discontinued about 1920. The reason they discontinued it was because the messenger boys made too much money that way.

There were times, however, when delivering a single message took so much time it was hardly worth the two cents we received. But I was interested in people then, as now. One message I delivered was an experience that has never left me. It was a telegram adressed to a Mr. Hedges, a traction tycoon, who was dining at Churchill's Restaurant.

Churchill's was on the corner of Broadway and Forty-ninth Street. I entered Churchill's and the headwaiter gestured toward Mr. Hedges' table. There were six or seven people sitting around it, and when I handed the message to Mr. Hedges I saw that one of the ladies was Lillian Russell. She nodded toward me while I waited for Mr. Hedges to reply to the telegram.

In our more sophisticated and cynical world, no headwaiter would ever direct a mesenger boy to an important man, for the waiter would never understand that the twenty-five-cent tip might be important to the kid.

I know there were sweatshops on the Lower East Side, and there were the miserable conditions always attendant on poverty, crowded tenements, child labor—conditions which had to be changed—but there were some compensations.

We led a more placid life. Headwaiters did not feel threatened by messenger boys; and Lillian Russell nodded to me!

The Irishman who deserted the messenger routes and the

grocery stores found a higher and more noble goal. He became a cop. To become a cop he had to pay a few hundred dollars to the Tammany district leader. A flock of relatives would help him get up this "fee." Many an Irishman put in an apprenticeship as a streetcar conductor to earn part of the money. The Irish were the first to learn about the virtues of running a streetcar. By the time the Jews and the Italians got wise to it, the Irish had skimmed all the cream off the top. The streetcar conductor always made himself an extra three dollars a day in filched nickels. Like a commission. The company knew he took it, but as long as he kept the car in running order and got the people where they were going, the company was content. There were occasional conductors who were greedy and the standard joke about them was: "He didn't even bring the trolley back."

Mike Gold, the leftist—author of *Jews Without Money*—used to harangue Jewish boys in Union Square about their stupidity in attending shul and maintaining the Orthodox rituals. Pious Jews used to warn their sons away from attending Mike Gold's meetings. Mike Gold was a pretty good writer, only he couldn't write a sentence without the phrase "class war" creeping in. I have heard in recent years that he is in Mexico.

Dick Husch worked in the New York post office for many years. Dick, along with Harry Armstrong, wrote "Sweet Adeline." Dick wrote over one hundred and fifty songs under the name of Richard Gerard but only "Sweet Adeline" was a hit. He sold all his rights to it for one hundred and fifty dollars. Later, when ASCAP came into being, Dick received royalties and continued to receive them until the day of his death.

This is part of the history of the public school I went to on Rivington and Eldridge Streets.

Across the street from P.S. 20 was a store called Cheap Habers', and on the corner was Max's saloon, and around the corner, next to Max's, was the livery stable on Forsythe Street owned by the father of Geraldine Farrar, the famous Metropolitan star. This wonderful woman was a prima donna in the grand manner. Kaiser Wilhelm, it is said, banished the Crown Prince to German East Africa to break up his romance with Farrar. Some years later Madame Farrar created a sensation when she appeared in the opera *Zaza*. The dowagers were shocked at the Farrar realism when *Zaza* powdered herself on stage as she awaited her lover.

In those days we kids could see Mr. Charles Broadway Rouss, the big blind merchant, get off the trolley and have his dinner every day in a tenement on the East Side. Charles Broadway Rouss was one of the greatest experts of fabrics in the world, and he could tell the value of every piece of cloth by his touch, so they said.

Murray Rosalsky, brother of Judge Otto Rosalsky, also went to P. S. 20. His family lived at the corner of Rivington and Allen Streets opposite the stairway to the Second Avenue elevated.

In 1904 the class was due to graduate but there was no commencement. Most of the students had perished on the steamer, *General Slocum*, which was carrying a Sunday school picnic from St. Mark's Lutheran Church. Even though most of those who perished were Christian, all the homes on the Lower East Side had pieces of black crepe hanging from the windows.

A few blocks away was Orchard Street, the Jewish Casbah. The pushcarts lined both sides of the narrow street, but we managed to play our games around them.

A cousin of my father's, A. Lindeman, had a dry goods store on Orchard Street. He went along for years making a nice living until his nephew became an accountant, put the store on a scientific basis, and discovered the old man, his employer, was bankrupt. The old man had used his own bookkeeping system for thirty years. It involved a little book in his back pocket which contained two columns—one marked "in," the other "out." When his nephew, the accountant, got through with him, the guy had to close the store. The nephew proved that he owed much more than he possessed. I still maintain that if there were no certified public accountants, Lindeman would still be in business.

In those days we saw Big Tim Sullivan who gave shoes to the poor, and Al Smith wearing his brown derby, and Jimmy Walker who visited with the Cooper Union Boys and sang with the Empire City Quartet every Friday night.

Eddie Cantor is now celebrating his seventieth birthday and this good man was one of the boys in that neighborhood. Eddie went to Riis High while I attended the University Settlement.

The kids in the Gus Edwards show, *School Days*—Georgie Jessel, Georgie Price, Walter Winchell, Herman Timburg, and Eddie Cantor—all came from the neighborhood. And so did Izzy Baline who played the piano at the James G. Blaine Club on East Broadway and who is known to us as Irving Berlin.

Katz's Delicatessen, which I last visited just a few weeks ago, is still going strong and it was Katz's who made famous "a shtickle for a nickel." On Saturdays when no cooking was done in the Orthodox Jewish home we were given a dime and went to Katz's. For a dime Katz's gave you a huge club sandwich loaded down with pastrami, corned beef, and salami, all the pickles you wanted, a huge plate of French fried potatoes, and a whole bottle of ketchup. Today Katz's charges you ninety cents for that deal, and it is still a bargain.

When my brother Jacob took over the Union Square Hotel, which became the "Algonquin" of the Yiddish theater, I was not at all concerned about the business prospects. But the evening Jack took title, I went around touching everything Bob Fitzsimmons had touched years before when he was the bartender, and I spent the first night in the room in which Henry George died while campaigning for mayor. But perhaps I have already written about this. Like writers and old men, I must beware lest I repeat myself.

America is still America

A YIDDISH expression "America bleibt America," or America is still America, means that all the years of hope and dreams wrapped up in the principles of America are still true. It also means that despite the assaults made upon us from time to time, from without and from within, and despite the strange doctrines introduced into American society by such people as Robert Welch, America bleibt America—America is still America.

I saw Jewish immigrants come off the boat without a dime. Their relatives who had preceded them to these shores by a year or a few months had saved up enough money to buy their passage and bring them over.

After a few appropriate greetings the newly arrived immigrant would borrow twenty-five dollars from the same relative or from the Hebrew Free Loan Society. With this money he went down to the wholesale district, which was then on Canal Street. He stocked up with sheets, pillowcases, blankets, and towels to the limit of his capital, and he began to peddle. The immigrant took his goods and began to walk in the direction of Long Island, or maybe up the Hudson Valley. Soon he'd be back, and now he had fifty-five dollars.

He'd buy more merchandise and repeat the process. First thing you know he had paid off his loan and had enough capital to open a bank account. Next another friend or relative advised him of an opportunity to open a store in Scranton, Pennsylvania, or Corpus Christi, Texas, or Albemarle, North Carolina, and soon this immigrant took his place as a substantial citizen of his community and received from his community exactly what he elected to put into it. This process was repeated not once, but thousands and thousands of times. This is the only place on earth where it could have happened, and we must remember: America bleibt America.

From Edward VII to Klein's

ON ONE of my trips to New York, I was the guest of Phil Harris who ran the world-famous department store, S. Klein's "On the Square." "On the Square" means across the street from Union Square Park, between Fourteenth and Fifteenth Streets on Fourth Avenue, at the northern border of the Lower East Side. A sale at S. Klein's is a signal for the local precinct to station twelve cops on Union Square. I visited Mr. Harris right after he purchased the Union Square Hotel which was adjacent to his department store. Ah, what an interesting story.

When it was opened in 1872, the Union Square Hotel catered to the aristocracy of the famous "Four Hundred." In the late

1880s they began to move "uptown" before great waves of immigration. The Germans had come first, then the Irish, followed by the Jews and the Italians. And now we have the Negroes and the Puerto Ricans.

Edward VII, when he was Prince of Wales, once slept in the Union Square Hotel. Richard Canfield, who later became our most famous gambler, was the night clerk, and Bob Fitzsimmons, who later became the heavyweight champion of the world, was a bartender.

Jenny Lind rested in one of its apartments between performances at The Academy of Music on Fourteenth Street, and Enrico Caruso is on the registration book of 1903. For years the Tammany sachems had their cold beer in one of the dining rooms after the July Fourth orations, and Theodore Roosevelt used the hotel for his New York headquarters when he campaigned for President in 1904.

But this hotel had greater significance to me because my brother Jack leased it in the early 1920s. He ran it during its last years in what was probably its most interesting era. The alterations Jack ordered were still in process and only the new beds had arrived when the members of the Boston Symphony Orchestra arrived and insisted on staying there. My brother sent me uptown to the old Normandie Hotel to borrow soap and towels for the musicians, who said they had never stopped anywhere else in New York.

Everyone connected with the Yiddish art world, which then was at its height, stayed there—playwrights, musicians, producers, actors, stagehands, extras—everybody stayed there, or at least received his mail there.

Now the hotel where Ruby Bob used to illustrate his famous solar-plexus punch, and where Charley Murphy outlined Tammany strategy, and where Paul Muni visited his mother, is gone. In the room where Enrico Caruso rehearsed for his American debut and where the future Edward VII drank champagne from the slipper of a charming girl, an IBM machine now impersonally adds up the day's receipts of S. Klein's daily housedress special.

What's the matter with New York?

TIMES SQUARE on a recent election night finally gave up the ghost. Not a horn, not a howl. "Blind beggars were able to tap their paths easily up and down the Square with no crush to hem them in," reported the New York *Times*. Where once one thousand, eight hundred policemen sweated desperately to keep the crowds in check, there were only two hundred and seven cops standing around exchanging precinct gossip.

I remember elections—even for alderman—that brought out cheering, pushing, shouting crowds. Election night meant Times Square with the little red or white ball atop the Times Tower, and the roar after the result was proclaimed could be heard across the water in the Jersey suburbs.

The break with this tradition is a piece of the "what's-the-use" attitude born of cynicism, corruption, and inefficiency.

They used to say of New York that the reason it was the romantic city was because all its citizens lived out of season. A fellow standing on a street corner on the hottest day in August was either an editor preparing a Christmas issue, a buyer thinking about next spring's fashions, or an impresario planning on what opera stars he would sign to sing for the Easter presentation of *Parsifal*. New York was a town living in the middle of the future, a town filled with anticipation.

So the question is why are people leaving this bright jewel of a city? The recent census shows that New York has lost in population and will consequently lose two congressmen. Before long, as every New Yorker knows, Los Angeles will surpass it as the nation's largest city, and California will become the nation's largest State.

Has the future given up on New York City; or has New York City given up on the future?

The truth of the matter is that New York has become a dinosaur. The dinosaur was the most powerful of all organisms developed on earth, but it led itself to its own extinction. It was a clumsy reptile and pretty soon it was so big it was all clumsy. It lost that delicate balance which alone sustains and nourishes the will to live and not just to grow. New York City, too, has lost its delicate balance.

It has let slums proliferate despite a massive slum-clearance program. Like the dinosaur, the city has lost track of its aims. The point of slum clearance is to house people, not to jack up realty values.

The slum-clearance projects only create more slums. Every time a block of houses is razed, in their place springs up a middle-class housing project with rents as high as one hundred dollars per room per month. The city has *got* to have these realty taxes, say the housing authorities.

It is a sad state of affairs. The slums of New York are far worse now than the slums I knew in 1910. There is neither hope nor optimism in these slums.

In Harlem there are many thousands who sleep in shifts because of inadequate housing. Mothers in the Negro and Puerto Rican ghettos stand guard all night beside their sleeping children to fight off rats. A New York *Post* survey some time ago showed that nearly 50 per cent of these ghetto tenements have but one toilet for every ten families.

The city has put up miles upon miles of office buildings and, despite the frantic program, it has lost industry. It has lost what has now become a major American industry—television—which has moved to the West Coast. And television moved despite the fact that all the actors, the directors, the cameramen, and the advertising agencies lived in New York.

Now, it is dangerous for people to walk in Central Park. In the hallways of Barnard College, printed signs warn girls not to walk along Riverside Drive unescorted. If I were the managing editor of the New York *Times* I would reproduce that sign and run it across five columns on page one.

Perhaps all of the people who used to care have left the city. The Socialists who used to agitate for a wages-and-hours law are now all Republicans living in tree-lined suburbs. Once upon a time Frances Perkins woke up Al Smith and took him on a dawn trip to see the children marching into the factories. But the girl who might take Miss Perkins' place is now a fashion editor maneuvering to take over the managing editor's job, or she is out in the suburbs, too, fussing with the electric can opener, and complaining there is no adequate ballet master in town.

"Don't be a litterbug" and "Cross with the green, not in between" are the only campaigns which have effect any more.

Is it any wonder Times Square no longer has its cheering crowds on election night?

The hope for tomorrow is what the city has lost along with its two congressmen.

Golf on the East Side

LIKE boys throughout history we were crazy about balls. Today you can buy a rubber ball for a nickel, perhaps, but when I was a kid, the balls were homemade.

You took a piece of wool or heavy flannel and crumpled it in your palm and wrapped a rubber band around it. You wrapped hundreds of rubber bands around it, all as tight as they could be, and in a month you had a pretty lively handball. Thin red rubber bands were sold fifty for a penny for this purpose.

We also used to play against the stoop. You threw the ball and if it struck between the bevel and the step and you caught it before it bounced, that scored one point. If it hit the bevel and you caught it, that was two points.

As for little girls, they played with dolls to some extent, but mostly they were helping their mothers and learning to be housewives.

The Wort, the Xort, the Zort

SOME of the small New York hotels had police troubles. Every time the reformers protested loudly enough, the police would raid a few small hotels, never disturbing the big ones, of course, where the real stuff was going on.

There was an old gent with a little hotel on Forty-sixth Street who was raided every few months. I remember his saying once: "Macy's sells these women lingerie; Liggett's sells them cosmetics; shoe stores sell them shoes and dress-shops sell them dresses and nothing happens to any of these merchants, but when I sell them a room, I get in trouble."

A raid necessitated changing the name of the hotel. Usually this was a large expense, since hotels were identified by a big electric sign and neon had not yet been invented. One fellow who had a flea bag of a place on a side street called it the Cort Hotel. Every time he was raided, he changed the top letter, and before he retired he had worked his way through virtually the whole of the alphabet. His hotel was called successively the Cort, the Dort, the Fort, the Lort, the Nort, etc.

By the way

A FAVORITE phrase on the Lower East Side was "by the way." I have described how the immigrant Jews picked up the necessary phrases like "Post No Bills," "working papers," and "enjoy, enjoy." "By the way" was also a favorite. The ability to use words in consecutive order delighted and pleased them because it indicated some familiarity with the language. They were becoming Americanized and this little colloquialism, synonym for "incidentally," became ubiquitous. My sister Matilda quit a guy once because every time he introduced her to someone, he would say, "By the way, this is Matilda."

The landlady

IN THE days before social security, I came across a breed of individual—sometimes an elderly man, but just as often an elderly woman. This elderly man got behind in the rent and one week led to another, and to consequent promises of his ability to pay—"I'm expecting a check" or "My daughter-in-law is coming to see me"—and first thing you knew he owed the landlady forty-eight dollars or eight weeks times six dollars.

And then I discovered the gambit that brought comfort to thousands of elderly men and elderly women. You told the landlady quietly that you had a little property which you could not turn into cash at the moment, but that you would make a will leaving it to the landlady to compensate her for her kindness, her generosity, and her understanding.

And you'd be surprised how many landladies fell for this idea, even though they might have heard it once or twice before. They did not dare take a chance, and of course, there is always what Lord Bacon once said, "The carrying of people from hope to hope is the greatest antidote to the seeds of discontent."

The estate of the elderly man usually consisted of several empty bottles of "Cream of Kentucky Bourbon" and a book, "How to Mark Playing Cards (for amusement only)" and a few yearning letters from a finance company.

In a willow basket

WHEN my mother went shopping she always carried with her a big basket. Her first stop with the basket was at the bakery on Broome Street where the bagels and pretzels hung on hooks and the rolls were heaped below. This must have been the first self-service store in the nation's history because I can remember her picking over the rolls, and the baker always handed me one.

From there she journeyed up Houston and Orchard Streets, which were lined with pushcarts. She stopped at the vegetable and fruit carts and then she went to the dairy for butter and milk. Our last stop was the fish market, where the purchases were always wrapped in old music paper. At the butcher's, the meat was usually wrapped in newspaper.

Very probably the shopping bag and the supermarket have taken all the adventure out of buying because they have robbed the consumer of the familiar. No peeks into a shopping bag has ever looked as inviting as my mother's big willow basket.

The Immigrant and the Children of Dixie

PELLAGRA was a special disease. In the South it killed seven thousand people every year and helplessly crippled a quarter of a million, mostly children. It reddened and cracked and peeled the skin. Pellagra was the scourge of the South, a curse laid upon its poor.

But in the American scheme of things it was no improbable accident that the man who banished it was born in Hungary and was brought to America when he was six years old. It has been said often enough that no nation in the world is as suspicious of immigrants as America, a nation of immigrants. It is equally true that no nation has ever offered as much of itself to the immigrants or received as much from them. It has been the most even "trade" of its kind in the history of modern civilization.

Joseph Goldberger, after being graduated from the New York University Medical School, entered the United States Public Health Service. The doctors of the United States Public Health Service are the policemen of illness, the detectives of disease. Goldberger not only wanted to cure disease, he wanted to conquer it, for it is written in the *Sefer Hassidim:* "Who is a skilled physician? He who can prevent sickness."

Dr. Goldberger worked in Mexico trying to seek new ways of controlling and wiping out typhus, and then he himself fell victim to the disease. For almost ten years afterward he worked in the government laboratories. In 1913 the Public Health Service ordered a new attack upon pellagra, the peculiar disease of the poor. It was known in every State and every village in the South. It made tired, listless dullards of children and weak oldsters of men in their prime. It was not a dramatic killer, only a cruel and a constant killer. It sapped the strength of the Southern people and undermined their will to achieve.

In 1913 a doctor in the South was a man in a silk hat, with a proper black bag, driving a buggy or a newfangled automobile. He had status in the community, he was respected, he was a man to reckon with. But Dr. Goldberger was none of these. He had neither silk hat, nor buggy, nor proper black bag. He had no status and you didn't have to reckon with him. He came into a town, usually on foot, a dusty, tired-looking man with a scraggly mustache, a worn hat, and a foreign-sounding name. Often the folks were openly suspicious of this "foreigner," particularly when he had forgotten the protocol of paying his respects to the local doctor.

Goldberger walked through Georgia, Alabama, Mississippi, everywhere knocking at the doors of crossroad houses and sharecroppers' cabins, asking, "Is there any pellagra in this house? When did you first notice it? Which members of the family have it and which haven't? How do you live? Where do you sleep? What do you eat?"

One day Dr. Goldberger's search brought him to a hospital for the mentally ill in South Carolina. He examined every patient in the institution. Pellagra was on every floor, in every ward. He asked permission to examine the staff of the hospital. None of them had the disease.

He found another clue in an orphan asylum in Mississippi. In every dormitory of the institution pellagra took its toll. But in every dormitory there were a few children who were free of it. Dr. Goldberger questioned the staff but there was no explanation. He questioned the children, and one boy offered his new friend his most precious possession—a secret.

"I get lots of milk," he boasted. "All I can drink. Maybe I can get you some."

Dr. Goldberger stiffened. Patiently, he got the story from his young friend. Two children were chosen as messengers for each dormitory. They went to the pantry every evening to draw a meager pitcher of milk. While they waited, they stole as much milk for themselves as they could, and they did not have pellagra.

The doctor was now convinced that the disease was not contagious nor communicable. But to substantiate his convictions, he inoculated himself, his wife, and his assistant with a solution of blood drawn from a man seriously ill with the disease. If pellagra was in fact a deficiency disease, he knew the blood would be harmless. None of them contracted the disease. This furnished his proof.

Proper diet was the preventive. The poor of the South ate sow belly, cornmeal, and molasses. They used their land to grow cotton instead of green vegetables. A diet which included greens of any kind effectively controlled and finally abolished pellagra.

When Dr. Goldberger died in 1929, after a bout with yellow fever, he left a wife and four children. There was no estate. But this Jewish immigrant from Hungary did leave a large legacy to his adopted land. Because of him millions of the children of Dixie grew up with clear eyes and straight legs.

The morning prayers in school

ANDRÉ MAUROIS, born Emil Herzog, now one of the great biographers of the Western world, went to a fashionable school as a young boy. Because he was Jewish, the teachers of the lycée excused young Emil from daily religious devotions in the Catholic chapel. Maurois describes how bad he felt about the exclusion and, not understanding the reason for it, how he would roam the school courtyard, making circles around the chapel where he could hear his classmates singing, "Lift Up Your Voices, O Israel." Inside they were lifting up their voices to Israel and here outside was the only Jewish kid in the school.

Much the same confusion has been engendered today by legal suits instituted by some organizations against the daily prayer in the public school assembly or classroom.

Those who want abolition of the prayer base their arguments on the traditional American principle of separation of church and state. They argue that prayer violates the First Amendment to the Constitution. But does it really?

Let me be quick to admit there are areas where this Amendment is indeed abridged. In my home city of Charlotte, North Carolina, there are daily Protestant devotionals held in the classrooms. These devotionals are denominational, and the teachers are paid not by the state or the city, but by the private Protestant organizations themselves. While Jewish, Catholic, Baptist, and Unitarian children are excused from participation, I believe that a violation of the "separation" principle is involved here. It is true that Bible teachers are not paid with public funds, but adherence to the Constitutional provision would require that they also pay the janitor and perhaps even build an edifice of their own.

Can we mount as good an argument against the prayer recommended by the New York State Board of Regents some years ago?

> Almighty God, we acknowledge our dependence on Thee, and we beg Thy blessings upon us, our parents, our teachers, and our country.

This prayer is simply an act of reverence. We live in a religious society. The state champions not one religion, but all religions. Common manners, common attitudes, and common acceptance are what keep alive our churches, synagogues, and witness meetings. All American institutions, including the city council and the Supreme Court, take for granted the existence of God, but none of these institutions carefully define Him. God can mean brotherhood or the metaphysical entity responsible for nature and love and the cosmos. What difference does it make? This prayer enforces no dogma. Few of us are so doctrinaire we would refuse to let a boy join the Boy Scouts because he would have to sing hymns at night around the campfire.

We have had religious wars throughout history. Thank God, this is behind us, in America at least. For the American Revolution did not despoil churches and religions when it succeeded. It is this we should remember when we talk of the "wall of separation." One of the earliest court decisions regarding the state and religion occurred in New York during President Washington's second administration. Parishioners went to court to challenge a Catholic bishop's right to dismiss a priest. The court decided the bishop's decision must stand since the government could not interfere in the internal organization of any church. In another case, the court in Virginia decided that an Anglican church was not a spoil of war, even though it had been established by the King, but belonged, rather, to the parishioners. These two decisions are but the first of many which enforce the American ideal that religion is a freely chosen way of life.

National organizations are challenging the propriety of school prayer in New York, and in Colorado they are urging a joint Hanukkah-Christmas celebration.

Over the last half century many Jewish boys entered Princeton, a Presbyterian school, Fordham, a Roman Catholic school, and Trinity, an Episcopalian school. In the main these students graduated and became lawyers and doctors and writers and teachers and Congressmen. Yet these lucky ones still eat matzohs on Passover and still join the shul in the community and bask when their son makes his bar mitzvah. And it was a healthy accident. The Jewish boys got a good education and the Presbyterian boys and the Catholic boys and the Episcopalian boys learned that there were such people as Jewish immigrants who could write essays on America and become Marines and paratroopers when the times called for these professions.

But above all, I think I would hesitate to fight a religious war over the heads of children. I have never yet seen a man turn his back on a publicly offered prayer at a luncheon meeting of a civic club, a city council, or an interfaith function.

If a man feels strongly about this, let him take up the cudgels himself, let him urge in public assembly that churches should not be tax-free institutions, that merchants refrain from using the public thoroughfare for Christmas decorations, that Sunday blue laws infringe upon his rights. This is a real fight, and while I will not join him, I will support incontestably his right to protest.

But you will win no battles of principle by keeping kids off the school buses or maintaining a moment of prayerful silence after the Pledge of Allegiance to the flag.

Will Detroit respond in time?

RELIABLE informants assure me that the teen-agers old enough to drive cars are now insisting they want an auto with a gearshift, a stick shift they call it. No more of these automatic affairs. There is something demeaning to a young lad to push a button or flick a switch to get a car from a parked position up to seventy-five miles an hour on the freeway.

The kid wants none of this, no denial of his potential virility; he wants to maneuver that engine and the chances are that he will get his way. Detroit was caught napping on the small cars which, until the auto capital manufactured "compact," it insisted were only snob items. But will Detroit bring back the stick shift in time? Will the Jaguar—which guarantees a boy a girl, particularly if the Jaguar has red upholstery—claim the lion's share of the market?

Let the motor run

IN THE American scheme of things, love is for some reason intimately related to the motorcar. One of the reasons Detroit took the gearshift from the floor and put it on the steering wheel was to accommodate college students all over the country.

Thus, the parked car is often a giveaway about love. But there are ways to combat this. One of the surest is to keep the motor running. Say you're visiting a married lady whose husband is away at work. You park your car but you leave the motor running and approach her house at a half run, as though you are in a hurry to reclaim golf clubs or collect the money she has made from the sale of girl-scout cookies.

No one covers himself with innocence better than a man who leaves his motor on. Neighbors who spy certainly don't think a man would let his battery run down for illicit purposes. When your tête-à-tête is through, go back to your car at a half run as though you still have to hurry to pick up several more checks for the local community-chest drive.

My daddy shot me

> O your heart must have been made of rock or steel
> You who can kill
> With your own hand your own fruit. . . .

Thus sings the shocked chorus in Euripides' tragedy *Medea*. Medea kills both her children to avenge herself for the slights of Jason who intends to leave her. Other crimes are more barbaric, others crueler, still others more deceitful, but no crime shocks us like that of a parent who kills or maims his child.

In Charlotte, North Carolina, a man is on trial, charged with having blinded his six-year-old son with shotgun pellets. The pellets struck the child when the father, allegedly in a rage, shot at the mother.

What can justice do that nature will not?

> Hark! Did ye hear!
> Heard ye the children's cry?
> O miserable woman! O abhorred . . .

The Jewish wedding

IN THE old days, the bride always remembered the wedding and could describe it accurately and in vivid detail to her grandchildren. But today it has all changed. I attended a wedding a month ago and did not hear a single mazzeltov (good luck).

The invitations of today are no doubt fancier, but also more forbidding. They must omit the names of the groom's parents and heaven help protocol if someone forgets the prefix "Mr." before the name of the groom. But it seems to me the folks do not understand that this attempt to reflect the culture of the surrounding middle class is less than convincing.

During the old-fashioned Jewish wedding, the pent-up anxiety and despair of everyday living were relaxed. People waited in hushed expectancy for the signal, "They are leading the bride." Everybody turned their eyes to the end of the hall where the bride, attended by maids and relatives and perhaps a dozen hangers-on, began her march to the wedding canopy.

Half an hour later, the cry went up, "The groom is coming." He was surrounded by at least two uncles and his father in addition to his brothers, friends, fellow workers, and perhaps the social director from the Settlement House. It was considered a formal insult not to invite all the neighbors to a wedding and all night long you heard the jovial mazzeltov.

Ah, what a joy and delight this would have furnished our fellow neighbors if we had maintained it instead of becoming so fancy.

The Jewish wedding had deep roots in history. One of the questions all Jews have to answer is: "In how many days did the Holy One, blessed be He, create the universe?"

The student answers, "In six days did He create the universe."

"And what has He been doing since then, up to now?"

And the answer, the only answer is: "Since then He has been arranging marriages."

God is a maker of marriages, but I wonder if He would bother to come to some of the affairs He has arranged?

Memories of the Twist

THE moralists among us—God bless 'em, they provide food for thought—have by this time expressed their abhorrence of the Twist. The gyrations of couples reveal our complete and progressing decadence, and the Twist will spin all the values out of life.

But I believe rather emphatically that the Twist is a return to Puritanism. Now it may well be that a body twisting to rhythms is suggestive, but so for that matter was the Puritan bonnet. As a matter of fact, I saw a dance not unlike the Twist on the Lower East Side of New York fifty years ago, and I saw it performed in our Orthodox shul. Our synagogue was a Hasidic shul.

The Hasidim is a religious sect composed of very pious Jews. The Hasidim believe that religious expression is a joyous expression, that faith is a matter of happiness and that fear and anxiety have no place in a synagogue. But their rules of decorum are strict rules and their inhibitions manifold. Yet on the holiday that marks God's gift of the Torah to the people ("Rejoicing in the Law") the Hasidim in our shul performed a dance resembling the Twist now performed at the Peppermint Lounges across the country.

The Hasidim moved in rhythm to the chant, and often abandoned themselves to the joy of its tempo, observing their prohibitions against touching or embracing each other. They were serving the Lord with gladness.

It would be foolish of me to maintain that the couples twisting are "serving God with gladness." I have no doubt they are glad, but I suspect that for most of them God is just a Sunday adventure. Their separateness, the fact that they dance without touching one another, is probably an indication of how remote they feel modern life to be. It seems to me the Twist is puritanical, because most of our dancers realize that people don't touch in everyday life, they do not communicate; and the dancers refuse to pretend by their dancing that they do.

This book was set in

Electra and Goudy Oldstyle types by

Harry Sweetman Typesetting Corporation.

It was printed and bound at the press of

The World Publishing Company.

Design is by Larry Kamp.